The Untravelled World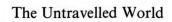

The Untravelled World:

A Memoir

Michael Adams

Q

Quartet Books
London Melbourne New York

First published by Quartet Books Limited 1984
A member of the Namara Group
27/29 Goodge Street, London W1P 1FD

British Library Cataloguing in Publication Data

Adams, Michael
  The untravelled world.
1. Adams, Michael   2. Journalists – Great
Britain – Biography
I.Title
070'.92'4   PN5123.A3

ISBN   0-7043-2449-0

Typeset by AKM Associates (UK) Limited
Southall, Greater London
Printed and bound in Great Britain
by Mackays of Chatham Ltd, Kent

For David and Paul

Contents

I am a part of all that I have met;
Yet all experience is an arch, wherethro'
Gleams that untravell'd world, whose margin fades
For ever and ever when I move.

Tennyson, 'Ulysses'

PART ONE
Gale Warning
(1938–39)

1

Down the long vista of memory I see a slight figure striding up through the pinewoods under a full moon. Presently the trees give way to Alpine meadows and the path threads its way on and up towards the highest of the ring of peaks on the horizon.

That figure is my youthful self and that peak, which is my objective for the night, is the Glandaz, 2,045 metres up in the Basses-Alpes south-west of Grenoble. It is an easy enough climb and what lends the Glandaz a special significance for me after more than forty years is not any glowing sense of achievement I felt in conquering it, but the unique circumstances in which I found myself on the top at dawn on one of the last days of August 1939. When the sun climbed over the broken range to the east and began to colour the mists swimming in the valleys far below me, I experienced (although I did not know it at the time) the last completely untroubled vision of my boyhood. Looking down from the crest, I felt a lightness of spirit which then seemed natural, instinctive, but which I would never recapture with quite that same full-hearted sense of identification with my surroundings. For me, as for so many others at the time, it was the end of the age of innocence.

Shivering a little, partly from the cold but also, I suspect, out of a kind of intoxication of delight, I ate the bread and cold meat I had brought with me. Then, turning my back reluctantly on that wide prospect, I raced down across the high meadows and through the trees and out into the little town of Chatillon-en-Diois and on by a side road to the old stone house in its tangled garden where I was staying. And it is only a little fanciful to say that it was like coming down out of paradise into the inferno.

The others – an elderly French widow and her sister who were my hostesses – were finishing breakfast when I arrived and I joined them round an antique 'wireless' set to listen to the news. As usual, it was bad. The Germans were stepping up the pressure on Poland, armies were being mobilized all over Europe, and while I had been running

down from the Glandaz, the British Ambassador to Germany, Nevile
Henderson, had been on his way to Berlin with a note for Hitler. No
one was optimistic about the response it would bring.

Already the fields about Chatillon were empty of men. In place of
the reservists who had been called to the colours, women and boys were
bringing in the harvest. The postman was doubling as town barber; the
baker's van and the creaking old local bus had been taken away to do
their duty for France. Of these details, of course, I remember little: I
have gleaned them from the diary I was keeping at the time. What I do
remember is the sense of oppression, the ominous cloudbank of
apprehension under which, in those leaden days at the end of August,
we sat impotent in the shadow of the mountains. No wonder that
moonlight assault on the Glandaz looms so large in my memory. It was
at once a physical relief, a necessary letting-off of youthful steam, and
an escape from the onset of the impending storm.

That storm had not blown up out of nowhere. In the spring of 1938
the Germans had occupied Austria. In the summer, against a background of German and Italian air raids in Spain (where the civil war
was entering its third year) and with a Japanese army advancing into
China, we had the first intimations of Hitler's designs against
Czechoslovakia. In September came the startling humiliation of
Munich – and after that the pace quickened, so that throughout 1939
our world seemed to be rushing headlong down the slope to disaster.

Each new concession by our own government became the prelude to
fresh impositions. No sooner had we acknowledged the victory of
General Franco in Spain than the Germans moved on from the
bridgehead they had established at Munich to occupy the rest of
Czechoslovakia. Before we had absorbed this blow, Mussolini –
encouraged earlier by the unconcern with which we had watched the
Italian assault on Ethiopia – sent his armies into Albania, on the first
day of an Easter weekend of breathtakingly perfect April weather.*
This series of shocks gave the *coup de grâce* to the policy of
appeasement and before the end of the month the House of Commons
agreed to the government's proposal to introduce conscription. At last
– although it wasn't easy, after all that had happened, to convince us of
their sincerity – it looked as though the men of Munich had decided to
draw the line. And about time too, we said.

* This prompted the observation in my diary that 'while Chamberlain takes a weekend
in the country, Mussolini takes a country in the weekend'. I think this must have been a
popular joke at the time.

'We' means my friends and myself in what we were coming to realize was a small and privileged section of Britain's pre-war society. Privileged, but not insensitive to the imperfections of the world about us, whose outward aspect was one of a stability, almost a serenity, that today seems legendary.

Looking back, it is the seeming changelessness of that world which is so striking; and that had aspects both good and bad. God knows, there were plenty of things about it that were absurd or pretentious. There was an ignorant and self-satisfied contempt for all things foreign, which were assumed automatically to be inferior. (I once heard an old lady in a Sussex hotel remark, after listening to the nine o'clock news from the BBC: 'I do think the news is so *dull* nowadays: all these foreign countries and their governments – and nobody cares two straws about 'em.') There was inequality, although its effects were softened by the tolerance and good nature which more often than not coloured relations between the classes; and there was much incompetence in high places, which was too often tolerated, and even admired, as an expression of the amateur approach so dear to English hearts.

On the other hand, there was an almost complete absence of corruption in public life, and there was above all a sense of community, which was shared to a remarkable extent even by most of those for whom life in pre-war Britain was least rewarding. If one tries to cast up a balance sheet between the casual and complacent thirties and our own feverish and uncertain age, it is this more than anything that we have reason to regret. This and a sense of the continuity of life in Britain which, with all its shortcomings, encouraged in my generation the belief that, taking things all round, as the tolerant and easy-going British tended to take them, there was nothing very much to worry about.

I see these contradictions reflected in the diaries I was keeping at the time and where, throughout 1938 and '39, islands of political comment stand up out of the general ebb and flow of my own preoccupations. And of all these islands, the one marked 'Munich' easily dominates the rest, throwing a long shadow forward over the lives of my contemporaries.

I was eighteen at the time and I had left school in the summer of 1938. After spending a few weeks travelling in France, I came back to England – a very rough crossing from Dieppe to Newhaven, I note – on 19 August. Next day I was in Sussex with my parents, who lived in Egypt and were spending their home leave in a cottage they had rented on the edge of Ashdown Forest. It was a Saturday, the weather was marvellous, and all that most people in England had on their minds that day was the final Test match against the Australians. We sat on the lawn listening through the open windows (no transistors in those days and the wireless was an ugly and immovable totem in the corner of the sitting room) to the mellow voice of Howard Marshall describing the first day's play at the Oval. And since the match was as remarkable in its way as the events that were to follow it on a wider stage, it is amusing to recall the details.

England won the toss and by lunchtime were 150 for one wicket. They batted all that day and all the next, by the end of which they had reached 634 for 5 (Len Hutton of Yorkshire 300 not out) and they finally declared on the third day at 903 for 7 (Hutton 364, Maurice Leyland 187, Hardstaff 168 not out) and took three Australian wickets for 130. On the fourth and final day, when – it is only fair to add – their great champion, the unforgettable Don Bradman, was injured and unable to bat, the Australians followed on 702 runs behind and were quickly put out again, leaving England victorious inside four days by an innings and 580 runs.

The glorious weather persisted almost without a break until the middle of September and it was out of these cloudless skies that the Munich crisis burst upon us. Suddenly my diary breaks off a chronicle of homely activities – games of tennis, walks in Ashdown Forest, an occasional swim off the rocks at Birling Gap – to record on 8 September that 'we seem to be in the middle of a critical week for Europe & the tension is acute'. The focal point was the Sudetenland, an area just outside Czechoslovakia where there was a large German population, one of the unfortunate legacies of the Treaty of Versailles. The German press was full of 'incidents' in which it was claimed that the Sudeten Germans were being victimized by the Czech authorities, and as a result:

France has put the Maginot line on a war footing & the smaller states of central Europe are all waiting to see which way the cat will jump. Italy, according to *The Times*, is not wholly in agreement with Germany this time; just now she is much occupied with measures against the Jews, in which cowardly & senseless purpose she copies Germany. War continues in Spain & China, & in each seems to be a long way from conclusion. Meanwhile, every day seems to bring it nearer to ourselves & rumours are on every tongue.

We were in the middle of the season of Promenade Concerts, which in 1938 were still held at the old Queen's Hall opposite Broadcasting House, and one night when the moon was full we listened to a concert of Mozart, with the moonlight flooding the darkened sitting room. But the next night it was not to a concert that we listened, but to a broadcast from Nuremburg, where a rally of the Nazi party was in progress and we heard Hitler's concluding speech, '. . . shouting, terrifying & enthralling – the speech for which the whole world had been waiting & which should determine whether it is to be peace or war'.

Hitler gave no clear indication of his intentions, but next day – another glorious day of Indian summer, when we sought out the shade in the garden and the valley below was filled with a blue haze – the Czech government declared a state of emergency in the Sudetenland and we heard with apprehension that at a cabinet meeting in London the defence chiefs had been in attendance. The atmosphere was electric and my brothers and I began to think and talk of war as something that could reach out beyond the headlines in the newspapers to affect our own lives.

Against the radiance of that seemingly endless succession of sun-filled September days, the idea of war seemed still barely more than a hallucination, a bogey thrust in our faces by that raggle-taggle figure with the toothbrush moustache whom we were only now learning to take seriously. By the middle of September, though, with Czechs and Germans coming regularly to blows in the Sudetenland, there were rumours that both the Germans and the French were starting to mobilize. The Russians were carrying out naval manoeuvres and there were consultations going on between the British and French military chiefs. Perhaps it was this that made me optimistic:

> War seems unlikely to me: Hitler is not likely to risk it in the face of the almost certain armed resistance of the democracies, of which up to now he has been doubtful. I think he will try to get another bloodless victory (as in Austria) or else to back out of the awkward position in which he finds himself. Of course he will not back down if he can help it [but] . . . if we stand firm, I think Hitler must accept defeat.

Before going to bed that night, I heard in a French broadcast the 'incredible news' that the British prime minister, Neville Chamberlain, was to fly to Germany to meet Hitler in Berchtesgaden. Only when *The Times* confirmed it next morning could we believe this, for in those days to fly to Germany was not the humdrum hop, skip and a jump that it is today, and certainly not for a sixty-nine-year-old prime minister, while the concept of the 'summit' meeting, which is so familiar to us, was unheard of in 1938. Chamberlain, in fact, had never been up in an aeroplane in his life and I was full of admiration, describing his initiative as 'a most striking & courageous one', which must reassure public opinion – although I did not expect it to do much more, since 'I can't think that Chamberlain will influence Hitler much'. The weather, I added, was still fine and I went out for a driving lesson.

For two or three days, while Neville Chamberlain came and went, we all breathed a little easier and one senses it in the fact that in my diary politics yield place to the more usual preoccupations of youth. I paid a visit to London, where I bought a pipe and smoked it for the first time (the sensation was 'disappointing'), saw a delicious new French actress, Danielle Darrieux, in *The Rage of Paris*, dawdled in the second-hand bookshops of the Charing Cross Road and went to someone's twenty-first birthday party. Even so, politics was never far away; after the birthday party my brothers and I went with a group of friends to drink coffee at the old Lyons Corner House at Marble Arch and had a furious discussion about the crisis and its implications; while on our return to Sussex we shared the experience, which must have been common to so many families in those days, of having an argument about Chamberlain and his policies which split the family down the middle.

When we listened to the BBC on the evening of 19 September, there were more or less open hostilities on the frontier between Germany and Czechoslovakia and 'the news seemed to imply that France & Britain (whose prime ministers were in conference together for nearly ten hours yesterday) are going to give way to Hitler once more. If they do, it will be the fault of Chamberlain, & this time it will be fatal . . .' On the 20th *The Times* published the outline of a joint Anglo-French plan for solving the Czech crisis which confirmed our worst fears. In return for a guarantee of their neutrality signed by Britain, France, Germany and Italy, the Czechs were to give up the areas along the frontier where the Germans could claim to be in the majority. After reading *The Times*, I was 'more angry than I have ever felt over politics' and when we heard next day that the Czechs, deserted by their friends, had accepted the terms of the proposed agreement, I knew for the first time the sensation of feeling ashamed of my own country.

The weather had broken at last and we were surrounded by nothing but gloom. I went morosely for walks in the rain, tried to read, grumbled about *The Times* ('which has lately adopted an attitude of disgusting & unjustifiably optimistic satisfaction over Chamberlain's "peace moves" ') and listened to the wireless, hearing at one moment the Mendelssohn violin concerto and at the next another of Hitler's extraordinary speeches in which (it was on 26 September) 'amid frantic shouts & applause he ranted as usual against the Czechs & the democracies and shrieked himself into a state of hysteria'. Unwilling to rest content with the humiliating terms imposed on the Czechs, Hitler was raising his demands every day, insisting now that the border areas which the Czechs were to cede must be evacuated immediately, that the elaborate fortifications along the old frontier were to be left intact, that the departing Czech civilians were to take nothing with them, not even their livestock or the food and furniture from their houses. Failing all this, Hitler said, the German army would move in at once, using force if necessary.

The 27th passed without incident and on the morning of the 28th, with the Czechs still standing firm and only a few hours to go before Hitler's ultimatum expired, war seemed 'absolutely imminent'; but I clung to the hope that 'Hitler might climb down, for the patience of Britain & France is exhausted & they uphold the Czechs in their refusal' of Hitler's conditions. And that afternoon it seemed as though the miracle had happened and Hitler *had* climbed down. Soon after the 2 p.m. deadline had come and gone, we heard that he had postponed the threatened troop movements and instead had invited Chamberlain to go and see him again in a four-party conference with Mussolini and the French prime minister, Daladier.

This time, of course, the rendezvous was Munich and with hindsight we know that this was to be the shameful end of the whole shabby story. But that was not how it seemed on that afternoon of 28 September, at any rate not to one optimistic eighteen-year-old enjoying, after a couple of rainy days, the very last of those fabled days of sunshine against which the Munich drama was played out through that September of 1938. To me it appeared, as I wrote in high spirits that evening, that Hitler had '. . . banked to the last on an eleventh-hour retreat on the part of the democracies, & as this did not happen he chose this conference as preferable to openly breaking his promise to the German people [that he would march tomorrow] . . . at last he realizes that he is up against a solid front.'

The optimism was short-lived, and the disillusionment that followed all the more crushing. Next day, in pouring rain, I packed my things and returned to London (where volunteers were digging air-raid shelters in Hyde Park) to hear the first reports from Munich, a sorry compound of relief and wishful thinking, on which I commented that

'I'm afraid it looks like one more triumph for Hitler & he does not seem to have reduced his terms in any essential.' On the 30th, the published results of the conference showed how completely Chamberlain and Daladier had given way. Aware that this was 'a fateful day', I took my camera and went out to photograph the trenches in the park and the newspaper posters reading 'NO WAR – *official*', and found myself at the end of the afternoon joining a crowd converging on Buckingham Palace, where Neville Chamberlain arrived hotfoot from Munich waving the piece of paper which promised, so he told us, 'peace in our time'.

When he appeared on the balcony of the palace, flanked by the King and Queen, there rose a roar of approval and there was no doubt that it expressed the mood of the majority in England that day. Down there in front of the Victoria Memorial, in the thick of a dense crowd in whose tangled emotions relief was certainly uppermost, I was conscious around me of something that was close to mass hysteria. 'London,' I wrote that evening, 'was rejoicing – but for me it is spoilt by the thought of the Czechs, who sent today a dignified & mournful acceptance of the Munich terms; they could do nothing else.'

Well, that was the end of it – for the time being. The reaction set in quickly enough and the debate that followed in the House of Commons, in which Duff Cooper (who had resigned from the Admiralty on hearing the news from Munich) joined Churchill and Anthony Eden in leading the opposition, showed how deeply the nation was divided. Unable to get into the public gallery, I stood outside the House to watch Chamberlain and the rest of them arriving for the debate; bought all the newspapers I could lay my hands on; saw a newsreel of the signing at Munich (that was our substitute for television in those days); and argued interminably with my brothers and their friends.

The Czechs who lived in the border areas were already moving out, in an astonishing display of self-discipline, with the German army hot on their heels. Churchill made 'one of his magnificent speeches' condemning Chamberlain's policy ('You had the choice between war and dishonour. You chose dishonour – and you will have war'), but there was nothing more to be done and as early as 4 October, in the midst of preparations for my first term at the university, I remarked bitterly that 'the crisis is now back-page stuff'. Two days later, after sorting out the pile of press cuttings I had accumulated, I packed a couple of suitcases of clothes, a new tea set and a print of Andrea del Sarto's *Portrait of a Young Sculptor* (it is in front of me as I write) and caught a train to Oxford.

2

Oxford, with all that it promised in the way of wider horizons, offered a heady release from these sombre preoccupations. From the damp autumn afternoon when I walked in through Tom Gate of Christ Church to find my little niche in this large new world, it was a fortnight and more before politics seem next to have impinged on my thoughts. They did so then only because there was a celebrated by-election in Oxford in that October of 1938, at which Quintin Hogg (now Lord Hailsham) and A. D. Lindsay, the Master of Balliol, fought a symbolic duel over the issue of appeasement.

We undergraduates had no vote, but we claimed the right (and clamorously exercised it) to make our preferences plain. Most of us were for Dr Lindsay, who was standing as an 'independent progressive', but I cannot pretend we took the whole affair very seriously. All I remember is that I attended one or two of Lindsay's campaign meetings and that on the evening of polling day a group of us joined the great crowd outside the town hall and tried to drown out the chant of 'H-O-G-G HOGG!' by shouting 'VOTE FOR HITLER, VOTE FOR HOGG!' (which I imagine was an unfair vulgarization of Lindsay's platform) and, less offensively, 'CHAMBERLAIN MUST GO!' – and trying to knock off a policeman's helmet or two into the bargain. To our disgust, Quintin Hogg won by a majority of 3,000 and Oxford appeared to have voted decisively in support of the Munich policy. 'I'm afraid,' I wrote disconsolately, 'that people do not understand its futility.'

Next morning my scout woke me up in triumph, observing that 'at last we can breathe again, Sir' – to which I made no reply. The truth is that I was much in awe of my scout, a man of enormous aplomb named Hicks. I could not disguise from myself the fact that it was Hicks who – with delicacy, but also with more than a hint of firmness when he felt it was needed – mastered me, rather than the other way round. And this, I was sensible enough to realize, was a sound arrangement, since I was little more than a schoolboy, while Hicks (who must have been in his fifties), quite apart from his familiarity with the environment to which I was a newcomer, was both wiser and far more articulate than I was.

Like a ground controller handling an inexperienced airline pilot, his instructions nudged me safely on to the proper glide-path for landing at an unfamiliar airport. It was Hicks who told me where to get a gown and when to wear it; who knew the college rules and when it was safe to break them; who had by heart the ritual for bump suppers and gaudies and summer balls; who knew the best recipe for mulled wine and could plan the menu for one of the luncheon parties we could still hold in our rooms – with Hicks of course playing the butler to perfection. Far more effectively than the shy don who was designated as my 'moral tutor', Hicks was in plain terms a counsellor where one was much needed. I shall always be grateful to him.

As undergraduates at Oxford before the war we shared what I see in retrospect as the besetting sin of our countrymen in that pre-war era: complacency. There was still a widely held assumption, especially among those who occupied the more favoured positions within it, that the British social system was the best that had yet been devised; that democracy was a British invention which no one else was quite capable of handling (though of course we could try to teach them); that the British legal system had no rival, and nor had the BBC; and that this effortless and presumably innate superiority extended equally to British engineering and shipbuilding and practically everything else you could think of, including – paradoxically – the British sense of humour.

If it is startling to be reminded of all this in an age when not merely most of the cars and cameras and transistors we see around us are foreign but even most of our shirts and shoes seem to come from Hong Kong or South Korea, it is worth recalling too that in 1938 these claims were not altogether ridiculous. Despite the shock of the abdication of Edward VIII in 1936, our social system stood up well enough by comparison with the picture in Mussolini's Italy or Nazi Germany – not to mention France in the closing stages of the Third Republic and the United States in the heyday of Al Capone and Huey Long and the Ku Klux Klan. British public life was exemplary and the lightest breath of scandal, whether domestic or financial, was enough to banish a man into outer darkness. And where British engineering was concerned, it was not unreasonable to take pride in an honours list which included Rolls-Royce and Alvis and Bentley – and even the ubiquitous Baby Austin – as well as Handley-Page and the Flying Scotsman and a fleet of ocean liners culminating in the *Queen Mary*, which was launched in

1936 and two years later captured the Blue Riband for the fastest crossing of the Atlantic (a record which remained unbroken until 1952).

None of these was a concern which figured prominently on our Oxford horizon, but each was a detail in the landscape against which our lives were lived; and they helped to provide my generation of young Englishmen with the luxury of growing up in an atmosphere of what seems now almost unimaginable security. Such at least was the case until the shock of Munich. And if Munich, in that autumn of 1938, sounded a warning note, it was some time before its implications came home to us, especially those of us lucky enough to be embarking on an Oxford career. Most of us felt, as I did, that the Munich policy was not merely ignoble, but misguided as well. And as the months passed and we discussed endlessly what had happened and what was likely to happen next, we could hardly fail to realize that it was ourselves and our contemporaries who would be called upon to pay the bill. At first this was no more than a shadow at the back of our minds, one that was to grow darker and more obtrusive throughout that last year before the war. Meanwhile, we were young and at Oxford, and there was too much else to delight and distract us.

I had come to Oxford from Sedbergh, an ancient and unpretentious public school in what is now Cumbria and was then a salient of north-west Yorkshire jutting out into Westmorland. It would be difficult to imagine a more striking transition. Sedbergh is of the north, northern, a small, solid market town in a moorland setting, the modest capital of a world in which the black-faced sheep grazing on the bare fells outnumber the human beings who raise and care for and make their living from them. And Oxford makes as good a symbol as any of that other world of the south, whose predilections and obscure intellectual preoccupations the northern countryman regards with a mixture of amusement and suspicion.

With its roots deep in that northern countryside of hill farms and rock-strewn rivers, Sedbergh had the reputation of being a hard school. And so it was, in outward appearances at least, with its cold baths and its passion for rugby football and its tradition of long-distance running over the open fells. When I first came to it from the south, it looked gaunt and more than a little forbidding. It had a compelling air of remoteness, of being – especially when the clouds came down on the surrounding hillsides – isolated from the world of ordinary men. When the snow came and the east wind blew down from the Pennines, Sedbergh could look and feel as bleak as anywhere I can remember.

That was one aspect – and even that one had its compensations. We used to go skating at Killington, high on the road to the Lake District, near where the finest stretch of the M6 now goes striding up the Lune valley; or we would toboggan down the steep slopes of Winder, which stands over the town like a monument to a patron saint. More often the wind was from the west and the fells were cloud-shadowed and in the rivers the water tumbled from one rock pool to the next, so that in spring and summer and all but the harshest depths of that northern winter we were in possession of as marvellously free and varied a physical environment as boys anywhere could want.

From this enclosed world it was indeed a long step to the wide horizons of Oxford; and Oxford, for all its other and varied attractions, could not rival the tranquillity and the sense of well-being that were the particular endowments of Sedbergh. Before long I was on my way back, on foot and in the company of my closest friend, Stuart Alexander (we had met five years before on our first day at Sedbergh and had stayed together ever since), on a journey which is closely linked in my mind with the next stage in the crisis that was overtaking Europe.

It was March 1939, Munich was six months behind us, and Stuart and I had set out to walk to Sedbergh at the start of the Easter vacation. The weather was pretty mixed as we made our way up through Derbyshire and along the Pennines, sleeping in country inns and holding wherever possible to the moorland paths. On the 14th, when we entered on the last stretch of our journey, we covered twenty-five miles through woods and by a stream and up over a high ridge to find shelter in the isolated Tempest Arms, on the edge of the moorland east of Nelson. In the bar the local farmers were discussing the prospects for the lambing season and we paid little attention to an uncertain report of fresh trouble in Europe. When we asked the landlady of the Tempest Arms about it in the morning, her reply was 'Ee, it's them Germans again'; and we had to be content with this when we set off for a splendid day's walking, up past Malham and across open country where our only companions were curlews and plovers and scampering rabbits, to drop down in the last of the afternoon sunshine into Littondale and the pretty little village of Arncliffe.

There we paused for a day's rest before the final march up and over the three peaks of Ingleborough, Penyghent and Whernside. After a lazy afternoon in the sunshine out on the hillside, we went back to our lodgings in the Falcon Inn and there read the first newspaper we had seen since leaving Oxford a week earlier.

From it we learned that it was indeed 'them Germans again': Hitler's troops had occupied the whole of Czechoslovakia and driven a coach and horses through the 'peace with honour' that Chamberlain thought he had won at Munich. It was a strangely inappropriate piece of news to pick up in those surroundings and when we walked off next morning into a snowstorm we pushed it to the back of our minds. We had more immediate concerns as we felt our way up the steep side of Penyghent and into the clouds. The snow turned to hail on the top and we ran quickly down for a lunch of bread and cheese in Horton-in-Ribblesdale, crossed the river and went on westwards to tackle Ingleborough. Now the clouds lifted and there was a gleam of sunshine as we reached the top to look back with satisfaction at Penyghent (which has a fearsome aspect from this side) and ahead to the friendly Howgill fells around Sedbergh. That evening, snug in the Hill Inn down by the old Roman road near Chapel-le-Dale, and again next morning as we battled on through renewed snowstorms over the top of Whernside and down into Sedbergh, not even Hitler could undo the sense of triumphant well-being that we felt.

In 1939, though, we could never escape politics for long. The summer term at Oxford had hardly begun when our attention was focused on a new development which closely concerned us all: the introduction of conscription. It was another grudging acknowledgement that the government had misjudged the pace of events, for only a short time before Chamberlain had pledged himself never to introduce conscription in peacetime, and he was now angrily challenged by the Labour opposition and the trade unions.

The Oxford Union was to debate the question on the 27th and everyone waited and watched to see whether there would be an echo of the notorious debate six years earlier, at the end of which the Union had resolved that 'This house will in no circumstances fight for King and Country'. Opinion among us was divided; but what must have seemed an amusing talking-point in 1933 was something very different in April 1939. We hated the idea of the loss of liberty – our liberty – and 'even a year earlier', I wrote in the eve of the debate, 'it would have been fantastic to talk of conscription in England . . . but this new policy of collective security calls for more than half measures and if conscription will show Hitler that we really mean business and that there will be no more Czechoslovakias, then I am all for it'.

When the debate took place, the chamber was packed and there were plenty of rowdy interventions, but the majority came down in favour of conscription. Late that night a group of us went on discussing its implications, as others must have been doing elsewhere in Oxford and all over the country. I was urging that the futility of the whole Munich approach was now obvious, that if only a firm stand had been taken a year earlier the war which seemed to be overtaking us could have been avoided, and that the next thing to do was to find 'better men than Chamberlain to guide us – Churchill especially'. It is sad now to record that when the war did come, I was the only one of those present who was not killed.

After that there was a lull as far as the political situation was concerned and undergraduate preoccupations reasserted themselves. All the familiar distractions were there, with new ones added which the summer brought: village cricket under the elms at Dorchester and Bourton-on-the-Water; punting on the river – with a musical friend sitting cross-legged in the bows, Puck-like, playing Debussy or Wolf-Ferrari on the flute; a game of bowls at evening in the Dean's garden, with the shadows lengthening across the lawn and Oxford's clamorous bells counting in the summer night; and talk – the endless, fanciful, discursive, egocentric talk of undergraduates in every generation about their hidden hopes and high ambitions. It was the perfect summer life, and if I was conscious, as I wrote late one night, that 'work is getting too little attention – there is too much else to think about', it was not surprising, for it was clearly an open question whether this first summer of ours at Oxford would also be the last.

The uncertainty about what might lie ahead did not prevent us from making our dispositions – or at least dreaming our dreams – about the future. I was sure of one thing: I had decided that I wanted to write – but the daunting problem was to know what to write *about*. Every now and then, usually when I had been subject to some particular emotional stimulus – hearing Solomon playing Chopin, or climbing through that snowstorm over the top of Whernside – I had felt the urge to try to capture the experience and to communicate it. But how to set about this delicate and elusive task?

Faced with this recurring problem, I thought it best not to pitch my sights too high. Later on, perhaps, I should learn how to handle the 'huge cloudy symbols of a high romance'; for the moment I should be content with a lower, a more mundane form of communication, using the same medium of words but to convey, not the quicksilver variations of emotional experience, but ideas which had a practical application to the needs of the day. If this meant becoming a tradesman, or perhaps a craftsman, rather than an artist, why that seemed an honourable alternative, and an exciting one in the context of the times. And so I find the idea taking shape in my diary throughout 1939 that the life for me – to start with, at least, and possibly as an apprenticeship to a higher destiny – was the life of a journalist, a foreign correspondent for preference, who would travel widely, meet everyone, have all sorts of adventures, become involved in events, and ultimately, the fullness of his experience, help to shape a better world . . .

In this expanding vision there were many ingredients. There was of course ambition: the ordinary desire of a young man to set his mark somewhere in the margin of history. There was the equally normal appetite for adventure, for a life of open horizons, in which it would be possible to travel and find out what lay 'beyond that last blue mountain barred with snow, across that angry or that glimmering sea'. There was a well-developed instinct for freedom, both personal freedom and that wider freedom which was under such constant threat in the world about me. And there was the strong sense (I mention it with diffidence and because it was characteristic of the environment in which I was growing up) of an obligation to render some service to society. This was not something we thought of as an incubus; if anything, it lent an additional zest to life. Nor is it easy to express in terms that are not pretentious. One could perhaps say that it represented the exact opposite of the idea that 'the world owes me a living'.

For the moment, though, as that summer term of 1939 drew to a close in a blaze of sunshine, I had nothing more momentous to decide than how I should spend the long vacation. I thought I would go to Paris for a week or so, after which an Oxford friend was to join me for a bicycle tour along the Loire; and when that was over, I planned vaguely to make my way further south and perhaps on into Italy, returning to England in September to collect my thoughts before the new term began. It looked an enjoyable prospect – and at the back of my mind was the thought that if the political situation came to the boil and I found myself stranded somewhere along the way, perhaps in Italy – which one had to assume would be on the opposite side if war should come – there might be adventure to be had as well.

So at the end of June I strapped a few clothes and Jolliffe's *Constitutional History of Mediaeval England* on to the carrier of a bicycle and rode clumsily off (perhaps it was Jolliffe which so upset the balance of the machine) towards Victoria and the boat train for Paris.

3

All went smoothly enough for a time. In Paris I met Pat Magee, a friend from Sedbergh who was about to enter the Church (and not long after that to find himself chaplain to a submarine flotilla), and together we explored the Louvre and Versailles and went to a rowdy music hall called the Alcazar and shared a last good dinner on the Champs-Elysées, with a bottle of champagne to launch him on his new life.

Next came the bicycle tour along the Loire, and that went off well enough despite the miserable weather that continued through most of that summer. My companion was Vic Ellis, one of the closest friends I had made during that first year at Oxford, and my recollections are of the two of us battling, heads down under our capes, into persistent head winds, or looking out from the battlements of this chateau or that over the rainswept countryside. But there were also the days when the sun shone and we would go spinning along through the summer landscape, and stop to swim in the river and eat our picnics of bread and cheese and peaches on the bank, with the towers of Amboise or Blois beckoning to us in the distance.

We came at the last to Tours, where Vic left me to return to England while I rode out along the quiet valley of a tributary of the Loire, itself confusingly called the Loir, in search of a *pension* where I had arranged to stay. In theory my programme envisaged here a spell of reading for my Oxford course, but circumstances were against me, partly because the *pension* was full of an assortment of students of different nationalities, but mostly on account of the personality of my hostess.

Madame Taunay was in every way larger than life and the atmosphere which she communicated to the *pension* and its inhabitants and everything about it was the atmosphere of the stage, or better still the opera. She herself operated, as it were, at full throttle the whole time. She would stride about the house in a *robe de chambre*, exploding with impatience, fury, surprise, amusement, her stout figure shaking with the vehemence of her emotions. To live at close quarters with her was invigorating; it was what Bernard Berenson – from a safe distance – might have called life-enhancing; but it was not conducive to the serious study of mediaeval history. Moreover, the weather had now recovered and for days on end there was not a cloud in the sky, while at night a great yellow moon would hoist itself into the sky to smile benevolently down on Madame Taunay's unruly ménage. With my attention so constantly distracted, it would have been difficult to maintain the pretence of working, even if there had been nothing else to divert me from my purpose. But there was something else, something that scattered the remains of those dutiful and (as it turned out) pointless good intentions and ensured my willing surrender.

Among the mixed bag of foreign students who had somehow floated into Madame Taunay's friendly net there was a young Finnish girl. She was a few months younger than I and even more unsophisticated. She spoke a little French and not a word of English and she was very shy. As the more boisterous of the students formed themselves into groups which romped and scrapped good-naturedly with each other, she and I found ourselves fitting into none of them but slipping instead into a kind of intimacy which was tender and inarticulate and as innocent as daybreak.

Sitting in the freshness of the morning under the trees in Madame Taunay's orchard, or slipping away to swim in the gentle Loir where it meandered among the buttercups, or whispering our shy endearments under the stars, we must have been like two children half conscious of some other, adult world beyond the boundaries of our inexperience. To say that we fell in love would be to misuse the term: we were neither of us mature enough to know what love meant. Our relationship (if I try to be objective about it) was insubstantial to the point of triviality – and yet it was marvellous too, because it gave us in our innocence just a glimpse of a realm we must one day explore more fully. It was cut short, when we went our separate ways soon afterwards, before it could be complicated by emotions we were not yet equipped to handle, and without exacting from us the price which life too often demands of pain or remorse.

Or so I thought when I looked back on the experience after we had parted. We had not exchanged assurances of eternal devotion; we were too timid or too wise to deal in such grand stakes. But we had spoken with the optimism of youth – and forgetting, in that summer brightness, the shadow that was creeping over Europe – of coming together again the following year, perhaps in Finland, perhaps in England, to take up where we had left off. But the following year was

1940 and by the time the next summer came around Finland had been
invaded and England was waiting her turn, and it was to be nearly ten
years before each of us could learn how the other had fared. When that
day came, there was a surprise in store for me: but that must wait its
turn.

Madame Taunay drove us both into Tours and under her benevolent
and humorous eye we said our farewells. While she set off for her
northern homeland, I turned my face south again, exchanging the
sunlit meadows about Ruillé-sur-Loir for a cloud-filled valley in the
Basses-Alpes and the old stone house under the shadow of the Glandaz
where I began this tale.

The house was called the Château Perdyer and it was in fact a small
mediaeval fortress set in a deep valley surrounded by mountains. When
I arrived, tired and hungry after an all-night journey, thunder was
rumbling among the peaks and the atmosphere seemed full of menace.
It was a far cry from the gentle banks of the Loir; and the change of
scene was accompanied by a sudden worsening of the political
situation. I had barely had time to refresh myself after my journey
before a report reached us from the neighbouring village of Menglon;
three classes of French reservists had been called to the colours.

This was on 21 August and next morning we waited impatiently for
the newspapers, which only reached the isolated Château Perdyer at
noon. When they arrived, they contained the startling news of the
non-aggression pact which was signed that day between Nazi Germany
and the Soviet Union. Here was the explanation for the rumours that
were reaching even our remote fastness. With armies being mobilized
all over Europe, with air-raid precautions and plans for the evacuation
of major cities, it looked as though the next few days must be decisive.

For three weeks my diary had made no mention of politics. Now I
tried, like everyone else, to understand the significance of this
unexpected development. Had the Russians betrayed us or had they
simply lost patience with the British and French, who talked of
collective security against Nazi Germany but could not bring themselves
to co-operate with the Soviet Union? Did the Russians imagine they
could trust Hitler, who had written in *Mein Kampf* that an alliance with
the Soviet Union would be 'a catastrophe for Germany'? And what
about his allies? The Nazi-Soviet *coup de théâtre*, I wrote (this was on
23 August):

. . . has provoked mixed reactions: the Japanese are annoyed & do not conceal it; the Italians swallow their surprise & hail it as a triumph for the Rome-Berlin axis, though what good it will do Italy it is hard to see. Perhaps a French commentator is right in saying that it is a desperate move by a Hitler who sees all other paths blocked . . . But then again, a desperate Hitler probably means trouble – & soon.

About one thing there could be no doubt: however cynical or misguided Hitler's move might be, its objective was to shake the resolution of the democracies and induce them to betray Poland as they had betrayed Czechoslovakia the year before. And, given the record of the democracies, it was impossible to be certain that he would not succeed. It looked as though at any moment the Nazis might stage a *coup d'état* and announce the annexation of Danzig. In that case, would Britain and France honour their obligations to Poland – and if so, 'perhaps we will wake up to a world war tomorrow?'

But the Germans did not move and the allied position seemed firm: French mobilization was well advanced and on the 25th we learned that the British fleet too was now on a war footing. What did it all mean: that war was now inevitable – or that at last, after all the shilly-shallying and the evasions and the appeasement of the last two years, the democracies had nerved themselves to call Hitler's bluff?

The date 27 August fell on a Sunday and for the first time since I had arrived in the Alps the weather was glorious. The mountains which stood over us, and which I had found so forbidding, lost their austerity. The air was sparkling and the overgrown garden of the Château Perdyer was full of the scent of pines and the sound of bees. Sitting there in the sunshine it was hard to believe that madness, like an uncontrollable tide, was creeping up on Europe and that far beyond our little tranquil world, under that same sun, men in half a dozen countries were on the march towards destruction. But so it was on that last long Sunday of peacetime: every time we turned on the wireless, the peace was shattered by news of preparations for war . . .

Feeling desperately in need of an escape from the tension, I determined that I would climb the Glandaz that night. The idea had been proposed earlier by André, the young nephew of my hostess. André was a climber and he had promised to take me up all the mountains around Chatillon; but within days of my arrival he had received his mobilization papers and had gone off to join his unit. Before he left, he gave me a piece of advice. Much the best way to climb

the Glandaz, he said, was at night and under a full moon. There was
nothing difficult about it: it was just a long steep walk, and that way
you could be on the peak at daybreak and watch the dawn come up
over the whole of the surrounding range. Now that the weather had
cleared, my opportunity was at hand – and the way things were going it
might not be there for long. What clinched matters was the fact that as
the clouds had cleared away the night before, I had seen the moon for
the first time in a week, and it was just coming up to the full.

After an early supper I set out for Chatillon with a blanket slung over
my shoulder and a pouch containing a thick crust of bread and some
cold meat. From Chatillon I found the path without difficulty and
followed it steeply uphill through pinewoods, with the moon glancing
in at me through the trees. Above the treeline the moonlight was so
bright that there was no mistaking my way and before midnight I was
on a plateau just short of the crest, where André had told me I should
find a shepherd's hut with a barn beside it where I could sleep. There
they both were, just as he had said, waiting to welcome me in the bright
stillness. And here, I thought wonderingly, as I looked round that
brilliant horizon and listened to the tremendous silence, was I, lifted as
far as I could well be above the clamour of that remote world of foolish
mortals into a real world of things elemental and eternal. Gratefully, I
cleared a space among the sheep's droppings on the floor of the barn,
rolled myself in my blanket and tried to sleep.

Whether from discomfort or excitement, I slept only fitfully and at
4.15 I saw the moon set. Then I dozed off again, and woke with a start
an hour later to find the shepherd standing over me in surprise.
Throwing off the blanket, I ran the few hundred yards to the summit,
with the ground grey at my feet and a great surge of brightness welling
up in the eastward sky. At first it was a pure white light, but with every
moment that passed there was more colour in it until, as I caught my
breath on the peak, the sun, that 'blood-red eye of day', seemed to peer
at me over the horizon and then shouldered its way up into the pale sky
and brought the world to life. That must have been the way of it, I
thought in wonderment, on the day the world began.

One can escape like that once in a way, but never for long – though I
don't suppose I realized it at the time. Down below again a few hours
later I was back in the confusion of that other world that was sliding
into disaster. The politicians went through their futile motions, the
headlines grew blacker and the preparations for war more frantic,

until, after breakfast on the morning of 1 September we heard the news that the Germans had invaded Poland and the Luftwaffe had bombed Warsaw. It was time to be on my way.

Quickly I packed my few belongings (I had left the bicycle in Tours and that was the last I would see of it) and arranged for a car to take me to Die, on the main line to the north.

The Paris train was crowded, but it left on time and ran through darkened stations where French soldiers waited for transport to the front. There was no certainty about onward connections and when I saw the barricades in the Gare de Lyon and the crowds of troops and evacuees I was prepared for every sort of delay. Instead, as though by magic, I caught a bus at once to the Gare St Lazare and jumped on a train just leaving for Dieppe; and at Dieppe I had barely time ⬤ cup of coffee and a croissant before the boat sailed in brilliant sunshine out into the Channel. The boat was packed and overhead squadrons of British bombers were heading for France. When we put into Newhaven, the sun was still shining on Beachy Head and the Seven Sisters, and then on the silver cloud of anti-aircraft balloons flying over London – the only indication that this calm evening of Saturday, 2 September 1939 was different from any other.

When we drew into Victoria, I was surprised to find that England was still at peace. My brother Douglas was just going out to supper with some friends and I joined them and ate heartily; I had had nothing but a few croissants and a bar of chocolate since leaving the Château Perdyer just twenty-four hours earlier. After that we made our way through the blackout in which cars and buses crept uncertainly through the darkened streets until, just before we reached home, a tremendous storm broke and the whole southern sky was illuminated by flashes of sheet lightning and a deluge of rain cleared the streets.

Next morning the skies had cleared again and London looked deceptively serene when we turned on the wireless to hear Neville Chamberlain announcing that we were at war. It was impossible not to feel a deep sympathy for him as he told us in an anguished voice that 'All I have wished for and aimed at in my public life has crashed in ruins' – but there was relief too in the knowledge that this was the end of the half-truths and the evasions of the past two years. Of what war really meant and how long it would take – and how it would end – we knew nothing. But there was something heartening in the thought that now, at last, we were out in the open, with a clear road ahead and no sophistries to confuse us or undermine our sense of purpose. When the air-raid warning sounded immediately after the prime minister's broadcast and we went a little sheepishly to find our gas masks and make our way to the basement shelter, it was almost a disappointment to find that it was a false alarm.

It was not to be the only false alarm before we got going on the road ahead.

PART TWO

Head in the Clouds
(1939–41)

4

Ten days later I went back to Oxford, where I was surprised (for the next term was not due to start for another six weeks) to find a number of my friends assembled on the same errand. With a wonderful conceit and unknown to each other we had come to the conclusion that the war could not be won without us and had arranged to see the joint recruiting board which had been established in Oxford to interview candidates for all three services.

We were all in high spirits. I don't know why this should have been so and I doubt whether any of us could have given a very clear answer. Partly, of course, it reflected the fact that we were young and there was the scent of adventure in the air; but there was more to it than that. There was the feeling that after all the uncertainties of the past year, after the humiliation of Munich and of having to look on passively while so much was done in our name that was shameful and degrading, things had suddenly come right side up again and the future looked clean and confident. And that seemed enough to go on with.

Something else which it is easy to forget is the fact that in 1939 Britain was not the little offshore island she is today, but a world power – in outward appearance *the* world power, the hub of an empire whose permanence we took for granted. She had at her command immense economic power, an unrivalled navy and a chain of colonial possessions strung out across the world. With these vast resources and the physical control we still exercised wherever it seemed most vital, from Gibraltar and Malta to Suez and Aden, and beyond to India and Ceylon and Singapore, there was an instinctive assurance about the nation's response to the Nazi threat. Now that an invigorating sense of a common purpose had banished the doubts and anxieties of appeasement, it was not surprising that young men should have been eager to join up or that, when the first urgent call went out for volunteers to act as air-raid wardens (for it was generally assumed that the country would at once be subjected to fierce attack from the air) individuals whom one had thought of as irrevocably idle or self-indulgent suddenly disappeared and, when next seen wearing tin hats and armbands, turned out to be working long night shifts on the roofs of hospitals or blocks of flats.

When nothing happened to lend colour to these expectations – indeed, when nothing seemed to be happening at all to justify the inconveniences and the restrictions which were imposed on us – it was no more surprising (although it was not very logical either) that the public's morale should sink as suddenly as it had climbed on the outbreak of war. The blackout was a nuisance; London's theatres and cinemas had all been closed (and there was no television); trains and buses were suddenly slower and dirtier and more crowded than they had been before; and in the first wartime budget, apart from all the usual tax increases on things like beer and cigarettes, income tax was raised by more than thirty per cent to a record seven shillings and sixpence in the pound. What was the point of it all, people began to ask, when the very next day Warsaw fell and Poland's brave resistance came to an end without our having lifted a finger to help?

It was out of the resulting mood of disillusionment that someone now coined the phrase which epitomized our discontents. I don't remember when we first began to talk of the 'phoney war', but it was an appropriately sceptical label for the period of inactivity which extended itself through the autumn of 1939 into an exceptionally hard winter and beyond it through the whole of the spring of 1940. During that time, people who had wound themselves up to a pitch of expectancy, who were prepared for a certain amount of self-sacrifice and were even ready to do their best (although they felt some embarrassment about it) to be heroic, were upset to find instead that they were merely to be inconvenienced. It was demoralizing to feel themselves suspended like this in a kind of limbo of indecision.

I was one of these. When my turn had come to face that recruiting board in Oxford, I had applied to join the RAF. 'Flying duties?' a brisk sergeant-major had asked before pushing me forward. 'Why yes,' I replied; it had not occurred to me that there was anything else to be done in the air force apart from flying. But during the few moments that remained before I was summoned before the board, I began to have doubts. I knew nothing of mechanics; navigation I felt sure would be quite beyond me; radio as far as I was concerned was a closed book. Perhaps, I thought doubtfully, they would let me be an air gunner . . . The sergeant-major settled the issue for me. 'In you go,' he said, 'I've put you down for a pilot.'

The board consisted of three retired officers, one from each of the services. They looked at me and grunted. 'Pilot, eh,' said one of them and he pushed a pad of paper across to me. 'Calculate the height of that hut by the sun,' he ordered, pointing out of the window.

Unnerved, I picked up a pencil, drew the hut, put the sun in one corner of what it would be flattering to call my sketch, and came to a dead stop. 'Well,' said one of my inquisitors with impatience, and I had to confess that I had no idea how to do it.

He seemed astonished and asked why I had not prepared myself for such questions. Because it had not occurred to me that they would ask me anything of the sort, I answered. He asked me what kind of questions I had expected to be asked. 'Oh,' I said, 'I thought you might ask me why I wanted to join the air force – that sort of thing.'

'And why *do* you want to join the air force?' asked the army officer, who was probably no more than a brigadier, though he might have been a field marshal for all I knew.

In my reply I made a tactical error: I told him the truth. I suppose I was too young to know how dangerous this could be, but I should have realized that my answer was not likely to win me friends in any quarter. I said that at school I had been so bored by the OTC (the Officers Training Corps) that I had promised myself never to have anything to do with the army; and that as I was often seasick I did not think I should be much use to the navy; which left only the air force.

My frankness provoked a mixed response. The soldier almost choked and the airman leaned back in his chair and rolled his eyes – but it was the sailor who saved my bacon by laughing, and five minutes later I was on my way with a slip of paper to say that I was 'recommended' – it seemed an unexpected word in the circumstances – 'for training as a pilot'. The RAF, I was informed, would communicate with me in its own good time.

I had to be content with that and I assumed, wrongly, as it turned out, that the period of waiting would be a short one. Back among my friends in the Mitre, I joined in the general euphoria as we compared notes about our interviews and forecast adventurous and distinguished careers for each other. My diary records it as a cheerful occasion and it was only when I was in the train on my way back to London that I felt 'rather depressed, as it was impossible not to wonder how many of these people I would see again'.

Such thoughts never persisted for long, however, and for the time being there were agreeable distractions. The authorities, aware of the need to bolster civilian morale, allowed places of entertainment to reopen and for a spell there were some good things to see and hear. I remember in particular what was probably the best production ever staged of *The Importance of Being Earnest*, in which Edith Evans as Lady Bracknell was backed up by Peggy Ashcroft and John Gielgud and Jack Hawkins; and then there were lunchtime concerts at the National Gallery, where for a shilling I heard Moseiwitch playing Chopin; and when the Queen's Hall reopened, there was a splendid inaugural concert in which Myra Hess played Beethoven's fourth concerto and the programme ended with Tchaikovsky's *Pathétique*, whose sad and searching melodies seemed attuned to the times.

As the weeks succeeded each other, though, and the RAF showed no sign of needing my services (what it was short of at the time was aircraft, rather than pilots to fly them), it became harder than ever to be content with such a butterfly existence. One by one my friends were called up, and then my brother Douglas, until, as I put it in my diary, 'everyone in London except me seems to be in uniform or bald – and some of course are both – but I am neither'. But then, just when I needed it, I had a stroke of luck. A master whom I had particularly liked at Sedbergh had recently been appointed headmaster of a school in Devon and the war had deprived him of two or three members of his staff. Desperate – I could only assume – he sent a telegram asking if I could help him out. I jumped at the chance and on 9 November, just after hearing of an attempt on Hitler's life, I caught a train to Taunton and then on through the sun-filled West Country, to find my way at last to West Buckland on the edge of Exmoor.

By this time the war was looking phoney indeed. While we had undertaken no offensive action of any kind, the Germans, having subdued Poland, had scored a number of successes at our expense. Before the war was a month old, their submarines had sunk twenty-six British merchant ships and the aircraft carrier *Courageous*. In October a U-boat penetrated the defences of Scapa Flow to sink the battleship *Royal Oak* as it lay at anchor, with the loss of 800 lives. Two days later came news of the first German air raid on Britain, when a dozen bombers attacked the dockyard at Rosyth. From time to time there were reports that the French were planning an offensive on what we rather self-consciously called the 'Western front' but this never materialized, and meanwhile the RAF confined its activities to dropping leaflets over Germany. There were even persistent reports about a 'peace offensive', in which the Italians as mediators were trying to persuade Britain and France to agree to a settlement with Germany which would recognize the disappearance of Poland from the map.

It was all both puzzling and dispiriting. Had the ghost of appeasement been finally laid or not? My diary shows that I was suspicious, but (on 1 October): 'I think it is pretty definite at last that Britain and France will never sign a peace treaty with Hitler.' One reassuring sign was the presence in Chamberlain's cabinet of Winston Churchill, who now began to emerge as the nation's conscience. There was nothing automatic or inevitable about this. Until the outbreak of war, a large section of British opinion had shared Chamberlain's antipathy for the man who had been his most relentless critic during the years of appeasement. It was by the speeches he broadcast during the winter of 1939–40, which gave us something to hold on to in the midst of so much uncertainty, that Churchill established himself as the leader who, when the moment came, would be able to steer us on to a more heroic course.

In this long period of inactivity and misgiving I was lucky to have work to do and I threw myself into it with enthusiasm. West Buckland was a small public school, splendidly situated on the southern slope of Exmoor. It was as remote as Sedbergh and we saw nothing whatever of the war. Almost our only link with the outside world was the wireless, from which we heard about the few developments of any significance in a war that seemed otherwise to have gone to sleep. We learned of the brave fight put up by the *Rawalpindi*, a P & O liner converted into a naval patrol ship, which was sunk by Hitler's 'pocket battleship', the *Deutschland* at the end of November; and a couple of weeks later the *Deutschland*'s sister ship, the *Graf Spee*, fought an inconclusive engagement with three British cruisers in the south Atlantic and ended up by scuttling herself outside Montevideo. Such excitements were rare and with one of the other masters who was a radio enthusiast I used to listen more to foreign broadcasts. From Boston I enjoyed hearing my second brother, David, who had emigrated to the United States a few months before the war began. He had found himself a job running the foreign news broadcasts for the *Christian Science Monitor* and took every opportunity to urge the United States to come into the war before it was too late. And like many other people in England at the time we used to listen avidly to 'Lord Haw-Haw', the German propagandist whose delightfully scrambled Oxford accent and garbled information provided some of the best entertainment available to us in that first unreal phase of the war.

In the way of real news there was one story in those last months of 1939 that had a particular significance for me. The Russians, after helping to carve up Poland, had turned their attention to the four small states on the Baltic and had forced three of them – Esthonia, Latvia and Lithuania – to sign treaties which led eventually to their being swallowed up into the Soviet empire, leaving the fourth in uncomfortable isolation. This was Finland, which refused to sign and instead mobilized its army, with the air of a tiny but very resolute David, to defy the threats from its giant neighbour. To the rest of the world it looked like a lost cause if ever there was one. After a month of steadily increasing pressure, we were incredulous when we heard at the end of November that the Russians had invaded Finland – and that the Finns were fighting back.

Like everyone else, but with a more personal interest, I thought the Finns must be romancing when they told us of ski patrols in white uniforms breaking up the Russian formations and taking large numbers of prisoners. We were sceptical when they claimed to have knocked out seventy Russian tanks in the first week of the fighting. We wanted – and I wanted more than anyone – to believe stories so hearteningly improbable. They offered a striking contrast with our own inactivity in the face of a slow series of reverses; but could they be true?

Amazingly, they were, and as the days stretched into weeks and the weeks into months, with the Finns still holding their own, we realized with astonishment that what we were watching was not a flash in the pan, but as disciplined a display of national unity as we were ever to see. And since I don't suppose many people today even remember that a war took place between two such disproportionate adversaries, I am glad to recall the extraordinary courage of the Finns and the example it provided for the rest of us at a critical time.

The term ended at West Buckland in the usual flurry of feasts and pillow-fights and much singing of *For He's a Jolly Good Fellow*, and I walked the six miles to the market town of South Molton for a farewell supper with some of the younger masters. It had been an enjoyable interlude and I had little to complain about when I went off to London to spend a cheerful Christmas with my brother (now a lieutenant in the Marines) in the unreal atmosphere of an old-fashioned pea-soup fog. I went to see the RAF, only to be turned away again empty-handed, after which I set out on a round of visits to friends up and down the country which brought me finally, as though drawn by a magnet, back to Sedbergh. As the year ended, I reflected remorsefully in my diary that in a year which, from Czechoslovakia to Finland, 'has seen some of the dirtiest work for a long time', everything seemed to conspire to see to it that I went on enjoying life. Nor was there much consolation in the fact that, apart from the sailors, who were having a hard time of it (by the end of 1939 the U-boats had sunk more than 100 British merchant ships), 'nobody else seems to be much more occupied than I am'.

Peering ahead into the gloom of 1940, I prophesied 'another year or so of war', glanced at the possibility that I might be killed, but decided that:

> . . . with all its drawbacks, I feel happier with the situation as it is than I did last Easter, when we were sitting in our gardens in the sun while German tanks were rolling into Prague and Italian warships were landing men along the coast of Albania. I used to feel furious then; and especially furious because nothing was being done about it. Our leaders pretended to be taken by surprise, they held up their hands and exclaimed with pious indignation – but they were accomplices and so were we, and I hated it.* Then, we were going down the ladder and we were very near the bottom, but at least now we are going up.

Sedbergh was at its winter best: hard frost at night and day after day of brilliant, still sunshine. The boys were on holiday and with a group of masters and their wives I would catch the bus (petrol of course was rationed) up to Lilymere, high in the hills towards the Lake District, and we would skate for hours, eating our picnic lunch on the bank with heather to cushion us and the bare trees pencilled against the clear sky. Under the midday sun the fells all round were golden and warm, and as the sun sank the colours deepened. When we walked down in the late afternoon, the western sky was a red and yellow tapestry and ahead of us Sedbergh was lost in a mist, rosy at first and then darkening as the light faded, until all the foreground was a soft blue, with the line of the fells above still glowing against the pale sky.

Back in London, there were burst pipes in my brother's flat and I was happy enough – for I had nothing else to do – to return to West Buckland for the new term. Here too the cold was intense, although we only learned afterwards (at the time the details were withheld on the eccentric ground that they 'might be of use to the enemy') that this was the severest winter since Waterloo.

Such weather made it a little easier to picture the conditions in which the Finns continued to resist the Russian invaders. By the beginning of

---

* When Arthur Koestler died in 1983, I was interested to read in one of the obituary notices this remark which Koestler made to Osbert Sitwell some time in the 1940s: 'As long as you don't feel ashamed to be alive while others are put to death, you will remain what you are, an accomplice by omission.'

February it was estimated that the Russians had suffered a quarter of a million casualties without seriously denting the Finnish defence line in Karelia. Held up on land, the Russians mounted heavy air raids, and learned – as others were soon to learn – that where the defenders were determined, bombing would only stiffen their resistance. Moreover, the outside world was now sending help to the Finns, though in very small quantities. There were Canadian and Swedish volunteers fighting with the Finnish army and when I heard that a British contingent was being recruited, I wrote to ask if they were accepting volunteers. On 28 February I received a cautious reply, telling me that no one under twenty-five was being accepted but that 'some exceptions' might be made and they would be glad to interview me.

Before anything could come of this, the Russians launched a fresh and what proved to be a final assault on the Mannerheim line opposite Leningrad. For more than a fortnight the fighting was on a scale which correspondents compared to the battles in Flanders in 1915 and '16, and the Russians as they advanced had to climb over heaps of their own dead. But the Finns were hopelessly outnumbered and by the first week in March the Russians were in the suburbs of Viipuri (Viborg), the second city of Finland, and the game was almost up. On 13 March came 'the news that I have been dreading: Finland has agreed to the Russian peace terms, which include the cession of the Karelian isthmus, including Viipuri' – and it was all over.

My diary had been full of little else for weeks and I was disappointed and angry. In a sense it was like Munich all over again, in that the Finns, who had resisted so indomitably, had been allowed to go under while the rest of us stood by:

> How many lives must have been lost in those forest battles, the story of which rang in the ears of the world? But now Finland has gone the way of Abyssinia, Austria, Czechoslovakia, Albania, Poland – and the dreadful thing is that in each case we might have helped had we been really determined and really unselfish. Will the world ever become a cleaner place?

And then, with a suddenness that took us all by surprise, the phoney war came to an end. On 9 April I was walking across Piccadilly Circus (the term had just ended at West Buckland) when a placard caught my eye: GERMANS INVADE, it said – and buying a paper I found that Denmark and Norway had become the latest targets for a German attack, and that Britain had promised any help she could give them.

At least this, with the heavy fighting that followed, seemed to put paid to the idea of a dishonourable peace. It also helped to make up my mind as to what I should do next. By now I was thoroughly restless and for weeks a contingency plan had been stirring in my mind. I decided to give the RAF one more chance and if they showed no sign of making use of me, I had something else up my sleeve.

I went back to see them and was directed this time to a depot at Uxbridge. There I was given a thorough medical examination and passed as Grade 1 ('like an egg', I remarked); and when I was sworn in and given two shillings (a day's pay, it appeared) I thought my hour had struck. When do I start, I asked – and was cast down to be told that when I was wanted, I should be sent for; and that would not be for at least another six months.

It was all I needed. I had not left Oxford to become a school-master. It was time to put my plan into action. Since the RAF had finally claimed me, I could not join any other service; but England was not the only country where the RAF maintained a presence. In the early part of 1940 a military build-up was taking place in the Middle East, in anticipation of an Italian attack from Libya against Egypt and the Suez Canal. My parents were living in Egypt; I was – technically speaking – a minor. What was there to stop me going to join them and trying my luck there? The RAF in Cairo might well be short of recruits. They would welcome me with open arms – and if not, why, there would be other avenues to explore . . . I managed to give the whole idea some sort of more or less plausible cover; but the fact is – and my diary makes it plain – that its chief attraction for me was that the journey itself promised to be something of an adventure. It would certainly be more fun than sitting around any longer waiting for something to happen.

There were obstacles, but they were overcome with unexpected ease. I needed an exit permit before I could leave the country; but when I explained that I was under twenty-one and wanted to join my family, one was soon granted. (I saw no reason to complicate matters by saying that I belonged to the RAF.) My resources were limited, but I had saved a good deal from the £4 a week I was paid at West Buckland and I found that if I travelled third-class by boat and train I could get to Egypt for less than £20. Visas for France, Switzerland and Italy presented no serious problems (it must have been very easy to be a spy in 1940) and if there were any other formalities, I have forgotten them. By the end of April I was ready to go. There was heavy fighting going on in Norway, in which the RAF was closely involved, but no sign of any unusual activity elsewhere in Europe – except that there were rumours that Mussolini might enter the war if the Germans came out on top in Norway. This lent an agreeable spice to my plans, for I intended to travel overland to Vienna and there take an Italian steamer to Alexandria. It was the most attractive as well as the cheapest route.

Finding that I had a few pounds to spare, I decided at the last moment to fly to Paris. After all, I had joined the air force: I might as well see what flying was like. In this way I embarked on 1 May 1940 on what I still look back on as one of the most enjoyable journeys of my life. Paris was looking its springtime best and I spent an agreeable day wandering about the city in the sunshine, until in the evening I climbed into a third-class compartment for the long haul south and east to Venice. At daybreak I breakfasted off fresh rolls and coffee at Montreux, looking across the lake at the Dents du Midi climbing out of the early-morning mists; then on out of the mountains and across the north Italian plain until at evening, a deliciously warm, southern evening, we came to Venice.

My joints were creaking after twenty-four hours on the wooden seat and I felt I deserved an escape from austerity; besides, I had never been in Venice before and could feel no certainty about when I might see it again. So I hailed a gondola and asked for the only hotel in Venice whose name I knew: the Royal Danieli. And so it was with the sunset colours warming the old façades that I had my first sight of Venice as I sat back on the cushions of the gondola, and my body as well as my soul, in Browning's phrase, 'smoothed itself out, a long-cramped scroll'.

When I had bathed and shaken out the creases in my best suit, I came down to dinner and found that I was the only guest in the dining room (in my memory it is all marble and chandeliers), so that the element of farce was inescapable. The air was full of rumours of war and here was I, looking, I imagine like just what I was: an English undergraduate, the next best thing to an enemy alien, fresh from my third-class carriage and hoping to suggest by the sophistication of my bearing that I was perfectly at home in the best hotel in Venice. The head waiter, combining the dignity of his office with the natural charm of the Italian, entered solemnly into the joke. Having nothing else to do, he hovered at my elbow, treating me at first with exaggerated deference and then, as we both succumbed to the absurdity of the situation, becoming a companion, a confidant, almost a conspirator (for he had no love for Mussolini) and entertaining me in my solitude with kindly humour. It was a delightful evening and as I wandered afterwards along the canals under a velvet sky I chuckled appreciatively at my good fortune.

Next morning the sunlight was sparkling on the lagoon and on the little Italian steamer which was to take me on the last stage of what an Italian would call my *scappata* ('a quick dash, escapade or prank'). There were few passengers and I shared a third-class cabin with a diminutive Italian who had served in the *Bersaglieri* in that other war twenty years before. He was full of self-mockery and contemptuous of Mussolini's posturing and of the whole ridiculous business of war. Keep out of it, he advised me, and let the politicians clear up their own mess – and we turned to more interesting topics as we strolled the narrow deck and drank our *aperitivos* in the empty first-class saloon and shared a bottle of wine with our spaghetti, paying little attention to the spluttering of the radio from behind the bar.

There is a gap in my diary here, for it had been taken from me when I left England and was returned only weeks later in Egypt. My recollection is of quiet days spent reading the *Kreutzer Sonata* as we sailed down the Adriatic and through the Corinth Canal to Piraeus. Then out into the open sea and across to Rhodes, where we stayed just long enough for me to make a reconnaissance which was to bring me back many years later for my honeymoon – and finally to Alexandria, where we landed in the late afternoon of 9 May 1940.

I stayed the night with friends in Alexandria and by the time I was up and about next morning my host had gone to his office. I followed him there to say goodbye. A secretary showed me into a waiting room where there was a ticker-tape machine against the wall. As I stood looking out into the bright Egyptian sunlight, the thing began to chatter to itself and I walked across to see what was on its mind. My thoughts were elsewhere and it was a moment or two before I was startled into concentration by the extraordinary message it was unfolding before my eyes. German troops, it said, had that morning invaded Belgium and Holland and the long-awaited offensive on the Western Front was under way. The Luftwaffe had bombed Rotterdam and its Stukas – dive-bombers – were in action at many points, while German paratroops had landed before dawn to capture vital bridges and airfields. The phoney war was well and truly over. From now on it was the real thing.

5

My parents were living in a graceful old house by the Nile a few miles south of Cairo and it was there that we crouched by the radio during the weeks that followed as the shocks came piling one on top of the other: the swift destruction of Belgium and Holland; the Germans' drive though northern France which brought them to the Channel coast; the disintegration of the French armies; and the British retreat to Dunkirk.

The men of Munich slipped away into the shadows and there was reassurance in the knowledge that Churchill had at last replaced them. Apart from this and the seemingly miraculous rescue of the bulk of the British expeditionary force, there seemed nothing to hold on to, no fixed point in the world that was crumbling about us. On 14 June I listened to a broadcast from Paris – where I had strolled in the sunshine six weeks earlier – as Nazi troops marched down the Champs-Elysées; and three days later came the severest shock of all when the aged Marshal Pétain, to whom France had looked for salvation, announced instead her capitulation.

Well, we all shared the dread of those dark days; but my own situation was now not merely frustrating but absurd. In fact, as I discovered when I presented myself at RAF headquarters in Cairo, it appeared in the eyes of the authorities deeply suspicious. Nor could I pretend that this was altogether unreasonable. As a member – however insignificant and inactive – of His Majesty's forces, I had left England in time of war, had travelled across potentially hostile territory and in a ship belonging to what had now become a belligerent enemy, to arrive in the nick of time on a safe foreign shore. If I had expected to be greeted with open arms, I was quickly disabused. The stern-faced officer who interviewed me said flatly that he did not believe a word I was telling him and that if my story were true he would have me sent home to England to be court-martialled as a deserter.

It was Mussolini who inadvertently rescued me from this ignominy.

Italy's entry into the war had closed the Mediterranean to British shipping and there was no way of sending me home (even if this bureaucratic approach had triumphed) except round the Cape of Good Hope. With shipping space at a premium and weightier problems to be resolved, even the stern-faced officer (his sternness, I soon realized, masked a deep sense of personal insecurity) could see that his suggestion was ridiculous. The court-martial idea was dropped and we turned to more realistic alternatives.

It appeared that there was only one RAF station within reach where I could be taught to fly and that was in Kenya. All sorts of difficulties were put in the way of my getting there, but by now I was almost in sight of my goal and I was not to be put off. At last it was agreed that I should travel to Nairobi as soon as transport was available. Impatiently, I occupied myself as best I could in a Cairo which had now become part of a war zone, with the Italians making threatening noises along the Libyan border. I found odd jobs to do in soldiers' canteens and around the office of the *Egyptian Gazette*, and the rest of the time I played tennis and bathed and walked with my father in the desert in the cool of the evenings, 'when shadows pass gigantic on the sand', and came back to sit after dinner on the roof of the old house watching the sailing boats sliding down the river in the moonlight. It was a life which would have been enviable at any other time but which left me restless for news of my departure.

Hearing none, I telephoned one day to enquire and was told that an aircraft had been chartered and was to leave next day; had I not received my instructions? I had not, but I hurried into Cairo and found there two other recruits with whom I was to leave at dawn for Nairobi. One of them was a member of the Palestine Police, and I recall this with interest because this was the first time I remember hearing about Palestine, where the Arab rebellion provoked by Britain's encouragement of Jewish immigration had been suspended on the outbreak of war. And the other, by an interesting coincidence, was a young Jew named Ray Shohet, whose father had been born in Turkey and had later moved to Egypt and acquired British citizenship. Between the two of them they gave me my first glancing acquaintance with a problem which was to monopolize my attention much later on.

Together we embarked on a kind of mad treasure hunt around the depots of Cairo in the course of which we accumulated a lot of thoroughly unsuitable equipment (heavy overcoats and boots in the relentless heat of the Egyptian summer) and learned that we were now aircraftsmen class V (there was nothing lower) and were told to stand by at dawn next day, 15 July.

The Palestine policeman for some reason fell by the wayside and so it was Shohet and I who at 6 a.m. boarded a little De Havilland Dragonfly for the first lap of our journey to Kenya. This took us for a thousand miles or so due south to Khartoum and of all the flying I ever did it was by far the most uncomfortable. The Dragonfly was a twin-engined biplane with seats for half a dozen passengers. It needed to refuel every two or three hours, so that we were forever climbing and descending through the bumpy desert air – and the journey took twelve hours. I was very glad when we reached Khartoum.

After a shower, Shohet and I went in search of supper and were directed to the airmen's mess – and this too was at first a disconcerting experience. Once you get the feel of it, an airmen's mess can be a vastly entertaining environment; but on first acquaintance, and especially on a summer night in the tropics, it can look like something out of Dante's Inferno. That night in Khartoum, still queasy from the day's buffeting, I found myself at a loss among the beer-stained tables, the greasy plates of fried eggs and baked beans on toast, and the sweating crowd of half-naked airmen swaying to the strains of 'Roll out the Barrel' vamped out *fortissimo* on the piano. But Shohet saved the day for me with a display of virtuosity which ensured him a place for ever in my memory.

Mumbling something about 'having a go', he edged his way through the crowd and waited until the reigning pianist, cigarette glued to the corner of his mouth, paused at the end of a chorus to refill his glass. In a flash, Shohet had taken his place and begun to play.

I marvelled at his presumption – but I had no need to worry. As he played, the tumult about him began to subside and there fell on that disorderly assembly a wondering silence. When he came to the end of his opening number – it was the *Rhapsody in Blue* – there were shouts of approval, which were hushed again as he switched to Schubert and presently to Chopin and Bach and the blues . . . It was like the immortal scene from the film *Genevieve* in which Kay Kendall, before the embarrassed gaze of her boy friend, plays the trumpet in a dance band. The airmen's mess had never seen anything like it: it was a triumph. Men queued to buy Shohet a drink, they refused to let him go, and when at last I prised him loose and we went off to find somewhere to sleep, I basked in his reflected glory.

Next day we flew on over the southern Sudan and into Uganda, the Dragonfly lurching as uncomfortably as ever as the pilot swung it from side to side to show us the game in the swamps below, until we fetched up for the night at a little airstrip at Tororo on the Kenyan border. And from here it was only a hop, skip and a jump next morning by way of Kisumu and a corner of Lake Victoria to Nairobi.

Our arrival coincided with a quickening of the tempo of the war in Europe. The fall of France, which gave the Germans control of the Channel coast, had put the Luftwaffe within easy striking distance of targets all over southern and eastern England. All through July 1940, while the U-boats were taking a heavy toll of British shipping in the Channel and the north Atlantic, the Luftwaffe carried out sporadic raids on coastal ports and convoys. Behind all this activity we could assume only that Hitler's next objective was the invasion of Britain.*

First, though, the Germans had to knock out the RAF, and this was Goering's aim when he launched his bombers against airfields and radar stations along the southern coast of England on 12 August, in what was the first strike in the Battle of Britain. In retrospect we can see the pattern, but at the time, and especially to an aircraftsman class V who was five thousand miles away, things were not so clear. My diary for 12 August is full of my own frustration at the fact that our flying course still had not started. Instead, I had a five-hour spell of guard duty at Nairobi airfield, which I occupied in reading and staring impatiently out over the dry grassland to the Ngong hills, wondering if I should ever cease to be a distant observer and become a participant in these great events.

Three days later the tone of the diary changes abruptly. With Shohet and twenty-three others I had been taken by lorry to a smaller airfield at Eastleigh on the other side of Nairobi, the training course had started, and at the end of our first working day I wrote: '. . . the change puts a completely new complexion on life. After spending a month at Nairobi throughout which my hands, metaphorically speaking, were never out of my pockets, I am as happy as a king at having work to do and at feeling that after all this time I am on the road to somewhere.'

How easy it is to get the best out of youth – if you only know how. For the next three months we worked harder than I have ever worked in my life. Our living quarters were spartan and the food indifferent. From reveille at 5.15 a.m. we were kept on the move with PT and lectures and navigation exercises – and in time with the flying itself – until we reeled off duty at six in the evening, our heads spinning with aerodynamic shapes and dihedral angles and the recoil action of the breech block on the Browning gun and I don't know what else; and if we didn't exactly enjoy it, it was still one of the most

* The invasion, as we now know, was scheduled to start on 15 September 1940.

satisfying periods of my life.

What made it so was the atmosphere at Eastleigh, which was quite unlike any RAF station I was to know later. The flying school was a tiny affair, improvised by a few individuals who had somehow found themselves a place under the protective umbrella of the RAF. The commanding officer was a South African and as good a leader as anyone could ask, and the instructors were a mixed bag of settlers and reservists who knew how to fly and had signed on for the duration. Discipline was strict, but it was administered with a sense of humour and relaxed as soon as we were outside the formal confines of the course. In the context of the times, it is not surprising that the whole thing seemed marvellously worthwhile, or that my unrest at last was stilled and I settled down contentedly to a life as different as it could well be from anything I had known before.

It was in many ways nasty and brutish: the airmen's mess was a very different environment from the JCR at Christ Church. And if one stopped to think about it, it was also likely to be short. The reports that now came thick and fast of the progress of the Battle of Britain made that plain enough. But there was companionship and an end in view and the sense (though of course we would not have dreamed of putting it like that to each other) that England needed us. Above all, there was good leadership – and on top of that the sheer fun of learning to fly, of straining forward towards the day when, our apprenticeship behind us, we would have earned the freedom of that wide African sky. After the long decline, my spirits soared.

Best of all was the company in which I found myself. Most of the other 'pupil pilots' were older than myself, farmers and colonial servants and remittance men who had forsaken a more comfortable existence in the East African colonies to sign on with the likes of Shohet and myself. We were to spend a year cheek by jowl with each other, undergoing many vicissitudes and celebrating our small triumphs together, and when I look back on our association it is with amusement and a wistful sense of affection. They were good friends to me, who must have seemed in their eyes very immature. I am glad I did not know that I should outlive all but a few of them.

By now there was no mistaking the importance of the struggle that was going on for control of the skies over south-eastern England. Its outcome, we all knew, must affect the immediate course of the war, and our own future as well, and every evening we crowded round the wireless in the mess to hear the tally from the day's fighting. The communiqués spoke (with exaggeration, as we now know) of twenty or thirty, or fifty – and on one day even a hundred – German planes brought down; but the fighter losses on our side were fearsome too, and there were anxious questions in our minds about the numbers in reserve, not only of aircraft but of pilots as well. On 7 September the Germans switched their attack from the Kentish airfields to London and we heard that 300 people had been killed and 1,300 injured in the first big raid on the capital. At the time no one had a clear idea of the effect that bombing might have on the life of a city or the morale of its inhabitants, and there was an uneasy undertone to the bravado with which, turning away from the wireless, we roared out our bawdy choruses in the airmen's mess. There was no difficulty about rousing us at 5.15 next morning for another day's work in preparation for the day when we would be needed to fill the gaps in the line.

That day seemed very distant but now my attention was focused as never before on the business in hand. In this I found myself initially at a disadvantage. When the instructor asked, at one of the first lectures of the course, whether there was anyone among us who did not know how an internal combustion engine worked, my heart sank when mine was the only hand to be raised. But such embarrassments were a small price to pay for the delight of being fully occupied at last; and when, after another week, we had our first taste of flying, I was relieved to find that I took to it as readily as anyone and was one of the first to attain the dignity of 'going solo'.

In that funny little circus at Eastleigh we had only five aircraft, four Tiger Moths and an ancient Avro Tutor. They had been acquired from private owners in East Africa and it was sternly impressed upon us that there were no replacements to be had between Cairo and Cape Town. We treated them in consequence with anxious solicitude, as one might treat the family pony or an ageing and well-loved fox terrier. No harm came to them at our hands, but one of the Tiger Moths had a narrow escape and it is amusing for me – now – to recall that my most alarming experience of the war, not excluding some later uncertainties, was in a Tiger Moth far removed from any scene of battle. It happened like this.

Once our flying training was under way, the day started with what we grandiloquently called the 'Dawn Patrol'. In plain terms, this meant that five of us would go off soon after sunrise to practise whatever was the latest manoeuvre in which we had been instructed. In a machine like the Tiger Moth, none of these presented much of a problem for a beginner, once he had gained a little confidence, for a Tiger Moth practically flew itself. If the pilot, in looping the loop or executing a slow roll, got himself into a scrape, all he had to do was to take his hands and feet off the controls and the aircraft would do its best to get him out of it. So when I flew off at six o'clock one morning in late September, I hadn't a care in the world. It was three weeks since I had gone solo and there was no reason for me or anyone else to doubt that forty-five minutes later I should be back to hand the aircraft over to someone else.

One of the great advantages of learning to fly in Kenya was the reliability of the weather, which was almost always perfect: clear skies, light winds and even temperatures. In the autumn, though, with the approach of the monsoon, clouds sometimes gathered in the early morning, to disperse after an hour or two in the warmth of the sun. Since we had no experience of flying 'blind' and since the Tiger Moth's dashboard was bare of all but the most elementary instruments, we were under the strictest orders to avoid going into or above the clouds.

That morning the clouds gathered as usual while I was going through my exercises and when I turned for home I decided, instead of going demurely home in their shadow, to climb into the bright sunlight above. Things happen quickly in the air and in a moment I found I was in the cloud – and out of control. For when you fly blind like that, all your senses betray you. You think you are climbing, until you notice that your airspeed is rising and you are travelling so fast that you must be in a dive. You feel sure you are flying straight and level, but the turn-and-bank indicator shows that your wings are at an angle of forty-five degrees to the ground, and you have to force yourself against all your instincts to throw the joystick in the opposite direction to right yourself. It is a hair-raising experience, which I can liken only to the sensation of walking blindfold and fast on a surface full of unpredictable steps and declivities – and of knowing that if you lose your footing and fall (in airmen's terms, if you lose flying speed and stall) there is nothing at all beneath you except several thousand feet of empty air . . .

It seemed safer to go up than down and cautiously I began to climb, forcing myself to disregard my own senses and put my trust in those impersonal dials in front of me. The cloud must have been thickening rapidly for it was a full fifteen minutes (and it felt like a lifetime) before the twilight about me began to lighten and presently, with a relief that I can still recapture, I broke through to see above me 'that little tent of blue men call the sky'. The sweat was pouring off me and as I levelled out and reviewed my situation I realized that I was not out of the wood yet. It was preferable by far to be above the cloud rather than in it, but there remained the problem of getting down again. On every side of me there extended an apparently unbroken sea of cloud and with the ground completely obscured I had next to no idea of my whereabouts.

For half an hour I flew backwards and forwards on opposite compass courses, making allowance for the wind and hoping in this way to stay in roughly the same place while I waited for the cloud to break up. Whenever I saw the semblance of a gap, I made for it and tried to spiral down through it, only to find myself almost immediately back in the cloud. To go on down was too chancy when I could see nothing in these depths of cotton wool, for somewhere close at hand were the Ngong Hills. Rather than risk running into them I climbed again on to that blessed blue roof of the world. But then there forced itself on my attention a new anxiety. I had been flying now for almost two hours. The Tiger Moth's petrol tank held nineteen gallons and we reckoned its consumption at seven gallons an hour. At most I could count on staying airborne for another forty-five minutes. Within that time I must do one of three things: make my descent through the cloud (avoiding the hills) and find my way back to the airfield; wait for another gap and go down through it and perhaps make a forced landing on whatever suitable open ground I might find; or bail out – leaving the faithful Tiger Moth to look after itself. Of the three, the last was the most unthinkable. It was not just that I was reluctant to jump off into space with my parachute – though I was. But how could I return to Eastleigh with my tail between my legs to report that I had lost, had *abandoned*, one of our precious flock? I had to get down.

For another twenty minutes I flew east and then west and then east again in that beautiful but relentless world of blue and white. And then, just as I judged that, come what might, I must take the plunge and go down out of it, I spotted a gap. It was small and when I came over it I could see nothing I recognized through the swirling edges of the cloud. Carefully, in a tight spiral, I circled down, to find myself in a valley whose sides were lost in the cloud, but where – a blessed sight – a road ran between cultivated fields. One end of that road must lead to Nairobi: but which end? I made my choice, noting an open field where I could return to make a forced landing if necessary, and set off to follow the road. Ten anxious minutes and I saw the suburbs and then the New Stanley, where we would foregather on our evenings off, and I knew I was home.

A few minutes more and there was Eastleigh and a crowd waiting to witness the return of the prodigal. I made a bumpy landing and clambered out on to the tarmac. I had been up for two hours and twenty minutes and there were between two and three gallons left in the petrol tank. The mixture of relief and satisfaction I felt gave way to apprehension as I saw the commanding officer approaching and braced myself for the blast. He looked at me sternly, but there was an encouraging twinkle in his eye.

'You must have had a sticky time of it up there,' he observed. And apart from a few explanations, that was that.

In the ideal conditions which Kenya offered, with clear skies and constant sunshine, we made rapid progress. Soon we were all flying 'solo' and the idea that in time we might actually make some contribution to winning the war began to seem less remote and fanciful. But learning to fly a Tiger Moth was only the first step, and the easiest one, on a longish road. Just as we were beginning to wonder where the next step would take us, we learned, in the wake of a visit from some bigwig from the RAF command in Cairo, that our destination at the end of the course would be 'somewhere in Europe'. This was not hard to identify, since in the autumn of 1940 there was nowhere on the continent of Europe where we could go without fighting our way ashore. It had to be England.

I was delighted. It was less than six months since I had left England for that carefree journey to Egypt, and I had never quite shaken off the feeling that I had as it were walked out of the house just a moment before the roof fell in. Dunkirk, the Battle of Britain, the Blitz – all these had gone on, and had involved my friends, while I was playing tennis in Cairo or kicking my heels in the sunshine of Kenya. My brother Douglas, now in charge of a searchlight battery at Portsmouth, would write to me casually mentioning 'two or three air raids today', and several of my Oxford contemporaries who had got off to a quicker start than I were already on active service. I was impatient to join them rather than remain any longer a mere spectator, and a distant one at that.

So at the end of October 1940 we climbed into a train for the long descent from Nairobi to Mombasa and the ship which was to take us home. We were not quite done with Africa yet, for when we awoke next morning five thousand feet lower, among palm trees and bright-green vegetation instead of the brown expanses of the upland savannah, and ran across the coastal plain to the sea, no ship appeared. Instead, we found ourselves installed in a marvellously improbable beach camp outside Mombasa, a group of thatched huts standing under mango trees and encircled by coconut palms, beyond which stretched the blue expanse of the Indian Ocean. And here we spent nearly a fortnight in comfortable suspense, half in and half out of the sea, savouring our indolence after the brisk routine of life at Eastleigh but fretful at one more bout of waiting (how much we still had to learn about war!) and a prey to contradictory rumours about our immediate future.

When at last we were assembled and told that we were to embark, there was a surprise in store for us. Instead of the troopship we expected, there before us at the quay was the *Athlone Castle*, flagship of the Union Castle line and one of the most modern passenger liners in the merchant fleet. No nonsense about hammocks in the hold; on the contrary, we found when we boarded her one steaming afternoon in early November that, apart from a handful of wounded soldiers bound for South Africa, we had the ship to ourselves, all 25,000 tons of her. Even the stewards were at their posts and seemed eager to look after us. And so it was that our little party of twenty-five 'pupil pilots', accustomed to a thirteen-hour working day against the bleak background of the barrackroom and the airmen's mess, settled down to enjoy what to all appearances was the most luxurious of pleasure cruises. Like most things that had happened to me since the war began, there seemed to be no rhyme or reason about it, but there it was, and we made the most of it.

The *Athlone Castle* was fast enough to be allowed to sail on her own rather than dawdle in convoy and she now made a quick dash down the coast past Zanzibar and through the Mozambique channel to Durban. Here, while some mysterious cargo was loaded, we went ashore and – once we had convinced the local population that we were not Australians (a contingent of Australian troops who had passed this way had left behind them a trail of destruction) – we received the friendliest of welcomes and went swimming from the finest beach I had ever seen, borrowing surfboards to ride the long rollers sweeping in from the south Atlantic.

The holiday-cruise atmosphere persisted until we had rounded the Cape. Then, as the outline of Table Mountain faded into the distance behind us and we headed up into the north Atlantic, with nothing but open sea ahead and on every side of us, more sober thoughts began to assert themselves. The war was still going badly: the Italians were advancing into Egypt and the day before we left Nairobi they had also invaded Greece; and while the Greeks were resisting bravely, this had meant the diversion of some of our own forces from North Africa. The

Germans seemed to have given up the idea of invading Britain, but the Luftwaffe was carrying on with its raids on London. Everywhere we were still on the defensive, and most of all in the theatre of war of which we now became acutely conscious: the war at sea.

At the end of 1940, while we were in no position to strike a blow of any kind at Germany, German submarines were as active and as successful as at any time in the war. In one week, we learned as we were leaving Mombasa, 198,000 tons of British shipping had gone to the bottom of the sea. A ship like the *Athlone Castle* could give the slip to a submarine – provided someone spotted it in time – but at the end of October the *Empress of Canada* and the Cunarder *Laurentic* were both sunk in the Atlantic. So when we were told that we should be required to do duty as look-outs during our passage up the coast of West Africa, we were ready and willing.

Beyond all this, we were not oblivious to what the future might hold for ourselves once we had completed our training, but we did not allow the thought to cloud our enjoyment of the moment. On 11 November, after noting in my diary that it was Armistice Day, 'the day when we used to think of the other fellows who died in the "war to end war" ', I went on to say that:

Today the world is very nearly perfect for twenty-five unprophetic airmen in the south Atlantic: a huge liner, a calm and vastly blue sea, books and deckchairs and a complete lack of the slightest need to *do* anything. This really is a delightful journey and as we plunge along at twenty knots in the face of a generous breeze there could only be one improvement: there's not a woman on board.

It was there on the deck of the *Athlone Castle*, with a game of poker dice in progress and a gramophone playing 'Frankie and Johnnie', that we heard that Neville Chamberlain had died. The news was like an echo from another world, stirring distant memories of that extraordinary summer two years before, in which the gaunt image of the old man in its wing collar was muddled up with the endless Test match and Hitler's rantings over the Sudetenland and men digging trenches in Hyde Park. It all seemed remote beyond belief. It would have been unreasonable to expect us, whose lives he had done so much to disrupt, to mourn Chamberlain for long; but at least I gave him the credit for having shown 'more honesty and determination than the rest of the company into which he threw himself at Munich two years ago'.

Her speed was the *Athlone Castle*'s only real defence. Her armament consisted of two ancient Hotchkiss machine guns – nothing more. We had no idea what her cargo consisted of, but the real prize for any marauder would have been the ship herself, and the knowledge lent urgency to our movements as we tumbled out of our bunks in the small hours, wearing a few more clothes with every passing night, to take our turn with the binoculars. To the crew and the handful of naval officers and seamen who reinforced them, all this was, I suppose, the merest routine. To us in our landlubberly ignorance it was novel and intensely dramatic, and when we ran into a gale off Cape Finistère it was exhilarating to stand on the bridge with the huge waves racing past in the darkness and the wind blowing clouds of spray in our faces – though I was glad enough when my hour was done and I could go back to my bunk feeling like Lord Jim and stay there until it was time for a late breakfast. It was sobering, though, to hear next day that a British ship had been torpedoed twenty miles behind us during the night or that a Greek steamer was breaking up a little way off our course – and that we would not and could not turn back to help either, for fear of the lurking U-boats.

On 8 December we turned due east, leaving the open waters of the Atlantic – and the U-boats – behind us as we made for the shelter of the Irish Sea. For sixteen days we had seen no land, so we felt excitement as well as relief on the afternoon of the 9th when a flying boat of Coastal Command came looking for us through the drifting rain clouds and an hour or two later we came in sight of the hills of Donegal and then the Mull of Kintyre.

The next morning dawned cold and damp and as we picked our way slowly up the channel towards Liverpool the docks ahead were wreathed in a smoky fog. After the lonely weeks at sea it seemed strange to be surrounded by other shipping: a convoy was assembling for departure and the grey sea was alive with tugs and tenders and grubby little tramp steamers, while a couple of destroyers raced officiously up and down like sheepdogs and on every side there were half-submerged wrecks to remind us that not everyone had been as fortunate in his landfall as ourselves.

6

In wartime nothing works out as you expect it to: you never know what is going to happen next and you soon learn to take life as it comes. When we left Nairobi, we were expecting an uncomfortable journey home in a troopship and instead we got that unlooked-for pleasure cruise in the *Athlone Castle*. As we approached England, we speculated optimistically about our chances of getting leave, at least over Christmas. Instead, after three days in the gloomy limbo of a transit camp, we were posted to a flying school at Cranfield, near Bedford, and went straight to work next morning learning to fly twin-engined training aircraft called Oxford Airspeeds.

After the clear skies of Kenya, the weather conditions were disconcerting. Three days out of four there was low cloud and if the fourth day was fine that usually meant frost at night and mist as the sun came up in the morning. Either way, the visibility was wretched and even when we could see the ground we were bewildered by the patchwork of fields and lanes below us, all so different from the open plains around Eastleigh with the Ngong Hills to give us a sense of direction. As soon as we had mastered the Oxford and were sent off on our own, we found ourselves getting lost and making forced landings all over the place.

More disconcerting still was the atmosphere of Cranfield, where regular officers of the peacetime air force maintained what seemed to us a stuffy and inefficient routine. At Eastleigh we had been kept hard at work but treated with friendly consideration. Here at Cranfield we spent much of our time sitting about in the crewroom waiting to hear whether we should be flying or not, and nobody seemed to care a hang what became of us in the meantime or made any effort to see that our time was put to good use. This was not merely tiresome for us. It was also demoralizing, and it seemed to us a funny way to try to win the war. Fortunately the bond formed between the twenty-four of us (poor Shohet had had to drop out after an accident) was a tight one and if the spectre of disenchantment was often in the air during the slow winter afternoons, enthusiasm and a sense of companionship kept it at bay.

Early in the new year I got a telegram from my brother Douglas, telling me that he had been posted overseas and would be having a week's leave before he sailed. I managed to get leave for the weekend and joined him in London, which I had not seen since I flew off to Paris in May, ten days before Hitler launched his onslaught on France. We saw Charlie Chaplin's *The Great Dictator*, had a slap-up dinner at the Trocadero, went to one more concert together (it was to be the last for me) in the old Queen's Hall, and spent the rest of the weekend calling on a succession of aunts and cousins, all of whom seemed to have been having a more dangerous war than I had. We listened to their bomb stories, saw where one had had an incendiary through the roof, skirted the fresh crater outside the front door of another, and were glad to find that none of them seemed much perturbed by any of this. Nor did anyone else and the atmosphere in London was much healthier than it was in the relative safety of Cranfield, despite the destruction of the Guildhall the week before and the empty shell of the Carlton Club and the gap where John Lewis had been in Oxford Street and the burned-out churches in the City . . . Despite it all, no one seemed to pay much attention when the sirens sounded. At the Queen's Hall, when an attendant held up a placard (the orchestra was in the middle of the *Après-midi d'un Faune*) announcing that the air-raid warning had sounded and asking anyone who wanted to leave to do so quietly, I wrote afterwards that 'nobody moved, and a little later Sir Adrian Boult announced with a deprecating smile, as though he felt rather foolish to be bothering us with something so trivial, that the "All Clear" had gone'.

If London was a tonic in that January of 1941, there was encouraging news from North Africa too, where Wavell had launched an offensive the day after we landed in Liverpool and in a month had driven the Italians out of Egypt, captured 100,000 prisoners and swept along the coast as far as Tobruk, which he was besieging while Douglas and I were enjoying that weekend in London. It was a comfort to know that at last our forces had gone on to the offensive somewhere – and had something to show for it. For us, in mud-bound Bedfordshire, the only enemy was the weather and in the way of servicemen anywhere our horizon was limited by our immediate preoccupations. We flew when we could, walked a mile down the road to the pub most evenings, and somehow fought off the boredom that hovered always on the margin of our very restricted lives.

The pundits were talking of the war now in terms of years – and if we stopped to think about it, it was hard to see how it could be brought to an end any sooner, if the end was to be victory. Hitler controlled the continent and even the most exciting successes in Africa could do nothing to alter that. For the time being, the only way of attacking Germany was in the air, and that was something that directly concerned us. Reluctantly we had accepted the fact, when we found ourselves flying twin-engined trainers, that we were destined to become bomber pilots. Not for us the glamour and the exhilaration of becoming the next generation of 'the few'. Our role was to be what we considered the much more mundane one of carrying the fight to the enemy in the primitive bombers of the day, the Whitleys and Wellingtons which were starting to go lumbering out across France and the Rhineland in night raids on German factories and marshalling yards.

It must have been a dangerous business flying about England in those days, with beginners like ourselves cluttering up the air and getting in the way of those more seriously engaged. There were plenty of hazards: the weather, the blackout, as well as the sheer volume of traffic round a busy airfield – and this might include enemy aircraft looking for an easy target. My first experience of night flying was eventful, for after making a few landings with an instructor I was about to take off by myself, had opened the throttles and was gathering speed, when a red light flashed in my direction. Guessing that someone was about to land on top of me (one of the main hazards), I swerved off the runway and hastily closed the throttles to lessen the risk of fire. Then I noticed that the lights of the flare-path were being extinguished and realized that there must have been an air-raid warning. A moment later bombs started falling on the edge of the airfield.

There was a steady stream of accidents at Cranfield, but not until the very last moment did one of them prove fatal. It was Easter Sunday and at dawn I had completed the hours of night flying I needed to qualify for my wings. We were all in tearing spirits as one after another we came to the end of the course. After breakfast we went to bed for a few hours and then returned to the crewroom to clear out our belongings – and heard the ambulance racing out on to the runway. We piled out and saw that two planes had collided. Now both were blazing in the middle of the airfield. We watched silently as the flames danced in the sunlight and the ambulance drove back to the sick bay. Presently word came that the pilot of one aircraft was unhurt, but that a Belgian officer who had been attached to our course was still in the cockpit of the other (it was the one I had been flying a few hours earlier). He had needed another hour and a half of flying time to complete the course; by the next day he would have been off on leave with the rest of us. We turned soberly back into the crewroom and gathered up our things.

There is a gap in my diary after that for more than a week and by the time I wrote again a lot had happened. I had got my wings, rushed off to London on leave, and moved on to Alfriston in Sussex, where I took a room in an old half-timbered pub, the Star, and spent three delightful days walking by myself over the South Downs and enjoying the peace and the beauty and above all the solitude. The sun shone, there was a breeze blowing in off the sea, and in the evenings the public bar was snug and friendly. The bombers went droning overhead, but no one was talking about flying and after dinner I would play a game of shove ha'penny and go to bed early and sleep like the dead in preparation for another day of perfect relaxation. I was to remember those days with pleasure in the time to come.

My apprenticeship was nearly over and in May 1941 I was posted to Lossiemouth on the Moray Firth. By now the war had taken another unpromising turn. At the beginning of April, Hitler had sent his troops into Yugoslavia and Greece and what had looked at first like an opportunity for us to break into Europe from the south-east turned quickly into another demonstration of Germany's superiority. British units which were sent from North Africa to fight alongside the Greeks were driven back and their remnant forced to withdraw to Crete, where the Germans followed them and in a series of brilliant airborne landings captured the island after a month of desperate fighting. What was worst of all was the fact that the transfer to Greece of 50,000 seasoned British and New Zealand troops so weakened the British army in North Africa that all the gains of the previous three months were lost. The Libyan front unravelled and German forces pressed forward to the Egyptian border, where they seemed poised for an advance along the coast to Alexandria and on to Cairo.

It is difficult now to recapture the mood of those discouraging days. Most of the time we were too busy with the job in hand to speculate about the future. Perhaps we were also too unimaginative as well. Whatever the reason, it is rare to find in my diary a passage like this one of 19 May, which followed a resumé of the gloomy facts of life in the late spring of 1941:

A propos of this question of winning the war, I must say that at present I can see no way in which we can gain the victory – yet I have confidence that in the end we shall. It is illogical, but not stupid, to my mind. *How* we can win is a question of strategy, & from that point of view a victory for us is impossible in the circumstances which prevail. *Whether* we shall win is a question of spirit, & in that respect I don't think we can be beaten. There are many faults in our war organization, just as there were in our peace organization. There are many profiteers and other disagreeable types, for whom this war is no great hardship. But the spirit of England is still great and the people have big reserves of spiritual power on which to draw. It is a pity that they will not draw on them until a crisis breaks . . .

I celebrated my twenty-first birthday at Lossiemouth, in the middle of the last stage of my training: six intensive weeks of lectures and night flying on Wellington bombers. It was absorbing, but Lossiemouth was no place to learn to fly at night, for as midsummer approached there was no real night at all in those northern latitudes. The first time I went night flying in a Wellington I noted that when we took off a little before midnight it was 'not much darker than a winter afternoon'. My instructor had been drinking and the cockpit smelled strongly of beer as I made my circuits and landings and then:

. . . flew off at 3,500 feet with the moon playing hide and seek behind towers of cloud; it was rather cold. We went back to the aerodrome but they had put out the lights [I suppose there had been an air-raid warning] and after circling for a while, trying not to collide with several other Wellingtons doing the same thing, the instructor told me to fly down to Inverness and back, and fell asleep. I flew off down the coast, the sea very calm and shimmering in the moonlight, the coastline easy to see for several miles, and when we got back the flare-path had been lighted again and we went in and landed. It was 3.45, so we packed up, after a night of most enjoyable – but only moderately useful – flying.

It appals me now, to think of myself at just twenty-one, with so rudimentary a training behind me, in charge of thirteen tons of valuable equipment and answerable for the safety of four or five other airmen as inexperienced as I was. But that is the way it was, and somehow most of us survived.

I had resigned myself to becoming a bomber pilot, although the sight of Spitfires sporting over the Moray Firth still set me longing for a livelier fate. Nor was it just a question of which would be more fun to fly – a fighter or a bomber. We had very little idea in those days of what effect the bombing of Germany was having and even less of what the strategy was behind it.* In theory, targets were carefully selected and there was no bombing of areas where civilians lived; but aircrews operating over Germany knew how inaccurate their bombing was (although senior officers were very reluctant to admit it) and that with the best will in the world they could not avoid killing civilians. While we were still training we knew nothing of the debate on these points; nor can I remember anyone raising issues of this kind with us. But as the day came nearer when we should be posted to operational squadrons, there must have been many who entertained doubts about the role for which we were cast. 'I don't relish the job,' I wrote early on in the course at Lossiemouth, 'and I don't think it does much good. "Military targets" are pretty comprehensive these days and I don't want to spend the rest of my days bombing civilians.' As things turned out, I had little to worry about on that score; but it was a dilemma which I should not care to face again.

In the few weeks I spent at Lossiemouth there was hardly one that went by without some startling development. On 12 May we were all set guessing by the news that Rudolf Hess – Hitler's deputy, no less – had landed in Scotland by parachute from one of the Luftwaffe's new twin-engined fighter aircraft, the Messerschmitt 110. Had he come with Hitler's approval, or was it a sign of dissension among the top Nazis? It provided an intriguing topic for discussion, but then Hess disappeared into the Tower and we heard no more of him until the end of the war.

Ten days later we were shocked to hear that the battleship *Hood*, one of the Royal Navy's most powerful capital ships, had been sunk with the loss of more than a thousand lives. If even at sea the Germans could get the better of us, people said, what hope was there of victory – until the navy in turn cornered the *Bismarck* four days later and sank her after her German crew had fought a courageous action against a circle of attackers.

At the beginning of June came the end of the affair in Crete, where the German triumph showed that on land the best that we could do was nowhere near good enough. And then, against this discouraging

* Both questions are discussed by Max Hastings in *Bomber Command* (Michael Joseph 1979), in which he describes how the argument about the choice of targets was conducted at the highest level.

background and just as I was putting in the last hours of my training at Lossiemouth, we learned with astonishment of the German invasion of Russia. Ever since the Nazi-Soviet pact in August 1939 had cleared the way for Hitler's attack on Poland, relations between the Germans and the Russians had been an enigma to us. We did not see much to choose between them, and while we accepted what Churchill said about being ready to ally himself with the devil if it would help to defeat Nazi Germany, we were not enthusiastic about our new friends. Besides, I remembered how the Finns had run rings round the Russians in the winter of 1939–40. The day after the invasion, I observed gloomily, 'I doubt if Russian resistance will have much success, though one cannot but remember Napoleon's experiences on the road to – and the retreat from – Moscow.'

The first reports of the Germans' progress seemed to justify my pessimism; but as usual it was our own more immediate concerns that preoccupied my companions and myself. In a spell of clear weather we jumped through the last hoops of our training, flying out night after night in that northern twilight on excursions for which, I reflected, 'we should have had to pay good money in other circumstances', and which I for one enjoyed without brooding too deeply on the purpose behind them. And when I was singled out, a couple of days before the course ended, and ordered to report immediately to 149 Squadron at Mildenhall in Suffolk, I liked the sense of urgency. After all, this was what I had been working towards for almost a year – not to mention all the frustrations before that; it was time to begin. 'It looks as though I shall be on operations within a week or so, which is both pleasing and, shall we say, disquieting. Anyway, here we go!'

7

It took me twenty-four hours to get from Lossiemouth to Mildenhall, a typical wartime journey of fits and starts, of changes in the middle of the night at ghostly stations where trains came and went unpredictably, while hopeful travellers dozed uneasily in the blackout. When I arrived, it came as no surprise to find that I was not expected. Despite the urgency with which I had been dispatched, the atmosphere at Mildenhall – outwardly, at least – was one of perfect relaxation. It was very hot, the placid Suffolk countryside was basking in the midsummer sunshine and in the sergeants' mess there was only one serious preoccupation: the acute shortage of beer in the local pubs.

Feeling like a new boy at school, I was taken to see the wing commander in charge of 149 Squadron and allotted by him to one of his flight commanders. Next day I was issued with all sorts of cumbersome paraphernalia – flying suit, inflatable life jacket (known as a Mae West in honour of Hollywood's reigning sex symbol), parachute, sheepskin boots – and for a moment it looked as though I should go right off on my first operation that night. Instead, at the last moment I was put on night duty in the control tower. It was there, as a spectator, but in the very front row, that I gained my first experience of the activity for which I had been so long in preparation.

It was a clear, still night after another perfect summer's day. The last of the daylight was fading as the sound of engines being warmed up and tested began to rumble over the airfield. The squadron was flying Wellingtons with the old radial engines and that grumbling roar as the aircraft lumbered from their dispersal points to the end of the runway was already the most familiar sound in my ears.

All the aircraft were in the air by 11 p.m., fourteen of them from Mildenhall joining forty-six from other stations nearby. Their target was the port of Brest, where three of the German navy's capital ships – the *Scharnhorst*, *Gneisenau* and *Prinz Eugen* – were in dock. As they set off for the French coast, even I did not have to be told that Brest was as

well defended a target as any on the other side of the English Channel.
I wrote in my diary next day:

Once they had gone, I spent the time dozing or yarning with a young
pilot-officer who was on duty with me, until 3.30 a.m., when the first
of them got back. After that there was a pause & then a period of
activity until about 5, during which eight more came in & landed
safely. Then followed an uncomfortable interval while we waited for
news of the remaining five. At last one more came in & at the same
time we got word that two others had landed at different airfields.
We waited a bit longer, until the sky was quite light, & then packed
up. The other two planes did not appear & I went to bed at 7 a.m.
with a feeling of distaste for the whole business, mingled with
surprise that I did not feel more deeply about it.

The squadron was in action again two nights later and this time I was
allotted as second pilot to the crew of 'Q for Queenie', whose captain
was a lively Australian named Les Dixon. Dixon was a pilot-officer
with a good deal of operational experience and a reputation, in the
slang of the day, for 'pressing on regardless'. He and the rest of his crew
were in high spirits and they made it clear to me that I was unusually
privileged. Not only was Dixon's among the most experienced crews on
the station, but 'Q for Queenie' was the first to reach Mildenhall of a
new type of Wellington which was just making its debut with Bomber
Command. It had two Rolls-Royce Merlin engines, which gave it a few
extra miles an hour (its cruising speed, if I remember rightly, was
something like 180 knots), and when we took it up in the morning to test
it we found that it also had a new gadget fitted on the instrument panel:
a curious little screen with a line down the middle of it. If we steered to
starboard of a given course, a series of dots appeared on the screen, and
if we strayed to port, a series of dashes (or the other way round – I
forget which). It was very 'hush-hush' – another favourite phrase at the
time – and I don't think any of us knew that we were trying out the first
direction-finding radar equipment which was to prove so invaluable to
bomber crews finding their way home in difficulties.
    And that was not all that was new about 'Q for Queenie'. She also
had the power to carry one of the new 4,000-pound bombs which were
just being introduced; and one of these monsters had been provided for
us to carry to Germany. To my relief, the target was the Krupps
armaments factory at Essen. I felt no reservations about helping to
drop nearly two tons of high explosive on so vital a part of Hitler's

armoury. It seemed as good a way as any of breaking my duck.

It was another very hot day and towards the end of the afternoon we stood in the shade of the wing and watched the armourers fitting the huge bomb to the fuselage of 'Q for Queenie'. It was an ugly brute, painted black and shaped, I observed, 'like an outsize dustbin'. It was so big that the doors of the bomb bay would not close and had to be taken off, leaving the bomb itself exposed a few feet above the ground. After seeing it securely attached, we went off with the other crews to be briefed for the night's operation: about the weather conditions we could expect, the course to be followed, the strength of the defences at Essen (which were second to none) and all sorts of other things which I have forgotten.

As often happens in life, this moment which I had anticipated for so long seemed now to have overtaken me with unexpected suddenness. A few nights earlier I had been taking off on one of our cross-country exercises out of Lossiemouth, with the familiar landmarks clear in that northern twilight, and with no doubt in my mind that in two or three hours' time I should turn in my log for the trip, eat a plate of bacon and eggs and go untroubled to bed. Now, as we left the briefing room and gathered up our equipment, everything looked much the same, but it was in fact quite different – and the difference was a crucial one. Soon after we had taken off we should find ourselves flying, not over the friendly Scottish Highlands but across the coast of France and into Hitler's stronghold, a target for the German anti-aircraft guns and perhaps for one of the new night fighters which the Luftwaffe had recently introduced. I don't remember how many aircraft were setting out from Mildenhall that night, but it would be surprising, after my experience two nights earlier, if it did not occur to me to wonder whether once again two of them would not return, and if so, which two . . .

My diary mentions no such forebodings, nor do I recall entertaining them. As we clambered aboard I remember only that I felt uncomfortably hot in my flying suit and found it difficult to avoid getting my equipment entangled with the knobs and levers that surrounded us in the cockpit. Next came the complex ritual of checking and rechecking that everything was functioning as it should. Only when all this was done and we were in position for take-off could I give my thoughts rein. Then I felt my excitement rising as we waited (we were to take off last because of our extra speed) and watched as the other aircraft taxied one by one to the end of the runway and roared off up the flare-path and into the night sky.

It was a quarter of an hour before midnight when we took our turn at the end of the runway and I said a quick prayer as I watched Dixon take a last look round and open up the engines. At once events took an unexpected turn. As 'Q for Queenie' gathered speed, she swung sharply to the right. Dixon fought to control the swing, but she pulled away again, this time to the left and across the line of flares, and I watched them flashing by underneath us, one under the port wing, a second just below my window on the starboard side and a third under the starboard wingtip. Then we were racing into the darkness, well up the airfield now and not yet off the ground. At last Dixon pulled the nose up and we were airborne – but the port wing dropped and I thought for a moment that it would touch the ground and we would go cartwheeling around it. Instead the whole aircraft fell heavily back to earth and, although Dixon at once cut both engines, went careering on at seventy miles an hour towards the edge of the airfield. I could dimly see a line of trees ahead; and now it occurred to me that just underneath us, sticking out of the bomb bay, was that ugly black canister containing a ton and three quarters of high explosive.

For the next few moments my diary tells me that I had:

. . . only a confused impression of being thrown about the cockpit – of Dixon's cool voice in the intercom saying 'here it comes, boys' – until a particularly violent bump made something give way & I was thrown to the floor by the bomb-aimer's panel. That's where I was when we came to rest, the air round me filled with dust and earth as the door had burst open beside me, and no sound except a strange whirring – which I took to be the bomb working up for a protest.

It didn't go off, or I should not be writing these words; and it had no business to do so, since it was not fused – but at a moment like this such reasonable arguments do not always seem perfectly convincing . . . and the bomb, like 'Q for Queenie' herself, had taken a beating. We didn't stop to investigate closely at the time but as soon as we had all scrambled out 'we legged it through the barley to the nearby road'. There we stopped, since there did not seem to be much point in running any further; if the bomb was going to go off it would 'blow the whole of Mildenhall sky-high', and presently 'the ambulance & the fire tender turned up, & then the wing commander and other officers, & soon afterwards we all pushed off to get some supper & then to bed, where I slept soundly for nine hours'.

We went back to the scene of the crime later in the day and it wasn't difficult to reconstruct the events of those few moments. The aircraft had crossed the edge of the airfield, missing the petrol dump by fifty yards (which made us glad it had swung so far to the left), had raced through someone's chicken coop and on over some allotments, before coming to a shallow bank. As it took the bank at speed, one leg of the undercarriage had collapsed and poor 'Q for Queenie' fell on her face in the barley and slewed round on her good leg – which was just as well as those trees I had seen were straight ahead of her. The whirring sound I had heard had come from the starboard propeller; with the aircraft on its nose and tilted to port, the tips of the propeller blades had been flicking lightly through the earth a few feet from where I lay on the floor of the cockpit. Miraculously, with the petrol tanks full, there had been no fire.

As an introduction to active service, this was not ideal; but it had its positive aspects. To begin with, perhaps because it had all happened so quickly, the episode had not seemed nearly so alarming as it sounds in retrospect. As I put it next day: 'Oddly enough – and I remember a fleeting impression of surprise at the fact – I was not frightened; and from what they said afterwards I am pretty sure none of the others were either.' Certainly none of us had any hesitation about taking to the air again a couple of days later, although now we had to make do with a plain old Mark III Wellington just like everyone else. As for me, I felt (for no good reason) that the episode had somehow advanced my status. It was as though, having applied for membership of an exclusive club, I had undergone a rather rowdy initiation ceremony and could now feel that I *belonged* in a way that I had not done the day before. I even found the experience oddly reassuring. Surely, I reasoned, if I could survive that, I should survive anything.

It was a classic case of *hubris* – and the gods at once cut me down to size. When we took up the replacement for 'Q for Queenie' and Dixon had carried out all the necessary tests for the next operation, he invited me to make my first landing at Mildenhall. Confidently, I assumed control and brought the Wellington round in a comfortable circuit until I was in line with the runway and ready to begin my approach. It was another glorious day in July. There was no wind and under that tranquil summer sky everything about us was perfectly still. When I throttled back, the aircraft came floating down as though it were no heavier than a glider. There is no more enjoyable sensation in flying than this, to come gently down with the roar of the engine almost silenced, allowing the natural force of the air over the wing surface to provide the right balance of lift and drag, so that the aircraft sinks gently, almost imperceptibly, to the point where you can cut the engine altogether and ease it on to the ground . . .

But gradually, as we glided on, a cold draught of anxiety seemed to blow down my neck. So imperceptibly were we sinking that already we were over the end of the runway and still a hundred feet or so above the ground. I throttled right back, but the aircraft went floating on as though bewitched, defying the law of gravity, as though it were not a great mass of metal, guns, instruments and fuel tanks but a piece of thistledown on the summer air. I was in trouble.

The fact is that I had forgotten to put the flaps down, so that the Wellington, all thirteen tons of it, was like a car which I was trying to stop without using the brakes. It was too late to go round again; there was nothing for it but to land and hope that there would be enough of the runway left for me to bring the aircraft to a halt before we ran off the end of the field. But there was not, and once we were on the ground and still travelling at forty or fifty miles an hour towards a line of light aircraft parked along the perimeter (one of them belonged to the station commander), there was only one thing to do. I kicked hard at the rudder bar to turn the aircraft to the left. For a moment, although I could feel the strain on the undercarriage, I thought I had got away with it. Then, with a horrible sound of rending metal, the undercarriage gave way and the Wellington slid sideways and came ingloriously to rest on one wing at right angles to the runway.

Everyone was very nice about it and after half an hour of the blackest despair the rest of the crew had almost managed to persuade me that it was 'just one of those things'. The authorities too, since they had no other aircraft to offer us – and probably would have been reluctant to let us near it if they had – decided that the best thing all round would be for Dixon's crew to take a week's leave. Within three hours I was off and on my way to London.

I could not feel I deserved it; but on the other hand, apart from those few days in Alfriston, I had not had more than a weekend of leave since we got back to England – in fact, not since I had drawn that first day's pay in Cairo almost a year earlier. And leave, in our circumstances, had an almost mystical significance. Like schoolboys released for the summer holidays, it was not just the liberation it gave us from a discipline that was irksome or from duties that were exacting; what we relished above all was the feeling that, however briefly, we could resume control over our own lives – even if it was only a matter of deciding for ourselves what we would have for breakfast – instead of leaving every decision to others of whom we knew next to nothing and who knew nothing whatever about us.

That was the secret of that week in July 1941 from which I was to recall long afterwards – as a painter might recall with affectionate care every detail in the image of his mistress – all the trivial accompaniments of days that were altogether unremarkable. Indeed, it was precisely because they were unremarkable, were humdrum and human and normal, that I was soon to spend hours conjuring them up in an intensity of nostalgia. And if that sounds (as I can see it does) over-emphatic, even ridiculous, I can only repeat that it is true, even though all that I did during that invaluable breathing space was to spend a couple of days in London, wearing ordinary clothes instead of uniform, sitting in the sun in Hyde Park, taking a girl out to dinner, and then making for the country to relax in the sunshine. I had no wish this time to be on my own and I found everything I was looking for in the house of old friends in a quiet village not far from Mildenhall. There I spent the days that remained to me in peace and utter contentment, helping to bring in the hay or just sitting in the garden (for that long spell of fine weather held through my leave and beyond), in an atmosphere that epitomized all that I loved about the old England that might or might not survive the war. At that moment it seemed serene beyond all challenge, or so I was made to feel. Perhaps my hosts, older and wiser than I, guessed, as we brought in the hay together on those long summer evenings, that time might be running out for me before long. Certainly they made much of me and I was to remember with gratitude and affection those gentle days in the sun.

I don't seem to have given much thought to the war during that week. It was only when I got back to Mildenhall that I took stock again, noting in my diary that the German advance into Russia seemed to be losing momentum, but that elsewhere we had little cause for satisfaction. There had been a revolt against us in Iraq, which had been subdued by a flying column of the Arab Legion from Transjordan under a British officer named John Glubb. The Germans under Rommel were threatening Alexandria. And in the war at sea, which meant more to me after that voyage in the *Athlone Castle*, the U-boats were sinking our ships faster than they could be replaced. If Britain had fought off the threat of invasion in 1940, we now had to face the equally grave threat that we would be starved into submission – unless we could mount a new offensive on some other front.

But there was no other front for us. The idea that the Russians might one day take the offensive against Germany would have seemed in that summer of 1941 absurdly far-fetched; and there was no sign that the United States was prepared to give up its neutrality. Unless the war was to go on for ever (and sometimes it looked as if it would), it was only in the air that we could carry the war to the Germans.

Bomber Command was very active during those summer months and the authorities were trying to give the public in Britain the impression that its raids (as I wrote – mistakenly) had 'reached a pitch of intensity rivalling that of the Luftwaffe's raids on this country last autumn'. The number of aircraft taking part was well publicized and so were the targets; but what the public was not told and had no way of knowing (and it was only now being reluctantly accepted by the senior ranks of the RAF itself) was that the raids, even when they were carried out by fifty or sixty or even a hundred Whitleys and Hampdens and Wellingtons, were doing very little damage to the German war effort – and were causing us casualties in both men and machines which we could not sustain indefinitely.

If the aircrews of Bomber Command had known how inaccurate and ineffective our bombing was, I suppose we might have been more reluctant to face the risks it involved. As it was, we carried on cheerfully and unsuspectingly, rather like the staff of a business enterprise which was outwardly prosperous but whose management was becoming aware (but did not inform us) of the unsatisfactory state of the books. When I got back from my week's leave, I noted remorsefully that I had 'missed a week of very heavy work at Mildenhall' and I welcomed the fact that Les Dixon's crew, with myself as second pilot, was down to take part in a raid that night on Bremen: 'There are 103 bombers attacking the railway yards there, while another fifty or sixty have objectives nearby.'

It was 14 July and the weather was as hot as ever when Dixon took us up to test our latest Wellington, 'O for Orange'. For a couple of hours we flew up and down across the East Anglian farmland until he was satisfied that all was as it should be. Then he got me to make two or three landings until 'even Freddie, the rear gunner, is convinced that I know how to land a Wellington without crumpling the undercarriage'. We handed the aircraft over to the ground staff to be fuelled and 'bombed up' while we joined the other crews in the briefing room before supper. And when that was over, I must have had a few minutes to spare because I wrote a page or two in my diary, mentioning that

Peter Edwards, a friend of mine from Lossiemouth, was already missing from a raid over Germany. 'A pity,' I wrote, 'as he was the most likeable chap I met up there & even younger than I am, only twenty. Let's hope he's a prisoner-of-war.'

8

We took off at 11.15 p.m. into a sky in which clouds were gathering, and circled the airfield once before striking out eastwards, climbing steadily. Soon after we had crossed the English coast we were in broken cloud and 'O for Orange' was bumping about a bit in the turbulent air over the North Sea. It looked as though the long heat wave was breaking up.

There was not much to be seen as we flew over Holland on our way to Bremen: through a gap in the clouds an occasional cluster of lights, which we took to be a German airfield, and now and then a few searchlights and shellbursts in the distance. We saw several other bombers on their way across, one only a couple of hundred yards away to the right of us. Then we were over Germany and the anti-aircraft fire grew heavier, but none of it came anywhere near us. We were flying at seven or eight thousand feet and still climbing between tumbled heaps of cumulus cloud. The moon, which was on the wane, came up soon after 1 a.m.

All this happened a long time ago and of course I don't remember the night's events in any detail now. But as soon as I was able to get hold of pen and paper, which was not for another ten days or so, I wrote down my recollections of the trip:

We reached Bremen round about 2 a.m. & recognized it by some waterways shining in the moonlight. Things seemed pretty quiet & we made a trial run over the town, untroubled at first by anything except a few wandering searchlights. Then the flak started to come up; I was standing in the Astro hatch, halfway along the fuselage, & the bursts looked like a cheerful display of fireworks. After this a long period of dark stillness; we lost the target & cruised around trying to pick it up again; searchlights & guns were inactive. Around 2.30 Jim Grace (the navigator) said he could see the target & Dixon turned for a bombing run. Then things did start to happen. One searchlight flicked on to us & held us, & at once a dozen more joined it, so that we seemed to be making our stolid progress towards the target in the glare of all the candles of heaven. Then the guns opened up & the firework display started again; but this time it was a freakish affair: all around us different-coloured bursts of fire & the whole sky, already blazing with light from the searchlights' beams, was filled with these clusters of sparks & coloured stars. I couldn't tell whether this was a heavy barrage or not, but I couldn't see how we could get through it unscathed, for some of the bursts seemed very close. I wondered why no shrapnel seemed to be hitting us – & then the aircraft started to lurch about in the sky, rather as though it was being pummelled by unseen fists.

There was quite a lot of chat over the intercom: the gunners commenting unfavourably on the nearness of the flak bursts, the navigator giving directions to Dixon (who had to hold a steady course all this time), & odd remarks of a general nature going to and fro. When at last we came over the target, the bombs wouldn't come off; I suppose the connections to the aiming panel were shot away. The flak was still intense & now it was simply a matter of getting out of it as soon as possible. Dixon jettisoned the bombs over a searchlight battery, but now the bomb doors would not close, reducing our speed seriously. At last, after about ten minutes of it, during which I had been ready to rush forward & take over if Dixon should be hit, we left the maelstrom behind & one by one the searchlights flicked off. The bomb doors were still open, as the hydraulics had been shot to bits, & the fuselage smelt of petrol now, so that things looked tricky for the return journey. I started to push out bundles of leaflets through the chute & when they had gone I went up to the front beside Dixon.

After a while he told me to take over & we changed places while he went back to assess the damage. The machine was still flying all right, which was very lucky, but the instruments had been damaged & the airspeed indicator was reading absurdly high. There was a big crack in the glass just in front of my face where a piece of shrapnel had struck & several holes in the fabric of the fuselage where I had been standing. The smell of petrol was very strong & there was a lot of oil slopping about on the floor.

I flew on over the Zuyder Zee & just before we left the Dutch coast two searchlights picked us up; one had another Wellington in its beam about 1,500 feet above us & to starboard. I did a few S turns to try to shake them off, but without success, & presently a few shells followed us, leaving a slowly sinking red glow in the sky. Then we were over the sea & the main petrol tanks were exhausted, so we switched over to the nacelle tanks. After a few moments of anxious popping, both engines picked up & we carried on. Height was 6,500 feet & I had the nose slightly down to increase speed.

Dixon took over again & presently announced that we couldn't make England and must prepare to come down in the sea. He was very cool & gave us all our instructions carefully. I was sent back to the fuselage to see to the dinghy release & the flotation gear (to keep the aircraft on the surface when we got out). Sandy, the wireless operator, & Fred, front gunner, joined me & we had a struggle to get the Astro hatch off – it was jammed tight – & then Jim Grace (the navigator) showed me just where the dinghy release was (I should have known but couldn't find it). Then Jim went up to join Dixon, & we waited. The petrol was finished & the engines were quiet now.

I hopped up in the Astro hatch to see how near we were to the water. We were only a few hundred feet up, so I stood by the flotation gear & told Fred to be ready to hop out first, followed by Sandy. I was still plugged in to the intercom & Dixon asked if I had everything ready. Just before we hit the water I pulled the three handles of the flotation gear, then caught hold of the dinghy-release handle.

We hit the water with a wallop (though our speed was down to sixty-five, Dixon told us afterwards) & seemed to stop dead. I was hurled to the floor & a surge of water which came rushing down from the cockpit covered me & whirled me round in the fuselage. For a moment I thought it was all over, but standing up I was able to get my head & shoulders out of the water. I saw Fred clambering out & Sandy waiting behind him. The water was rising, but they got out quickly & I fought my way through the water to the Astro hatch, gave another pull at the dinghy release to make quite sure, & pulled myself up through the hatch into the air. The others were all out, so we clambered into the dinghy and pushed off.

There were several things we would have liked to get out of the aircraft, but already she was settling in the water and it didn't seem worth the risk. After about ten minutes, she sank. So there we were in the middle of the North Sea, six of us in a rubber dinghy about seven feet across & shaped like an ancient Briton's coracle. We felt pleased at getting out with so little trouble, and since Sandy had sent out SOS messages in plenty of time there did not seem to be any reason for anxiety. It was 5.15 a.m. & we reckoned that by lunchtime we should have been picked up & returned to England.

At that moment (though I did not learn of it until long afterwards), two thousand miles away in Egypt my mother woke my father to tell him that I was in trouble. In a dream, she explained, she had just seen the pilot of an aircraft – she was sure it was me – looking anxiously from side to side as though lost. I was safe, though, she insisted – and continued to insist, even after the arrival of a cable announcing that our aircraft was missing and all through the uncomfortable interval that followed.

The date was 15 July 1941: twelve months to the day since I had first put on my RAF uniform in Cairo. It seemed like longer. Most of it had been spent in uneventful drudgery, but I seemed to have made up for that in the last ten days. Looking round the empty expanse of the North Sea, I wondered what would happen next.

The sea was a bit choppy but we drifted about peacefully enough, waiting for the sound of the aircraft (or would it be a launch?) coming to pick us up. As the morning passed, we began to wonder whether our SOS had been received; and when nobody appeared throughout a long hot afternoon, we had to admit to ourselves that something must have gone wrong. (In point of fact, no one had heard anything from us after we left Bremen and the radio transmitter had no doubt been damaged along with almost everything else when we were over the target.)

And so nightfall found us out on the open sea. We took it in turns to rest, two at a time, in the well of the dinghy, while the other four sat round the inflated rim, their legs jumbled up with the bodies of the two who were 'sleeping'; but none of us slept much that night.

Next morning we tried to persuade each other that we might still be picked up, that even now the air/sea rescue people were combing the North Sea for us. But we did not believe what we were saying and with every hour that passed it became more obvious that we might be in for a long wait. At that stage we did not put it any more bleakly than that.

We had only a rough idea of our position, since few of our instruments had been working when we limped out over the Dutch coast and we could only guess how many miles we had covered before we hit the water. The North Sea is a hundred miles wide and it soon became clear that we were out in the middle, in what was effectively a kind of no-man's-land; for we neither saw nor were seen by the ships of either side, which clung to the safety of their respective coasts. Much the same was true of aircraft, of which we saw none by day and surprisingly few by night – when they could not see us and had in any case no means of identifying us.

In this state of uncertainty we drifted helplessly for six days and nights, our spirits rising and falling in tune with the weather. When the sun shone and it was calm, we stripped off our clothes to dry them – and after sitting with the summer breeze playing on our skins it was easy to fancy at evening that we could make out the coast of England there among the sunset clouds. When the wind rose and the waves ran high and it rained, our mood changed accordingly. We had of course no protection from the weather and we were more or less wet through all the time, which seemed to do us no harm, but it was not easy to remain philosophical if you were resting 'below' when a wave came over the side and went straight down your neck.

The dinghy may not have been very commodious, but it proved strong enough to withstand for a week the shifting and heaving of six uncomfortable bodies. Only a single skin of rubber separated us from the sea below and this skin did indeed spring a leak early on; but we plugged the leak with a curious cone-shaped wooden peg supplied for the purpose and this clumsy repair survived (much to my private surprise) to the end. If our masters had only provided us with a mast, we could have improvised some sort of sail and at least made a bid for freedom. For mere survival proved to be no problem (I should not care to repeat the experiment in winter) and it was frustrating to be able to do so little to help ourselves.

It was interesting to discover how little seemed to be necessary for survival. The dinghy contained a set of iron rations designed to keep a crew going for twenty-four hours or so. Fortunately, Dixon took charge of this and doled out the contents to us in realistically small amounts: a couple of biscuits a day or a piece of concentrated chocolate, with a few raisins and one or two Horlicks tablets. Water presented a more serious problem. There were three safari bottles, each containing a pint of water, and a fourth bottle filled with rum. Without argument we agreed to Dixon's suggestion that we restrict ourselves to a mouthful of water each morning (sometimes we had a second mouthful in the evening) – and when it rained, as it did throughout the last day, we laboriously washed the salt off a parachute harness and funnelled the precious rainwater into one of our bottles. When our spirits were low because it was raining or the sea was choppy and the waves were splashing in over the rim of the dinghy, we allowed ourselves a swig of rum, and very comforting it was on the worst nights.

On this regime we got by without much difficulty and were none the worse for it afterwards. In fact, thanks to Dixon's foresight, we still had two thirds of our food supply left after six days, and the three water bottles were full. In purely physical terms, we could have carried on for another two weeks.

Psychologically, I am not so sure. The mind is less docile than the body and I was aware of a limit somewhere in the offing beyond which survival in this sense could not be taken for granted. At the outset, it seemed absurd and melodramatic to suppose that we, who felt so much alive, could in a day or two be dead: and dead, not in a blaze of gallantry, but merely faded out of existence . . . But then there were times, as we stared out over that limitless vista of sea and sky, in which we ourselves were the only living creatures, when it seemed that we were destined to float on, unremarked and helpless, until we went mad or died.

We didn't talk about this aspect of our situation. Most of our communication was in the superficial tone of service banter and we would tantalize each other by picturing the amount of steak and kidney pudding and Scotch ale we would consume when we got the chance. It seems odd, for there must have been more serious thoughts going through all our minds. I don't remember, though, that we gave expression to them, nor does the account I wrote of our adventure suggest it. I do remember that I prayed, and that I derived much comfort from doing so; and I dare say the others did the same. If so, we kept the fact to ourselves, with an instinctive reserve which none of us knew how to breach.

It was in the middle of the afternoon of our sixth day at sea that there came a break in the monotony. We had spent the morning collecting rainwater and Dixon and I were resting when we heard what might have been the distant hum of aero engines. We held our breath and listened, each thinking that his imagination might be playing tricks, as the sound grew louder – and presently one of the others sitting above us called out that he could see four aircraft, twin-engined, which looked like . . . Messerschmitt 110s, the latest fighter plane of the Luftwaffe.

The news seemed to promise us no advantage. Enemy fighters could do us no good (we thought) and much harm. It seemed best to keep our heads down and hope we would not be seen. No sooner had we come to this conclusion than one of the German pilots spotted us and broke away from the formation to take a closer look. Down he came in a steep dive until we could see the shark's teeth painted on either side of the nose of the aircraft and the pilot's helmeted face behind the windshield and for a moment there was a chill in the air – for, however much or however little you know about the pilot's intentions, it is an uncomfortable experience to find yourself in the sights of an enemy fighter. But with a roar and a whoosh he was over us and climbing again, and when his companions followed his example and dived at us one after the other, the whole encounter had an unmistakably friendly context, so that Sandy, our rear gunner, even waved at the last of them and got a wave from the Messerschmitt's rear gunner in return; and presently they all made off to the east, leaving us to speculate about their intentions.

They were back again before dusk and it was with mixed feelings that we saw that they had brought with them a seaplane, a Heinkel 115, which flew low over the sea towards us with the evident intention of putting down on the water. But the sea was choppy and after two or three attempts the pilot gave up the idea and climbed towards the Messerschmitts circling protectively above. Then he flew directly over us and dropped what turned out to be another dinghy, which fell into the sea beside us and exploded on impact, although it floated long enough for us to seize hold of it and salvage its contents. These included a Verey pistol, a compass and a mast and sail, but disappointingly little to eat or drink. We transferred all this gear into our own boat, which began to take on the appearance of a crowded village store, and as the seaplane and its escorts droned away over the horizon we fell to discussing this confusing turn in our fortunes.

We were not sure whether to feel relief or disappointment at the seaplane's failure to pick us up. On the one hand, we had narrowly escaped capture; on the other, we had lost the only chance that had come our way of being rescued. And now we must decide what to do next. If we could find some way of rigging up the mast from the German dinghy (which we had no way of fastening in our own), might we still be able to make our way to where, somewhere beyond the westward horizon, lay the elusive coastline of East Anglia? Would it be quite sporting (I swear we solemnly considered this point of etiquette) to take advantage of the Germans' generosity to make good our escape from them?

These were knotty problems to resolve; but as it turned out, the decisions were taken out of our hands. As darkness fell, the sea grew rougher and as the dinghy climbed each wave and then slid down into the trough on the far side of it, we had enough to do to stay afloat. A lively west wind was blowing spray all over us and there was no question of getting the sail rigged, even if we could find a way of stepping the mast. With nothing that we could do for the moment to take control of our own destiny, we settled down to see one more night through, two of us resting as usual in the well (though it was anything but restful that night, with a couple of inches of sea water slopping to and fro between us), while the other four huddled miserably on the rim, wet through and listless – for by now we were not in the best of shape – trying to ride the dinghy over the waves so that as little water as possible came over the side and talking intermittently, and then generally of food . . . It was as disagreeable a night as I can remember.

At daybreak the sea was quieter and there was a ship on the horizon. It looked hardly bigger than a tug, but it was still something for us to get excited about. And then the Messerschmitts appeared again, and presently the seaplane as well, and it was obvious from their movements that they were looking for us. Before long someone had spotted us and the seaplane came gliding towards us to make an uncertain splashdown on the waves. To our surprise the pilot taxied right over our dinghy and a trapdoor opened in the belly of the aircraft, from which strong arms emerged to haul us up, one by one, to safety. The whole operation took only a few minutes.

So our future was decided, all in a moment and over our heads, you might say. I should have liked to find out whether our captors knew who we were before they rescued us, but we had no German and they no English. If they were surprised, they showed no sign of it, nor of disappointment either. They covered us with blankets, changed our torn wet socks, and gave us a swig of what I suppose was brandy. They could not have taken better care of us if we had been members of the Luftwaffe like themselves. As for us, I suppose we could have tried to resist capture, but we were so weak that a child could have overcome our resistance. As it was, a wave of relief swept over us as someone else took over the responsibility for our survival and we were able at last to relax, lying flat on the floor of the seaplane.

After twenty minutes in the air we came down again to find ourselves at Amsterdam, where we reeled drunkenly along the quay – for we had lost all control of our leg muscles – to a waiting truck. The truck took us to a hospital, where they put before us slices of brown bread and liver sausage, with a mug of watery *ersatz* coffee. It was a far cry from the sort of self-indulgence we had promised ourselves, but it seemed a banquet in its way. And then, without further ado, we were put into a kind of black maria and whisked off to a military prison somewhere in the heart of Amsterdam. Here, each in his solitary cell furnished only with a plank bed and a straw mattress, we slept on and off for three days and ate whatever we could lay our hands on, which was not very much.

One hot afternoon as I lay on my mattress staring at the ceiling, I heard music. The cell had no window, only a skylight high in the wall, and it was through the skylight that there came now out of the torpor of the afternoon this blessed sound. I've forgotten what the music was. I only know that I listened to it, isolated in that narrow cell, in perfect contentment. Then the music stopped and after an interval the door of my cell opened and a young German stood smiling in the doorway. Without language, it was not difficult for the two of us to make contact of a sort, with the music still sounding in our ears and stretching an invisible line of communication between us.

For a few minutes we gestured and hummed and laughed at each other, as we might have done if we had met on holiday, in a youth hostel, or in my rooms at Oxford. But then a brusque interruption brought us down to earth and reminded us of the very different circumstances in which we had met and of the quite different behaviour that was appropriate to the relationship between us: reminded us, in short, that we were enemies and had no business to pretend that we were or could be friends. At least, that was what I took to be the message roared out by an officer who found the door of my cell open and looked in to read the riot act to the young German, and who seemed, justly, I felt, to be including me in his remonstrance.

So my friendly young enemy disappeared and the officer slammed the cell door and I went back to my pallet to reflect on this encounter which for a few moments had broken the monotony of my day. And then, very softly now, I heard the music again. This time it was a popular song of the day, one I knew well – I even recognized the recording (it was by Duke Ellington) – but I could not put a title to it . . . until suddenly it came to me and I chuckled appreciatively. It was 'In My Solitude', and I can hear the melody now and feel an absurd sense of nostalgia for that moment in the half-remembered limbo of a Dutch gaol forty years ago.

Limbo is an apt image for those few days in Amsterdam, for we were in every sense disengaged, rootless, suspended. Behind us and separated from the present by that interminable interval in the North Sea, was a life which already seemed indescribably remote. Ahead lay a huge uncertainty, a country, as it were, to which we had no maps. It was a restful pause, a moment – and how rare this is – of utter and enforced irresponsibility. We had no duties, no obligations, no property: no hostages at all to fortune. Even our personalities seemed pared down to the minimum, for we were under orders to disclose nothing to our captors beyond our names and numbers. Everything else was on the scrapheap, or in cold storage; and the completeness of the break with the past was symbolized by the fact that we retained from it absolutely nothing but the clothes we stood up in. Even our flying boots we had jettisoned, for they took up too much space in the dinghy; and our pockets were empty, for it was a rule – more practised in the breach than the observance, I dare say, but I had obeyed it with a novice's thoroughness – that before setting out on an operation we must remove from them anything, even if it were no more than a bus ticket to the nearest town, that might provide information to the enemy.

Before I left that first prison, the Germans gave me a pair of boots. And from somewhere I acquired a matchbox which bore the legend: 'Carlton Hotel – Your Home in Holland'. I treasured this for some time, in the way that a child will treasure a button or a broken toy, and for the same reason: that it was all I had.

PART THREE
Brought Down to Earth
(1941–45)

9

It was in this condition of comparative nakedness that I embarked on a new life, without surprise – for a war soon teaches you to take things as they come – and with a good deal of curiosity.

I had very little idea of what to expect as a prisoner-of-war, and the same was true of most of my companions. Strange as it seems, the idea of captivity was not one to which we had paid much attention. Indeed, we used to give surprisingly little thought to the future, partly because we were young and in general optimistic, and partly, I dare say, out of a kind of protective escapism. The idea that we might be killed was one which we could hardly avoid altogether, but we tended to keep it at arm's length, clinging to the assumption – which was really more of a superstition – that whatever might be in store for others, we ourselves were marked down for survival. And between these two alternatives, of sudden extinction and an immortality which the statistics (if we paid any heed to them) must have told us was highly improbable, it hardly occurred to us that there might be a *via media*, a compromise which was neither quite one thing or the other.

So it was with a lively interest that I looked about me a few days later when I was taken with the rest of our crew and put aboard a train at Amsterdam (smiles and winks from the Dutch commuters at the station) for a journey up the Rhine valley to Frankfurt. There we spent a couple of weeks in the deceptive comfort of a transit camp and interrogation centre for air-force prisoners, before travelling on eastwards for a day and a night until we reached a little station called Kirchain, where we tumbled gratefully out of our 'express goods' train at dawn and marched stiffly off through cobbled streets to find our new home.

It was called Stalag IIIE and at first sight it looked pleasant enough, apart from the barbed-wire fence that surrounded it, with watch towers at the four corners, and the red and black swastika flag flying over the gate. Inside the fence, three red-tiled bungalows stood in a field about the size of a football pitch, and opposite them was a row of single-storey buildings which turned out to include a primitive wash-house (eight or ten cold-water taps over a zinc trough), a cookhouse and the offices of the camp staff. It looked in the August sunshine like a holiday camp; and that, in a slightly sinister way, is what it was. It had been built a few years earlier as a summer camp for the Hitler Youth.

There were fifty-two of us and we were the first inmates, the founder-members as it were, of Stalag IIIE, so that we had to start, in the most literal sense, from square one. When we arrived there wasn't so much as a football in the place, let alone a book; and since there were no facilities of any kind for educating or entertaining ourselves, we had absolutely nothing to occupy our minds. Nor – and this was crucial – had the camp been hooked up to the vital network by which the Red Cross maintained a channel of communication between prisoners-of-war and the outside world and through which alone we could expect eventually to receive mail or parcels, or indeed anything at all that might help to improve our situation.

So we were thrown back on our own resources entirely; and our own resources were extremely limited. We were all sergeants (the officers had been separated from us at Frankfurt and sent elsewhere) with an average age of twenty-two. With very rare exceptions, we had no qualifications of any kind, except that we had been taught, in something of a hurry, to fly an aeroplane or plot its course or maintain its communications system or its defences. Beyond the very limited horizon which our training had opened up to us, we knew little about anything and had no experience whatever of managing our own affairs. What faced us now was an interesting challenge.

The first need was to organize ourselves into some sort of functioning community and this we achieved after some untidy skirmishing. Accustomed to a rigid chain of command in service life, the fact that we were all equal in rank meant that there was no ready-made formula to hand. We reverted instead to the most rudimentary and absolute form of democracy, electing a leader and defining his responsibilities and the limits of his authority in the light of our unfolding circumstances.

That sounds very neat and orderly – but in practice our unwritten constitution was hammered out only in the course of a series of disorderly meetings; for we were unversed in such matters and this was very much democracy in the raw. I have in my mind's eye a clear picture of how I would look down (my bunk was the top of a three-decker at one end of the hut) on these assemblies, at which, instead of points of order, ribaldries were exchanged which enlivened but also held up our deliberations. Had it been like this in Athens, I wondered, before they got the hang of things and while they were still trying out this idea of democracy? And there were after all resemblances, for the fifty-two of us in that hut and even the 200 or so which Stalag IIIE eventually held could all meet in a single assembly, like the population of a small city-state, without having to delegate responsibility for our affairs to a deputy or an MP. I wouldn't want to press the parallel too far, but it was an interesting introduction to political science.

On the whole, democracy proved itself; but the Germans at Stalag IIIE, though inadvertently, gave it a useful helping hand. The camp was run by the German army, a fact we had noted with dismay when we arrived from Frankfurt. For there was known to be ill-feeling between the army and the Luftwaffe, and this ill-feeling was reflected in their contrasting attitudes towards the growing number of RAF prisoners in Germany. The Luftwaffe, with an agreeable echo of the chivalry with which the air forces of both sides had treated each other during the First World War, behaved during the second almost invariably with consideration towards its prisoners. Not so the German army, who showed towards us even at that early stage in the war (later on, as the bombing of Germany was intensified, this was understandable) an often petty sense of resentment and hostility. And this attitude was especially marked in the treatment we received from our army guards at Stalag IIIE.

The first intimation of this came soon after our arrival, when our newly-elected camp leader presented on our behalf a list of complaints about our living conditions. We were at once paraded in front of the camp commandant, who gave us a spirited harangue in German, from which we gathered only that he regarded us with extreme distaste. Presently he switched to English and told us that as Englanders we should expect no special treatment, that escape from this camp was out of the question and that – using a phrase which found a permanent place in our vocabulary – if we did not behave ourselves 'we will put a strain over you'. They did, but not immediately.

During the weeks that followed, and as more prisoners arrived to fill up the remaining bungalows, our thoughts turned insistently to the idea of escape. We lacked experience and any sort of equipment and the primitive ideas we tried out ended in failure, though fortunately without attracting the attention of the guards. It was only when a final party of prisoners arrived and had to be accommodated, since all three bungalows were full, in an empty shed close to the building where the

Germans themselves lived, that matters were carried a stage further.

Dark and dismal, this shed had only one quality to appeal to its inmates: it was built into the wall which on that side bounded the camp, taking the place of the barbed wire which ran along the other three sides. One evening towards the end of September, after we had amused ourselves with a lively sing-song (it was the only kind of entertainment we had so far devised), we were counted and locked as usual into our huts and presently went to sleep – only to be awakened after an hour or two by the guards. They were all smiles and in the best of tempers. It was nothing, they said, just some absurd story of an escape and they had orders to count us again; it would take only a moment. They had already been through the other two bungalows and when we had been roused and marshalled into some semblance of order (for with half a dozen Germans in the hut as well as the fifty-two of us there was barely room to move at all), they quickly counted us and showed no surprise, but just a hint of relief, at finding us all present and correct, and then moved on to the shed opposite us.

There (as we learned from its occupants next day), the prisoners seemed to be sleeping very deeply. Still good-humoured, the Germans waited while their leader routed them out of bed. Sleepily, they assembled and the count began; but as the tally mounted it began to look as though something was amiss. The shed's full complement was thirty-two and here were twelve . . . fifteen . . . eighteen – but what was this, only twenty in all? The leader was apologetic; there must be some mistake ('keep in line there, now, once again'): ten . . . fifteen . . . no, twenty it was – and no one seemed to have any idea of the whereabouts of the other twelve. It was only then that one of the guards noticed a hole in the wall . . .

Next day the shed was locked up and its twenty remaining inhabitants distributed between the three bungalows, which were now more overcrowded than ever. The rest of us sat in the sun, glad of something fresh to talk about and wondering if this was the end of the matter. In the afternoon it became clear that it was not. The cry of 'On Parade' went up and we assembled outside our huts as though for the usual roll-call. But presently the commandant appeared, followed by an interpreter and several minions carrying sacks. And there followed a scene so bizarre that if I hadn't written an account of it soon afterwards I should have imagined my memory had played me false.

The sacks were opened and proved to contain dozens of pairs of wooden clogs. Our boots were taken away from us and we were each given a pair of the clogs. It was explained to us through the interpreter that because we had not revealed our comrades' intention to escape, we were to be punished; and as soon as we were all reshod we were marched into an adjoining paddock where for the next hour and a half the guards solemnly drove us round and round, shoving and shouting at us as we went slipping and sliding on the uneven grass, while a group of soldiers and bottle-washers looked on: 'the riff-raff of the establishment', as I wrote, 'assembled to witness the humiliation of the Englanders'.

That was the start of what came to be known as the Great Strain, a serio-comic milestone in the chronicle of life at Stalag IIIE. (It was a year or two later, when I was reading *Othello*, that I found that Shakespeare had anticipated the Great Strain. In Act I, scene iii, Desdemona's father remarks: 'For they escape would teach me tyranny/To hang clogs on them.') It was an incident that would have been unthinkable in a prison camp run by the Luftwaffe; nor did we ever experience again anything quite so petty or so absurd at the hands of the German army. The only significance of the affair was that it set an enduring tone for our relationship with the Germans at Stalag IIIE; for, whoever had planned it (and how were we to know what trouble he had been having with his digestion or whether his wife had been unfaithful to him?), we never quite forgot that he had found willing hands to carry out this dingy revenge.

Once the clog-march was over, we were locked into our huts – and there we remained for the next week of unbroken sunshine, allowed out only in ones and twos to go to the wash-house or the latrine. While we had been outside getting the feel of our clogs – the only footwear we were to be allowed for the next six months – the guards had been through the huts and had removed two pocket chess sets and half a dozen tattered books which the prisoners who came after us had brought with them, so as to leave us with nothing whatever to do but sit and stare out at the sunshine.

The very day on which the Great Strain was lifted and we came blinking out into the sunshine, the weather broke; and when all twelve of the escapers were recaptured, a certain gloom descended on the camp as we settled into the routine of life as prisoners-of-war. We were still out of touch with the world; no mail or parcels had reached us and we were struggling along on the minimal rations which the Germans provided. With very little to eat and nothing to do, and without much idea of what was happening outside except that the war was going badly for us, it was a discouraging period – and yet it is interesting to recall that the possibility of defeat seems never to have crossed our minds.

I know that this was so because from somewhere I had managed to acquire an exercise book and a pencil and had begun to keep a diary again. I have it still, to remind me of much that I have forgotten about that outwardly dismal phase of apprenticeship. For some time, I find myself preoccupied with mundane details of our physical environment: with the rations, in particular (one fifth of a loaf of bread and a pound of potatoes a day, with a watery vegetable soup for lunch); but presently I see myself in those laborious pages beginning, really for the first time in my young life, to think. And at once the horizon, which had seemed so inescapably close, begins to recede as I realize that there is no reason for my imagination to be confined along with my body.

I was more fortunate than most of my companions in that my mind was well stocked with images from an unusually varied upbringing. Tramping round the paddock in my clogs, I could with a little effort picture myself back on the fells above Sedbergh, with the cloud shadows racing over the bracken; or standing on a balcony over the flooding Nile where tall sails battled with the current; or parking my bicycle outside the cathedral at Chartres to go in and walk among the shafts of coloured sunshine slanting down from those incomparable windows; or riding at sunset across Venice in a gondola, with the waters of the Grand Canal lapping, gently caressing, against the steps of the palaces. Or there was the memory of that last dawn of the old world when I stood on the crest of the Glandaz and looked down over the cloud-filled valleys of a world on the brink of war . . .

And if it was only now that I came to appreciate my own good fortune, I was struck too, when I looked about me, by the resilience with which the great majority of my companions could adjust to a change in circumstances so swift and so far-reaching. Everyone in that camp had arrived there after an experience of some moment. Some had been shot down, some had crashed, some had bailed out and floated down on their parachutes into the hostile darkness. Many had been injured, some seriously, and perhaps had seen their companions killed; and not in every case had the circumstances of their capture been as amicable as in ours. Yet, meeting them, you would have seen little to distinguish their bearing and attitudes and reactions from those of any other group of airmen on active service. We had all been in captivity for nearly six months when I wrote this: 'There are men here – boys, rather – of the age of twenty who, after being shot down (in itself a harassing experience), have been half-starved for months, kept in mental and physical inactivity, bombarded with news of the war which is naturally one-sided – & the result is that when told of the fall of Singapore they sing "Salome".'

'Salome' was one of those elaborately obscene songs for whose composition the other ranks of the regular air force had developed a positive genius, and which they had taught us amateurs almost as a formal part of our training. By some sort of spontaneous combustion the chorus of 'Salome' would start up whenever our situation appeared to be especially unfavourable: when the news was bad or there was nothing left to eat, when there was a 'strain' or a search or some other unwelcome interruption to the tedium of our lives – and it seemed an admirable and in its way sophisticated expression of our defiance and of the sense of solidarity which it was so important for us to maintain.

I expect that German prisoners devised similar techniques; but this kind of collective self-defence must have been harder for them as they came to doubt the cause in which they were engaged. And that, of course, was what saved us. We felt sure of our ground – and the more we found ourselves under pressure, the easier it became for us to maintain a united front. Our circumstances as prisoners-of-war in Germany were as a rule barely uncomfortable enough (they were positively luxurious compared to those endured by prisoners in the hands of the Japanese) to keep us up to the mark in this way. But for those of us who started life in Stalag IIIE, and especially during that first winter of 1941–42, there was just enough both of physical discomfort and psychological pressure to encourage in us the kind of obstinate unwillingness to co-operate which is both seemly and stimulating in the prisoner-of-war.

There was the hostile atmosphere engendered by the Great Strain, which continued to find expression in a series of searches and petty restrictions. There was the spartan accommodation and the lack of any distractions for either mind or body: with no footwear besides our wooden clogs, no kind of physical activity would have been possible, even if we had had the space and the equipment for it. These limitations became doubly irksome as the winter set in – and proved to be the harshest winter that any of us had experienced. For six weeks we had temperatures of between –5° and –15°C; the cold-water taps in the wash-house froze up, and when they were thawed out the drain remained frozen, so that the waste water simply ran out of the open doorway (there was no door) and froze there, making access to the wash-house hazardous for us in our clogs. As for the 'open plan' latrine, which was also virtually in the open air, it posed a challenge which I suppose would have been more acute if we had had more to eat . . .

Apart from washing ourselves, there was the problem of washing our clothes – and having washed them, of getting them dry again, for we had nothing else to put on. So it was not altogether surprising that as the winter set in one or two prisoners reported finding lice in their clothes. With the threat of typhus in the air – and the camp had not even the most rudimentary sick bay – the Germans took this seriously and as the first snows were falling at the beginning of November they announced that we were to go *en masse* to a big camp further north which was equipped for this kind of thing, to be formally 'deloused'. The episode stays in my mind as one of the most disagreeable of my whole life.

It was an hour before dawn on Guy Fawkes' day when we set off through the snow in our clogs, carrying (this presented no problem) our few belongings and two days' rations: two fifths of a loaf of bread each and a piece of blood sausage. The Germans made one concession to the weather and issued us with French army greatcoats, insubstantial things in a pretty shade of blue; but I was glad of one since my wardrobe still consisted of the shirt and battle-dress in which I had fallen into the North Sea in July. Thus equipped, and probably (I don't remember about this) humming 'Salome' under our breath, we marched off in the darkness to the station and stood there among the snow-covered piles of coke while a freight train was marshalled, each truck bearing the familiar legend *40 hommes, 8 chevaux*.

In we piled, and off we went, jerkily, into the reluctant dawn. At first we joked bravely about square wheels and how lucky it was that we were not horses; but gradually we relapsed into a state of frozen misery as we tried alternately to sit on the dirty floor, with the cold air whistling through the cracks in the floor-boards, or to stand stamping our feet and rocking against each other as the trucks clattered and clanked over endless unseen points. The journey lasted six hours but eventually, like all things good and bad, it came to an end and we found with relief that our frozen limbs were still serviceable as we stumbled out on to a station called Luchenwald and marched off under a grey sky into the unknown.

After a mile or so our destination presented itself, in the snow and the mud and the grey November twilight, as the most depressing place I had ever seen. (Years afterwards, when I read *One Day in the Life of Ivan Denisovich*, it recalled for me at once that camp at Luchenwald in all its grey wretchedness.) It looked to us, accustomed to our tiny back-water, enormous, a kind of gigantic slum, and it was in fact an agglomeration of separate camps whose size and variety bewildered us. Within the outer fence of barbed wire there were internal divisions, each a world in itself, in which there hurried through the muddy snow soldiers of various nationalities, dressed in queer polyglot uniforms: Frenchmen, Serbs, Czechs, even – behind their own special wire but in full view of the rest of us – Russians, whom none of us had seen before.

We did not learn all this at once for first we had our own unwelcome appointment to keep. From the main gate we were marched directly to a long one-storey building where we were separated from our belongings, told to strip, had our heads shaved and went on to be. . . I suppose the word is fumigated . . . to find ourselves at the end of the process shivering naked in an unheated passage, sans clothes, sans hair and feeling acutely ridiculous. My diary records:

> . . . a strange spectacle: sixty men, naked & shaved to the scalp, hop around in anxiety in the bare passage trying to find the clothes that belong to them – or, failing these, the best of the remainder, for the Frenchman running the establishment had mixed up all our clothes, & passed them back for us to fight over. After a six-hour journey in a cattle truck & nearly four miles of marching through the snow in wooden clogs & a couple of hours waiting about in the November gloom, it wasn't easy to see the funny side of it . . .

Once the delousing was over, though, and we had found a place to sleep, we set out to explore these unfamiliar surroundings and the visit began to take on a more agreeable tone. For one thing, it was invigorating to have our narrow horizon so suddenly and unexpectedly extended. Instead of our own narrow little world, with its uniform population – all English, all young, all aircrew – and its lack of any but the crudest essentials of life, here was a positive metropolis of a prison camp, housing men of all ages from a dozen countries, many of whom had acquired in more than a year of captivity aptitudes – and possessions – of a sophistication at which we, like bumpkins from the village, could only marvel.

I got off to a good start when I fell into conversation with a couple of Frenchmen, one of whom as we parted pressed into my hand a scrap of paper and told me to take it to the cookhouse. When I did so, I found that it entitled me to his ration of soup – and then the fellow handing out the soup, who turned out to be a Yugoslav, noticed my uniform and invited me to visit him later in the evening, remarking that he had a brother serving with the RAF in Egypt. When I followed his directions I found him already entertaining several of my companions from Stalag IIIE with a liberality which was astonishing to us. For a couple of hours we exchanged news of the war and compared our experiences as prisoners, and in general enjoyed – for it was the first time for months that any of us had encountered anyone whose background differed at all from our own – what seemed like a tremendous social occasion.

Our host was one of a party of Serbian air-force officers who had been captured when the Germans invaded Yugoslavia two or three months before I had been shot down. At first sight they looked, with their resplendent uniforms, like the 'chocolate soldier' whom Bernard Shaw made the anti-hero of *Arms and the Man*; but like him they were full of surprises. Apart from their immediate advantage of living in a camp which was far better organized than our own, with a flourishing black market and all sorts of clandestine contacts with the outside world, their situation was far from enviable. Their country was under occupation, many of their families had been wiped out (especially those of the officers), they could not even be sure that an independent Yugoslavia would survive the war; yet they were courteous and debonair and extraordinarily generous to us in this fleeting encounter. Above all, they gave us the feeling, there in the unexpectedly warm heart of this forbidding place (and the same was true of the Frenchmen) of being part of a wide and ultimately indomitable fraternity for whom the present, with its attendant ills, was no more than an unpalatable interlude. It was a considerable achievement.

There was one group of prisoners at Luchenwald, though, who were rigorously excluded from this fraternity and whose situation left an indelible impression on my mind. These were the Russians, of whom I wrote at the time that in the midst of all this:

... the wretched state of the Russian prisoners was terrible to see. Other prisoners were not allowed to communicate with them at all. Their rations were a tenth of a loaf and a little soup a day – nothing else; just half the amount that had made starvation seem a reality to us – and there were unpleasant stories of men being shot out of hand when they picked up packages of food or cigarettes thrown over the wire by Frenchmen. They were bullied by the guards, cowed and weak from starvation: altogether a pitiable sight and one that made my blood boil. I stood in a light fall of snow watching them in line for their midday meal. Guards were shouting at them in German and when they obviously did not understand, the guards would seize them by the arms and hustle them about. Insufficiently clothed, terrorized and weak, they tried to avoid the guards but when they had received the meagre amount of soup in their billycans, the guards would chivvy them about again, no doubt hoping to see them spill the soup, and the Russians would shamble off anxiously, trying to save the precious food.

That scene stays in my mind as the epitome of war, with its squalor and degradation and the hateful power it has of bringing to the surface in the most ordinary men patterns of behaviour of which normally they would be incapable. You can explain it, as some do, by saying that there is in every one of us a brute just below the surface and restrained only by the conventions which civilization imposes on us; or (as I prefer to believe) that war disorients us and thrusts us into what, psychologically speaking, is uncharted territory, so that we act and react irrationally in circumstances for which we are unprepared. Whatever is the truth of it, I know that the impression I received that day in the mud and the snow of Luchenwald had its effect on the way I was to react in a comparable situation more than a quarter of a century later.

After the unforeseen distraction of the delousing expedition, we went 'home' to Stalag IIIE with mixed feelings. That glimpse of a wider and a more complex world than our own had been stimulating but also disturbing. On the whole it was with relief that we settled back into our own familiar backyard – especially as our lives now took a turn for the better.

Just before we set out on that dismal journey in the cattle trucks, the first mail from home had found its way to us and when we got back we found that we were firmly on the map. Not only were there letters for most of us, but even parcels: both the food parcels sent by the Red Cross and the personal parcels in which our families were allowed to send us, once a quarter, clothes and everyday things like toothpaste and razor blades which people tend to describe as necessities but whose existence we had practically forgotten.

It is difficult, perhaps impossible, to convey what all this meant to us after four months of isolation. The letters of course had been censored at both ends and sometimes there was not much left of them – but even the envelopes had their value for us. The familiar handwriting was like an embrace and the postmark, with its commonplace 'London SW, 4.30 p.m.', would throw open a whole compartment in the memory that had grown musty with disuse, out of which would shape itself a picture of a London street in the gathering dusk, the plane trees all bare and a group of people waiting at the bus stop, past which a figure went hurrying towards the pillar box on the corner . . .

It was a funny business, being a prisoner. In one sense we had all grown up quite suddenly; in another, we had reverted to a kind of childhood – and it wasn't the easiest thing to get used to. We had at the same time to rely on ourselves and to accept the fact that we were dependent on other people for our simplest needs. Unless someone fed us, we should starve. Unless someone provided us with clothes, a comb, a pencil, shoe-laces (not that we had any use for these while we were restricted to our clogs), we should have to make do without them and the other trifles which we would once have considered indispensable. And when you came right down to it, there was precious little that really *was* indispensable, apart from food – and there was something to be said for an experience which could teach you to distinguish it from what was merely desirable in life.

This was the valuable aspect, the pearl in the outwardly unpromising oyster of life as a prisoner-of-war. If you were ready to learn, it had a tremendous amount to teach you: first, about human nature and about the qualities and characteristics which made one man rise and another sink among his fellows (for here we started out equal, not just in rank and age, but in the fact that we owned, every one of us, precisely nothing); and then, most valuable of all, about yourself, your aims and motives, your weaknesses and the inner resources by which you might overcome them and devise out of all this a scale of values which was truly your own, distilled, sometimes painfully but (speaking for myself) more often out of a mixture of surprise and relief, from your own experience.

Quite early on I find in my diary a passage where I asked myself what I really missed about the life from which I was temporarily cut off. After freedom itself – and that had already been curtailed once we were absorbed into service life – and the comfortable background of family and friends, it was remarkable how much of the baggage of 'civilization' I found I could discard without much sense of loss. Diversions like the theatre, the cinema and the dance hall, which had seemed so alluring as an escape from the barrackroom at home in England; even the pub, to which we had gravitated almost automatically on our free evenings; all these I now found I missed, not for themselves but only as symbols of that lost freedom ('I've never suffered the least anguish at having to do without my pint, but oh to walk once again into a friendly English pub, a free man!'). Physical exercise I missed, but again more for the freedom it presupposed than for itself – but then our skimpy diet left us with little energy to spare. Privacy, or rather the lack of it, was at first a hardship, but not a major one, not at that age; life in a prison camp, after all, was in this respect not far removed from life in the sergeants' mess – and the sergeants' mess not altogether unlike a boarding school, except that there were fewer holidays (and none at all, of course, in a prison camp). Even music, to my surprise, I hardly missed, although once other wants had been supplied it was something I came to long for.

Being a prisoner was in fact not unlike going back to the days before the industrial revolution, both because we had to learn to manage without any of the mechanical and technological aids invented in the last two hundred years and because the prisoner must put up with a lack of mobility which is more or less absolute. The first of these disabilities is easy enough to cope with – even tempting: witness the popularity of camping and climbing and sailing holidays among people eager to step back into an environment more natural as well as more exacting. But the lack of mobility: that is an altogether more formidable challenge. So instinctively have we come to take it for granted that we can jump in the car, or take a train or a bus, not to mention an aeroplane, and exchange our own environment for a completely different one in the space of an hour or two, that it is difficult to put ourselves in the shoes of our ancestors, for whom the stage coach existed (if they could afford it) but who, in nine cases out of ten, could seldom travel more than a few miles from the place where they were born.

In our own case the contrast was even more marked. A few weeks before I was taken prisoner, when I was rounding off my training at Lossiemouth, I had been flying with a crew of young men like myself all over the Highlands and the Western Isles. When we had a day off we could explore the glorious countryside around Elgin and Forres; and in the endless twilight of the northern summer we could walk the sands of the Moray Firth, and take a wee dram from time to time and in between watch the aircraft of coastal command going out to look for German submarines. Now I was confined with a couple of hundred others to an area the size of a football pitch, and it took a little time to adjust our sights.

For this necessary exercise I had an invaluable ally in my father. A contemplative man, largely self-educated and widely read, he now made it his principal concern in life to satisfy my wants, so far as this lay within his power. Not my physical needs, to which my mother and those faithful aunts gave their attention, but the no less pressing demands – in the long run they were more pressing by far – of my mind and spirit.

When the first parcels arrived at Stalag IIIE, there were two for me. The first contained clothes: a Jaeger pullover, fresh shirts and socks, with a toothbrush, and a brush and comb to mock my empty scalp, and these were welcome indeed. The other was a wooden box, perhaps twenty-four inches long and fifteen across, which when it was opened in front of me (such was the rule) caused me to gasp in wonder and anticipation. Apart from a stray copy of *Ivanhoe* and some dog-eared mystery story, I had had nothing to read for three months, and this was a deprivation for which I had found no solace or remedy. But here, tight-packed in that magic box which had found its way to me by God knows what uncharted route (it had come from Cairo, where my parents were still living) and presently spread out before my disbelieving gaze, was a whole library in itself.

My father was always a man to take the long view and when he pondered on the composition of that box of books for me, he took no chances. With Rommel on the move in North Africa and Hitler's men marching deeper into Russia, there was no knowing how long the war might last and my father, as though planning for another Thirty Years War, made sure that I should not go short of reading matter. He started off, uncontroversially, with a complete Shakespeare, sonnets and all, on India paper. Then came Milton, in the splendid Nonesuch edition, and after him Browning, another thousand pages to help me remember, as I noted in my diary, 'that the name means poetry as well as machine guns'. Next, the collected works of Voltaire: and who better than *Candide* to remind me of the many evils from which I was immune? In addition there were four of Trollope's novels, ideal reading in a prison camp because Trollope, like the Dutch painters of the seventeenth century, paid such leisurely attention to detail, to the textures and nuances of everyday life. For us in our isolation that was enormously attractive, and reassuring too, in that it gave us the feeling of being at least vicariously in touch with a world familiar but become suddenly as remote as the Egypt of the pharaohs.

Here were rich pastures and I decided to keep what used to be called a commonplace book, noting in it anything in my reading that seemed to have a special relevance to my situation; and it is interesting to see what kind of ideas struck home most immediately to an imagination so eager for inspiration.

The earliest entries point clearly to a state of mind where survival was the foremost preoccupation. Subconsciously, perhaps, I was building up my defences – and for that purpose, as he must have foreseen, my father's selection (with others that were to follow) was an inspired one. From *Paradise Lost*, for instance, on the very first page of this homely anthology, comes Milton's reminder that no external force can bind a man into submission against his will, since:

> The mind is its own place, and in itself
> Can make a Heav'n of Hell, a Hell of Heav'n.

Just over the page, from a reading of *Richard II*, what I record are not the poignant words which Shakespeare put into the mouth of the poor self-pitying king, but the stern and heartening injunction of Carlisle when he tells Richard:

> My lord, wise men ne'er sit and wail their woes,
> But presently prevent the ways to wail.

And next to it stands the passage (it is from 'Bishop Blougram's Apology') in which Browning offers what I have always found as good a guide as any to the wise acceptance of life as it is – with the proviso that we have it always in our power to make it a little better:

> The common problem, yours, mine, everyone's
> Is – not to fancy what were fair in life
> Provided it could be – but finding first
> What may be, then find how to make it fair
> Up to our means: a very different thing!

That lesson was soon learned and before long, as the range of my reading was extended, the tone of the entries becomes more varied. I was still on the look-out for those sudden shafts of insight with which an imaginative writer could light up some aspect of our own condition. Charlotte Brontë, for instance, might have had us in mind, whose lives had been transposed so abruptly from the active to the passive mood, when she wrote in *Villette* of '. . . lapsing from the passionate pain of change to the palsy of custom'. But now it was in a spirit of pure appreciation and not out of any need for reassurance that I would single out a phrase like this one from *The House of the Seven Gables*, in which Nathaniel Hawthorne epitomized the enemy we had to contend with: '. . . the cold, sunless, stagnant calm of a day that is to be like innumerable yesterdays'. If on such a day I felt any inclination to weaken, there were always people like Conrad to remind me that 'As long as there is any life before one, a jolly good fright now and then is a salutary discipline' . . . and Samuel Butler put the same idea into a more sophisticated frame when he remarked in *The Way of All Flesh*: 'We have so often found life to be an affair of being rather frightened than hurt that we have become like the people who live under Vesuvius, and chance it without much misgiving.'

Samuel Butler made a marvellously astringent companion for me at a time when the foes I had to fight off were boredom and self-pity. My father had clearly been influenced by him at some stage in his life and the letters he wrote to me while I was a prisoner carried frequent overtones of Butler's distinctive blend of cynicism and clear-sightedness. But they carried echoes too of so many other writers, and strayed so beguilingly over a whole wide range of human thought and experience as well, that I treasured the growing pile of these letters as much as the books themselves, and they did more to equip me with the philosophical outlook I needed than the contents of all the parcels I was to receive. It is a tribute which I suppose only a fellow-prisoner could appreciate to the full.

I say I treasured my father's letters and whatever else I might have to abandon when we were moved from place to place, I never let them out of my grasp. Looking through them today, when my own sons are as old as I was when he wrote them, what strikes me is the extraordinary sensitivity with which he was able to judge what to say and what not to say. There is almost playful acknowledgement of the fact that my situation leaves something to be desired; but there is also the unspoken assumption that I should not want him to waste time on commiseration, as though I were a hospital patient condemned to a diet of slops, but shall look to him for more substantial nourishment.

From the outset he is looking ahead – happily neither of us knew how far ahead – to my return and is laying plans for the holiday with which I shall celebrate my recovered freedom. As with that first parcel of books, he is thinking on the grand scale. A year, he suggests, would be an appropriate term for this holiday, and he starts to consider the relative merits of the Pyrenees up towards Andorra – 'fine mountain country, with gentians peeping out of the short grass high up, and fast-flowing agate-green mountain streams with trout in them' – and of central Italy, in 'the little hill towns about Perugia, with landscapes just like the wistful backgrounds of the renaissance painters'.

He judged rightly that to read about places I knew and others I had yet to see would keep my imagination on the move, even if my body for the time being was immobilized. So he drew on his own memories of Chartres, where 'I shall never forget my first glimpse of the windows on a dull and rainy spring day, when they hung like heavenly jewellery high up in an almost dark cathedral'; or recalled a journey he had once made with Howard Carter, the discoverer of Tutankhamun's tomb at Luxor, when they left the ship at Naples and drove to Pompeii, then on to the sea at Salerno and back by the coast road to Naples: '. . . one of the loveliest drives in the world: the road runs high up on the mountains bordering the sea, which lay then all rippling hundreds of feet below, while the roadsides were smothered in flowering shrubs and fruit trees in blossom . . .'

His memory for the detail of places was remarkable, and when he was short of memories he had only to look out from the roof of the old house by the Nile to find much to delight us both. When he first sat down to write to me in Germany, resuming our correspondence as he remarked 'after a certain rather uncomfortable interlude' (for a full month he and my mother had known only that I was 'missing, believed killed'), the river was starting to flood: '. . . and the moisture in the air brings the light-blue morning mists, in which faery boats drift along and are swept out farther and farther by the swirling brown current and the waters begin to creep over the flat lands bordering the road'.

As the seasons began to roll past, there was always this pageant at hand and in between stories and recollections he would include every now and then a vignette of the Egyptian countryside which I had known as a child, with 'a frieze of sheep and goats tap-tapping along dusty canal banks against a sunset glow and the endless fields of *durra* rustling gently in the wind'.

There was a fine discretion about his handling of this theme of travel; he never forgot that, however invigorating it might be to me, it could be tantalizing as well. When he described his own garden by the river's edge, where date palms grew out of the lawn and in the evening 'the setting sun turns the bunches of dates golden-brown and the palm stems sway lazily in the breeze – if there is any', he added as though in an afterthought that he too was pinned down by the war. (In nearly four years he had been no further afield than Alexandria.) So it was ostensibly on his own account, but really on mine, that he quoted what he called 'the encouraging assurance that change is an easy panacea; it takes character to stay in one place and be happy there'. If there was not much to please the eye in my terrestrial surroundings, he added, I could always look up at the changing patterns of the sky; and he recalled from somewhere the story of the philosopher showing a friend his garden. 'It isn't very big,' remarked the friend. 'Not if you look this way,' agreed the philosopher, pointing horizontally; 'but this way' – pointing upwards – 'it reaches heaven.'

It was the happiness which these letters exuded that reached out a helping hand to me; and it was unclouded by the anxieties which he and my mother kept to themselves, with three sons engaged in the war (for my second brother, David, had now signed on with the Canadian air force) and the war itself on their own Egyptian doorstep. They were eager, of course, to know something of my circumstances, but since there was little that I could tell them that would be reassuring, and less space in which to tell it, I thought it sensible to confine myself to the barest outline. When his questions went unanswered, my father was quick to take the hint, observing coolly that 'while we naturally hanker after more details, it is easy to forget that there are in all probability few to give and that your existence is not such as to lend itself to far-flung description.' As it was, he wrote, he pictured me with 'Milton and Shakespeare and tinned beef and boots mixed together under a straw bed' – which was a pretty accurate vision. 'Never mind', he added in a perceptive aside, what one might think of as the normal comforts of life 'will one day' – not 'soon', you notice, or 'by Christmas', or any other of the deceiving phrases with which others sought to keep up our spirits, but just 'one day – be yours again and so cherished that they will never again be lightly held'. And there he hit an important nail on the head.

Of the war itself he wrote little. There were, to begin with, those censors to be propitiated, one at his end and one at mine. One of his earliest letters had been returned to him, 'shipwrecked on the reefs of indiscretion', and after that his references to the progress of the fighting were few and indirect. He knew that any news he might give me would in any case be out of date by the time I received it – letters took as a rule two or three months to reach us – and he was shrewd enough to guess, as he once hinted, that 'possibly you hear more than I suppose'. (By the time he wrote that, some of the more technically ingenious among us had indeed put together a radio receiver which kept us often more accurately in touch with events than our captors.) Only as it affected my family and friends was he careful to keep me posted about the course of the war; and since he was in Egypt, where throughout 1942 and much of 1943 he was close to the only front on which our own forces were active, he had in this respect plenty to tell me.

His was indeed an admirable listening post and a number of my pre-war friends fetched up in Cairo on their way to the front as it swung to and fro across North Africa until the 8th Army moved on into Italy in the summer of 1943. My parents were happy to provide a base for them where they could rest and wash the sand out of their hair, and from their comings and goings I gained an idea of the way the tide of the war, which had been running so strongly against us when I was captured turned gradually in our favour. Mostly, on this personal

level, the news was good and for a long time those of my friends who
were with the army in the Western Desert seemed to enjoy a wonderful
immunity; whereas my companions in the RAF, those who had come
with me from Kenya and with whom I had speculated so carelessly
about our common future in those sun-filled days on the deck of the
Athlone Castle, were shot down and killed one after the other, until
only a handful remained.

While they survived, they used to write to me and their letters, so
casually recording that so-and-so had 'bought it' or 'pranged', or using
some other of the cheerful euphemisms that masked another tragedy,
were almost as precious to me as my father's. But it was from him that I
received the blow I most dreaded, when he wrote in his tone of gentle
realism to tell me of the death of Stuart Alexander, with whom I had
walked in all weathers over the hills about Sedbergh before we went up
to Oxford together in that last year before the war.

A few months earlier my father had written to say that Stuart had
turned up 'in some not very distant quarter where there is good
bathing' and hoped to come and stay when he got leave. He was to
bring with him, if he could find her again, 'a young lady of whom he has
made frequent mention'. After an interval there came a letter from
Stuart himself, looking ahead to the time when together we might
resume some more fruitful existence, but providing about himself only
the laconic information that 'I am still a bachelor, though recently I
have had rather a narrow escape.' After this, a long silence during
which I reflected enjoyably on the celebration there would be in the old
house by the Nile when Stuart arrived, as the most welcome of guests
and the closest possible reminder of the happiness which for all of us
was in suspense. When it came, the news that instead his jeep had been
blown up by a mine shortly after the battle of Alamein gave me my
blackest day in the whole of the war.

10

By that time our own situation had improved dramatically. At the end of April 1942, when I had been a prisoner for nine months, news reached us that we were to be transferred from our little outpost to the main camp for air-force prisoners, Stalag Luft III. There, we were given to understand, we should find ourselves living in conditions of almost unimaginable luxury: there would be a library, sports facilities, room to study, to organize classes and lectures and plays – everything, in short, that our hearts could desire (except freedom). Perhaps we should even be able to have a hot shower once in a way . . .

We did our best to look enthusiastic about these breathtaking prospects, and indeed we were delighted at the thought of being able to stretch our wings in a cage less cruelly confined. And yet . . . if the guards who brought us this information had been more observant, they must have noticed that our smiles were forced, that there was something that seemed to temper our rejoicing. And so there was, for since the beginning of March we had been engaged in the building of a tunnel which we had hoped to have ready by the end of June; and here were the Germans telling us on 28 April that the first party (which was to consist of 100 prisoners, including me) would leave for Stalag Luft III in a week's time, to be followed a week later by the remaining ninety odd. It was a critical situation.

As soon as the Germans were out of earshot we put our heads together to see what was to be done. The key figure in the enterprise was a Welsh miner (I have forgotten his name, for of course there was no mention of any of this in my diary, apart from a brief résumé of the facts once the episode was behind us) and to his knowledge and technical skill we all deferred. The tunnel by now was some eighty-five feet long, but there was still thirty or forty feet to go before it would reach the perimeter fence. It was out of the question that we could complete it within a week, said the master builder, but just possible that it could be done inside a fortnight. If we all buckled to, he was ready to have a go.

We had no alternative – and it was always possible that the move would be postponed – so we got down to it, and for the next week the tunnel dominated our lives. It was not easy work, for the camp was built on sand with only a shallow top-dressing of soil, and every foot of the tunnel had to be securely buttressed with timber (to be precise with the bed-boards from our wooden bunks, which became increasingly insecure and uncomfortable as the work progressed) and it had to travel straight and at a constant depth. Such subtleties were the responsibility of the Welshman and a few chosen experts. The rest of us, the brute labour force, apart from contributing our bed-boards, were merely employed in shifting the sand from the head of the tunnel to the starting point and dispersing it as inconspicuously as possible about the camp.

Even this was not as easy as it sounds. It meant that a steadily increasing number of us would go down for a shift of forty-five minutes, which we would spend on all fours, head to tail like a mule train, pushing boxes of sand between our legs to the next man, hoping that no one would faint (for the air grew very foul, despite the ventilation shafts which were cautiously driven up to the surface at intervals) or by a clumsy motion knock out of place one of the timbers and provoke a landslide.

I don't remember much about it now, but I do remember thinking that here was one more illusion gone. Looked at from outside, as I had considered it when I was first taken prisoner, the idea of building a tunnel out of a prison camp had about it the aura of romance. It must be exciting, stimulating, an experience to savour; and so it might seem – until you came actually to find yourself engaged in it. Then, like almost everything else connected with war, it turned out to be both disagreeable and dangerous. With sand in your fingernails and grating against your knees, breathing that filthy air, you found yourself praying for the end of the shift and reflecting that it would be hard to imagine a more dismal end than to be buried alive by a fall of sand six feet underground at Stalag IIIE.

We went at it as fast as we could and by the time our advance party left for Stalag Luft III, the tunnel was more than a hundred feet long; it was touch and go whether it could be completed in time for the rearguard to make use of it. As we rattled eastwards by train and then when we were installed in our new quarters, we waited breathlessly for news. When it came, it was vastly satisfying. The tunnel had been finished with two days to spare (it was 163 feet long) and that night fifty-two prisoners had escaped through it, the last of them as day was breaking. The whole neighbourhood had been thrown into confusion as troops were brought in from elsewhere to search for the missing men; and one could only speculate about the fate of the staff of the camp when the Gestapo arrived to investigate the affair, and to enquire how it was that those who were recaptured were found to possess maps, compasses and all manner of things which they had no business to have in a well-run prison camp.

In these joys we could share only vicariously; and there followed, as generally happened, the disappointment of hearing that, one by one, the escapers had been recaptured (and in one case shot). But as a skirmish, a minor engagement on the part of a resistance movement in which we could claim a modest share, it left us with some sense of fulfilment. At the very least, it represented an appropriate farewell gesture to our hosts at Stalag IIIE, who had made our lives there much more uncomfortable than they need have been.

At Stalag Luft III, by contrast, we now found ourselves living in conditions which, if not luxurious, were certainly far more congenial. The basic pattern was the same; the barbed wire, the searchlights at night, the miserable ration of bread and potatoes and watery soup; but the atmosphere was radically different. Not merely did those promises (which we had instinctively disbelieved) of 'amenities' turn out to be true, so that we could, after a fashion, study, play games, organize concerts and plays and at intervals wash both ourselves and our clothes in hot water, but – and this was crucial – we were now in the hands of the Luftwaffe, who on the whole treated us with respect, losing their tempers with us only when, out of boredom or a vague sense of obligation, we provoked them by insubordination or the kind of practical jokes which enlivened our existence.

We soon learned how far we could go without running into danger. It was fun from time to time to disrupt one of the parades at which, morning and evening, they counted us. It was even more fun, when the guards were pacing up and down our ranks trying to maintain order, to see if one of us could plant a lighted cigarette in the barrel of a rifle slung over a man's shoulder. If we were caught in this or some other misdemeanour, the penalty was a week in the 'cooler' on bread and water, and we accepted our punishment (unless of course we could evade capture and merge into the ranks of our fellows, who would mount diversions and hide us and generally confuse the issue) with the good humour of schoolboys convicted of some formal breach of discipline. It was not in their interest or in ours to let these pranks provoke a formal confrontation between us, nor did we try to do so unless some wider issue was at stake and we felt it necessary to stand on our few rights. On the whole, the Luftwaffe played the game with us and we with them, in a spirit of not unfriendly tolerance.

There were exceptions, of course, but at Stalag Luft III in 1942 they were not many and most of them were of our making. In Sergeant-Pilot (later Warrant Officer) 'Dixie' Dean, we had elected a 'camp leader' of altogether outstanding ability and under his direction we organized our affairs to a remarkable degree. There was an escape committee whose consent and supervision was required for any attempt to break out of the camp. There was a school – you could almost call it a university by the middle of 1943 – in which I learned Italian and shorthand and at the same time (for my year at Oxford made me in that company almost a professor) taught history and French. There was an amateur dramatic society whose productions would not have disgraced a provincial repertory company in England (I like to remember that I acted in one of them alongside Roy Dotrice) and a debating society, which gave me a valuable grounding in public speaking. In fact almost any activity, legitimate or illegitimate, could be catered for, since there were between two and three thousand men in our compound (there was a separate officers' compound next door) who possessed between them an extraordinary variety of skills. And where technical ingenuity by itself could not provide something we needed, it was not long before we found ways of supplementing it, by theft or bribery and ultimately in a few cases by blackmail, so that soon we possessed a radio (from which a summary of BBC news bulletins would be circulated from hut to hut), and later on a highly developed unit for forging German identification papers and any other aids that might be needed for escape plans which grew steadily more complex and sophisticated.

All this was a far cry from our narrow existence at Stalag IIIE. It was not a life which anyone would choose for himself and I felt its shortcomings as keenly as anyone. But it was a pattern of existence in which it was possible, for much of the time, for anyone who wished to do so to engage himself in some useful activity. And here, I came to realize, lay the key to happiness.

Sometimes, inevitably, this was not enough and I felt, as on a day in September 1943, 'all the boredom and the greyness of this life closing in on me'. But in Flecker's *Hassan* I had come across the remark that 'Allah . . . gave men dreams by night that they might learn to dream by day', and I set out to develop day-dreaming as a conscious technique, a deliberate form of exercise for the imagination. And my dreams took the form now, not of nostalgic recollections of things past but of a fierce determination to live more fully in future: 'One of these days I'll go on my travels again and know the pleasant anticipation of a new port and the joy of exploring. And I'll have my eyes open and make up for two or three years among barrack huts and barbed wire – by God I will!'

Looking back now, I can think of all this as a vital part, perhaps the most vital, of my education. The difficulty about it was that its lessons were soon learned and that with the slow – the infinitely slow – passage of time they became repetitious. After a year at Stalag Luft III we were moved to a new camp at Heydekrug in what was then East Prussia and is now well inside the frontier of the Soviet Union. Up there near the shore of the Baltic, a thousand miles from England, we spent another year, in conditions closer to those we had known in those early months at Stalag IIIE, until in June 1944 the long-awaited news of the allied invasion in the west seemed at last to promise us salvation. But before the promise could be fulfilled, we still had a long way to go.

Two weeks after the invasion, the Russians mounted an offensive in the east and our spirits rose still higher at the thought that the fighting was taking place only some 250 miles from us. When the Russians broke through and seemed to be heading straight for Koenigsberg ('just round the corner from here'), the excitement mounted and all the expectations which we had learned so painfully to hold in check found free rein. During the first half of July the Russians advanced at an astonishing rate. On 10 July there was a tremendous electric storm and lying in my bunk that night I wrote that:

. . . the Russian armies are pressing straight towards us through White Russia; Minsk was captured a week ago and now they are fighting in the streets of Vilna – about 150 miles from here . . . It is impossible to say where we shall be in a week's time. We might be marching west across East Prussia, or in cattle trucks jolting through the Polish corridor into Germany proper. We might be piled into lorries heading east into Russia – or we might still be here on the border of Lithuania. Taking it all in all, there is a delicious uncertainty about it all, which acts like a tonic after the past thirty-five months . . .

For another four days the uncertainty persisted. Rumours flew and contradicted each other, and every day we expected to find ourselves on the move westwards; but with each day's delay the hope grew that the Russians could cut off our retreat along with that of the Germans. Then on 15 July – three years to the day after I had been shot down – we were bundled off on foot on the first stage of a journey which was to carry us right across Poland and Germany. At dawn next day we crossed the river Niemen at Tilsit (where I peered out from our cattle truck at the island where Napoleon had met the Tsar Alexander in 1807) and rolled on past the battlefield at Tannenburg and across the Polish corridor, to arrive in the evening at Thorn. Here we paused – and a couple of days later heard confused reports of the attempt on Hitler's life when Colonel Von Stauffenberg brought a bomb in his briefcase into the command headquarters – but when the Russians developed a new thrust towards Warsaw we were soon back in the cattle trucks again for another forty-eight-hour journey which took us to Fallingsbostel, a little country town near Hanover. And it was here, as the euphoria of that summer of 1944 faded, that we settled down to endure one more winter in a country that was starting visibly to collapse.

It was a hard time for us, as it was for the Germans. The relentless allied bombing deprived us, as it deprived them, of food supplies and coal and mail. What was more important was the fact that, although the end was almost in sight and despite the furious attacks in the east and in the west, not a single allied soldier was yet on German soil, and it was sobering to sit down at eleven o'clock on the morning of 3 September and reflect that '. . . in 1939 most of us thought the war would last six months or a year – and now, after five years, here we are back where we started territorially, with the winning still to be done'.

For us, though, there was the compensation – which was denied to the Germans – that as the situation worsened, so our hopes grew. Now, too, we felt in touch with events. By day and by night the bombers roared over our heads and on a clear day we could see them, like great shoals of silver fish against the blue sky, while more than once at night we could feel the reverberations as the bombs fell on nearby targets. There were endless rumours and false alarms and if, as autumn shaded into winter, our hopes began to seem agonizingly deferred, just over the horizon of our lives lay freedom. The thought was intoxicating.

Meanwhile, though, our immediate problem was to survive. We had next to no food, for we were beyond the reach of the Red Cross and the Germans had cut our rations and were to cut them again, until we were living on 200 grams of bread a day and a few potatoes, with a thin soup of boiled swedes ('Jesus Christ,' we used irreverently to say, 'the same yesterday and today and for ever') at midday. The stoves in our barracks were for the most part as empty as our bellies and the roofs leaked until the frost came to seal them. With the war visibly in its last stages, there was no point in trying to escape, even if we had possessed the strength for it, into the chaos of a country disintegrating before our eyes. Survival had become a sufficient objective in itself.

My own survival kit was the remains of the library I had built up at Stalag Luft III and which I had taken with me to Heydekrug. There was not much left of it now, for when we marched out of Heydekrug in July 1944 we had been able to take with us only what we could carry. At first sight it seemed absurd in such a situation to weigh myself down with books; but there had been willing hands to help me carry a few of them and now, in this final emergency, they proved their worth. During that last winter of the war, alongside the breathless accounts of the progress of the fighting in the east and in the west (where the front crept slowly towards us) my diary reminds me that I read as widely as I have ever read before or since, and with a total absorption which few of us can know after the age of fifteen or sixteen.

All through a dark December day, for instance, I lay in my bunk reading Conrad's *Typhoon*:

only occasionally conscious of barrackroom, cold, hunger and the rest – I saw that dark hold where the coolies were flung to and fro as the ship was battered by the storm, and the chartroom like an island where Captain MacWhirr planned his campaign and the giant waves beat on the windows – an experience like this makes one *feel* the value of books as few others could.

After that came *War and Peace*, spread over a fortnight this time – and in the middle of it the Germans launched their counter-offensive in the Ardennes. I hardly knew which campaign was which during those two weeks as the tremendous sweep of the narrative, with all its variety of character and situation, took hold of my imagination and I was transported into a world so powerfully visualized as to blot out our own predicament. I knew exactly how Pierre felt, though, when at the end of his first day as a prisoner he was given a potato baked in the ashes and thought that with a pinch of salt it was better than anything he had ever eaten . . .

It wasn't always easy to concentrate. Eighty young men living in one room can make a lot of noise, and that same barrackroom was the scene of some very varied activities. One evening I broke off from *War and Peace* to watch: 'an American disembowelling a chicken on the floor beside me – a distasteful process which I have not witnessed before. The chicken is for sale, having been bought from a German; I could have it myself if I could afford 180 cigarettes.'

And there were the lights (four twenty-five-watt bulbs to each barrack) which came on at dusk, by which time it had been too dark to read for a couple of hours, and went off again whenever there was an air-raid warning (usually two or three times every evening) and out for good at 9.30 p.m. So we had twelve hours or so of darkness to pass somehow; but I found that my reading generally started some train of thought which I could pursue when the lights went out, and which helped to shut out the ugly world about me. One evening in the early spring of 1945, for instance, it was a line from Macbeth – 'So fair and foul a day I have not seen' – which set my imagination going. I had always wondered why Macbeth could not make up his mind:

> . . . but clearly it was such a day as today, with reminders of winter alternating with intimations of approaching spring . . . The wind is soughing in the pine trees which border our compound, so that one might almost be in Euston station with one of the big engines letting off steam before it goes roaring into the north; or one can fancy oneself in a cabin on board a liner, with a high sea sweeping past the porthole and the spray driving over the decks. Again, on one of my brief trips into the open air I felt it to be a Sedberghian day and could imagine how invigorating it would be to run down from Calf into the arms of that wind, and how good a bath and a brew would seem when I got back – in fact Macbeth and a gusty March day seem to have taken me quite a long way from a prison camp in north-west Germany.

While the daylight lasted, I ranged eagerly through the books that were left to me: Milton and Samuel Butler and George Meredith. Someone lent me *The Good Companions* and I wished that J. B. Priestley could have seen the enjoyment it gave me. On another day, when I had been to the cookhouse to collect the midday soup for our barrack and seen a gruesome still life of horses' heads on the table (we had a few pickings of horse meat in the soup on Sundays), I was amused to come back to my bunk to read Bernard Berenson on the *Italian Painters of the Renaissance* . . . and in the midst of it all I must have had at hand a volume of Ogden Nash, for when the Germans, in reprisal for some offence on our part, took away from us our palliasses of wood shavings, I noted these apposite lines:

The only troubles of the rich are the troubles that money
   can't cure,
Which is a kind of trouble that is much more troublesome if
   you are poor.

By now – we were in the middle of March 1945 – there was no
doubting that the end was in sight. One night I came in out of a storm to
write that 'It's a roaring, tearing, terrible night and the Russians are less
than fifty miles from Berlin!' In the west the allies were rumoured to
have crossed the Rhine, the last great barrier to their advance, and
seemed to be heading straight towards us. And then, as our excitement
mounted, there came a reminder that we were not yet out of the wood.
A party of prisoners arrived who had been evacuated from a camp near
Stettin at the last moment before the Russians overran it. They had
been on the road for thirty-five days and they were in poor shape. There
was not much we could do for them; but when I gave one of them a
spare pair of socks and a razor blade, apologizing for the fact that I had
nothing else to offer, his reply (he turned out to be an American from
San Antonio, Texas) earned him a place alongside Conrad and Ogden
Nash in my anthology: 'It's amazin',' he said, and I guessed from the
way his beard was stirring under the tired eyes that he was smiling,
'how well you kin git along on nuthen', if that's all you got.'

Would the Germans try to march us off too when the allied armies
approached our camp? What point would there be for them in doing
so, when the game was so obviously up? As the allied advance crept
towards us (and the rumours ran ahead of it), I discussed these anxious
possibilities with one of my closest friends, a New Zealander named
Neil Guymer. We had been together since we had been captured within
a few days of each other in July 1941. We had nothing in common
except the experiences we had shared: he was a pessimist, I am an
optimist, he had barely opened a book in his life before he cut his teeth
on my copy of *Candide* at Stalag IIIE. Even in our service life we stood
at opposite poles, for I had been shot down on my first trip, Guymer on
the last of the standard tour of thirty operations, after which a man
earned a respite in some safer billet – a characteristic blow, as he saw it,
from a malignant fate. If the friendship between us was an improbable
one, it had, for me at least, the firmest possible basis: I knew I could
depend on Neil in any emergency. So when we determined that if we
were to move in any direction from Fallingbostel it would be
westward, the bond was sealed – and as though to confirm our resolve
it was at this very moment that I took down the old volume of
Browning and my eye fell at once on this message from 'An Epistle':

I have shed sweat enough, left flesh and bone
On many a flinty furlong of this land.
Also the countryside is all on fire
With rumours of a marching hitherward.

As Easter came and went and we seemed to be forgotten, our hopes rose. The birds were singing again and it seemed a good time to be thinking of going home to England. And then, early on the morning of 7 April, the Germans burst into the compound and told us to be ready to march in forty-five minutes' time. It hardly came as a surprise and our preparations were soon made – but we tried every trick we knew to postpone our departure. We got in the way when we were not wanted, and when the Germans came looking for us, we were somewhere else, so that it was late afternoon before they had us marshalled and ready to go. They gave us a loaf of bread each to see us into the uncertain future and off we went, like a tribe of nomads on their spring migration, with our tattered uniforms and each of us carrying his few possessions in a blanket roll slung over his shoulder. In mine, along with the loaf of bread and a spare pair of socks, were the diaries I had kept since 1941, a wallet containing my father's letters – and Browning.

It was exhilarating to be outside our cage at last and on the move; but there was one thing wrong. I recalled a quotation I had noted more than three years earlier, at Stalag IIIE. It was Oliver Wendell Holmes who had written: 'I find the great thing in this world is not so much where we stand as in what direction we are moving.' Now we were moving in the wrong direction. There was only one thing to do and Neil and I laid our plans.

It had been raining in the morning, but by the time we were on the road the sun had come out and it was a perfect spring evening. Now we saw the value of the hours we had gained. Whatever destination the Germans had in mind for us that day, we were not going to reach it before nightfall. As dusk fell and the darkness swallowed up the fields and woods about us, we began to look for our opportunity; and when the road ran through a thick wood, where pine needles carpeted the verge and the trees almost met over our heads, blotting out even the pale starlight, we saw it. I touched Neil's arm and we ran silently under the trees, dropped to the ground and lay unmoving while the tramp of a thousand feet echoed through the still woods. When the end of the column passed and the silence came stealing like a tide in its wake, we stayed motionless until all we could hear was the sound of our own breathing.

So we were free – but there was no time yet to think about it. Our first preoccupation was to get away from the road and find somewhere to hide. After crashing clumsily about among bracken and dead branches, we emerged on to an uneven heath and stumbled across it for an hour before lying down to sleep in a hollow among some bushes. We were awake long before dawn, stiff and cramped and cold, but as the sun came up in a clear sky we set out – westwards.

I cannot remember much now about the days that followed, for amid other preoccupations my diary was no more than a few hurried notes on the inside of a cigarette packet, on which after all this time the pencilled characters are almost indistinguishable. But I remember the whole adventure as the holiday of a lifetime, in which we walked in perfect April weather through the thickly-wooded countryside of the Lüneberger Heide, slept in barns or under the open sky – and were as happy as I have ever been in my life.

Two moments I do remember vividly. The first was towards evening of the next day, when we had been resting in the loft of a barn and planned to move on through the night. We were assembling our belongings when Neil's firm hand suddenly gripped my arm and I turned to find him staring purposefully out through a small hole which served as our window on the world. Immediately outside, and framed in the aperture, was a German officer, his eyes searching, his whole body motionless except for one hand which was lightly tapping his boots with his swagger stick. Neil and I sank, infinitely slowly, into the straw and lay there hardly daring to breathe. A moment later we heard his slow tread as he sauntered through the barn just below us. I remember thinking that if I put my hand out over the edge of the loft I should be able to touch his cap.

We stayed there that night and in the morning, before moving on, we decided to hide everything that we did not absolutely need for our onward progress. It was absurd, even I could see, to go tramping about Germany carrying Browning and all my diaries, as though this were some undergraduate expedition. We both felt amateurish enough as it was, having no grounding in such escapades, but we tried – a little self-consciously – to suit our behaviour to the occasion. And so Browning and the diaries, with the thick packet containing nearly a hundred of my father's letters, were buried under the straw in a corner of the loft. It was a wrench, for between them they represented the distillation of nearly four years of hard-won experience. I told myself it was just conceivable that one day, when life had settled down to a more orderly pattern, I might retrieve them. The thought seemed frivolous and out of keeping with our new seriousness of purpose, and I put it aside.

Soon after we had left our hiding place in the morning, we heard the tramp of feet along the road where it ran within a few hundred yards of our path, and knew that another contingent of prisoners from our camp at Fallingsbostel was on its way eastward to an unknown destination. Our destination too was uncertain; but we knew in which direction we were moving . . .

The other moment came towards the end of a day when we had been walking all afternoon on soft turf under the trees – a pleasure beyond imagining after the years of confinement – in the unfailing sunshine. The air was perfectly still and there was no sound except our own footsteps on the grass and our own breathing – for we were tired – and the small noises of life in the forest.

Presently we came to a clearing. In front of us the forest stretched away, close-packed and seemingly endless, the land falling gradually towards the plain that lay beyond. As the sun sank and the shadows lengthened, we stared out into that distance, straining to see what we knew were there: the spearheads of the British 2nd army. But the stillness was complete and there was no hint of movement in that wide landscape. We might have been alone in the world. Gratefully we unslung our blanket rolls and spread them on the ground while we built a fire in a hollow tree stump and boiled a billycan of water from a stream nearby. We made tea and ate a thick slice of bread with it, then lay on our backs and looked up at the clear sky, pale now in the twilight – and felt suddenly so perfectly and wildly happy that it was all we could do not to shout aloud.

Freedom at last was a reality and we experienced a kind of intoxication in which we had no thought for what might lie ahead, but felt only that we had shrugged off the whole dark burden of disappointments and longings and endurance that had weighed us down for so long. There was nothing rational or responsible about it, just a miraculous sense of release, so that we seemed no longer earthbound but felt that for a moment we were at one with the sky and the stillness and the spirits that seemed to whisper among the leaves.

The magic of it lasted, I suppose, only a few moments before we came down to earth and set about making our dispositions for the night. Close by, where a fringe of pine saplings lined the edge of the clearing, we found a stretch of turf just wide enough for the two of us, smooth and soft, well hidden among the trees and sheltered by their branches. Some of these we stripped off to make a bed and then we rolled ourselves in our blankets, lying close for warmth, and stared up through the branches at the sky. It was dark now and the sky, still clear, was full of stars. Out of the west we heard the faint hum of an engine, which grew until presently a single aircraft flew low over the forest, its outline sharp against the night sky. When it was gone, the stillness returned and shrouded everything, and imperceptibly, our hearts still buoyant with this unfamiliar, breathtaking freedom, we drifted into sleep.

A week later we were in the hands of the 2nd army and freedom was unqualified. In the interval there had been incidents of which my memory is confused and unreliable. We had been discovered, recaptured (here I have an uncomfortably clear recollection of lying in some bracken, looking up the barrel of the rifle of a young soldier who had just spotted me) and liberated again – and fed – all in a daze of unreality. But there was one thing I had to do before it was all over.

A war correspondent, wearily questioning freed prisoners, showed little interest when I tried to enlist his help. I was insistent, though, and at last Neil and I climbed into his jeep and set off up the road along which we had marched out of Fallingsbostel – could it be only a week before? All about us forest and heath and forest again lay brilliant and serene in the spring sunshine and we searched in vain for a landmark we could recognize. The correspondent was apprehensive, for we were close to the front line: were we nearly there?

'Just over the ridge,' I said hopefully – but it wasn't, and when I said this for the third time, the correspondent put his foot down. He was going no further. I pleaded in vain, but as we argued, six Germans created a diversion by emerging from the trees to surrender to us, and before we had finished with them another jeep came round a bend in the road behind us. It stopped and a British major got out, red-faced and genial. I switched my attention to him and when he promised to act as our escort the correspondent reluctantly agreed to drive on.

After another mile or so, suddenly we saw the farm, standing back from the road on the edge of the wood, just as Neil and I remembered it. I shouted and a moment later we all piled out, the major swinging his revolver and the correspondent nervously bringing up the rear. Together we crossed the farmyard, skirted the stables and entered the barn where Neil and I had hidden. Eagerly I climbed up into the loft – and there in the corner, all undisturbed, lay Browning and the rest of our modest possessions, just as we had left them. Carefully, I handed them down, while the major asked questions and the correspondent blinked. Then we went back to the jeep and the major, when we had thanked him, drove off on some errand of his own. The correspondent took us back the way we had come and parted from us with evident relief. All this fuss about a few books!

But it was Browning who put the thought into my head:

> O the little more and how much it is!
> And the little less and what worlds away!

PART FOUR

On the Move Again

(1945–51)

11

Six months later I was back at Oxford and the whole sombre world of the prison camp was no more than a storm cloud drifting away to the horizon.

How soon a smile of God can change the world . . .

It was as though Browning had anticipated my exact circumstances and mood when he went on to write:

True, I have lost so many years: what then?
Many remain: God has been very good!

During the interval between my return from Germany and the day I went back to Oxford, great events succeeded each other. I ought to remember them, but I have only an uncertain memory of VE day, when we danced round a bonfire on a village green in Sussex; of the incomprehension and the vague sense of unease we felt on hearing that some monstrous weapon had been exploded over a Japanese city whose name we had never heard before and were never to forget; and of the strident election campaign after which Winston Churchill, so long our idol and our talisman, was so unceremoniously bundled off the political stage. But in that summer of 1945 the luxury of being alive and free so disproportioned everything for me that there is no period of my life of which I have a more indistinct and shadowy recollection.

It was natural enough. Like someone recovering from a long illness, what interested me was not the sweep of great events but the tiniest details of everyday life. To take a walk, to talk to a woman, to see flowers, to drink fresh milk, to have a bath: all these had become now delightful exercises in self-indulgence and I used to chuckle every night, I remember, as I climbed between the sheets of a real bed.

While I was still a prisoner I had decided not to go back to Oxford. I had left it at nineteen, I was now twenty-five, and I had no wish to reappear as some kind of Rip Van Winkle. What saved me from a decision I should always have regretted was the realization that my father, who had sacrificed more than I knew at the time to send me to

Oxford before the war, would be disappointed if I did not return there now that it was over. Since he had done more than anyone to keep me mentally alive in the meantime, it seemed churlish to deny him this satisfaction. When I did go back, I found that I was not alone in bridging so wide a gap; and the new generation, to whom we must have seemed like the survivors of some antique breed, did their best to put us at our ease.

Our own presence in these familiar surroundings inevitably reminded us of those others who were absent and would never return. We were not sentimental about them, who had been less fortunate than ourselves, but we did not forget them either and to this day I cannot pass the gates of Worcester College without an affectionate nod in the direction of Stuart Alexander, whose body lies far away but unforgotten in the Libyan desert.

In every other respect, if one wanted to recapture the world as it had been before the ugly interruption of war, there could have been no better place to make the attempt than in Oxford, where on May morning the madrigal singers still climbed to the top of Magdalen Tower; where outside the Sheldonian the busts of the Roman emperors looked out across Broad Street at Blackwell's; and where every night at five past nine o'clock, for some forgotten reason, Great Tom boomed out from under its cupola over the main gate one hundred and one deep strokes.

I loved especially the tolling of the old bell, a nightly reminder to me of my good fortune and of how as a prisoner, one winter's night, I had been reading *Zuleika Dobson*, in which Max Beerbohm made such engaging fun of Oxford life. The action centres on Christ Church and I can still remember the pang of homesickness I felt as I lay in my bunk and read his description of the sound of that great bell pounding out into the night: 'Stroke by stroke, the great familiar monody of that incomparable curfew rose and fell in the stillness.' How vividly that sentence had brought to my mind, there in a prison camp in East Prussia, the very essence of the Oxford I had known and which seemed at the time so tantalizingly remote! It felt good to be back within the scope and sound of that 'incomparable curfew'.

Outside it was the real world, and that was changing fast, in ways which were to transform the social landscape in which I had grown up. The Labour government of Clement Attlee, who had taken Churchill's place as soon as the war was over, was driving through parliament the series of social reforms which laid the groundwork of the welfare state. I cannot pretend that at Oxford the social revolution that was going on around us occupied the forefront of our thoughts. We saw it and were aware of it; it provided a kind of ground bass which we could not ignore, but against which we still felt entitled to improvise our own self-indulgent arabesques. And I was as self-indulgent as any in the pursuit of those ambitions and desires which had occupied my dreams in the lean years just behind me. I worked just hard enough to get an adequate degree, played games, joined in the mock-serious frivolities of undergraduate life – all with just a little more discrimination than my companions and I had shown before the war, but with no anxious thought for how I should make my way in the world.

Whether I deserved such a carefree existence or not, I enjoyed it to the full. And when it was over and I went out into the world at the ripe old age of twenty-seven, I realized that Oxford, whatever else it had done for me, had given me back my youth. It was a prize to treasure.

12

The war had left me with an intense appetite to be on the move: to travel, to take in the world, to shake off that sense of confinement which for so long I had been able to escape only in dreams. Like Ulysses I had known:

> How dull it is to pause, to make an end,
> To rust unburnish'd, not to shine in use!
> As tho' to breathe were life.

Now, with the world become suddenly my oyster, I was impatient to be up and off and to explore that world and make myself a part of it – or it of me.

At the end of 1947 I sat my finals at Oxford and started to look about for some way of earning a living. As it had always been, journalism was what I had in mind, but in 1947 the approaches to Fleet Street were strait and narrow. Like so much else, newsprint was severely rationed and the newspapers were flimsy affairs of a few constricted pages. With experienced journalists coming home from the war, nobody had any use for the uninitiated like myself. Finding no encouragement, I cast my line a little wider. I sent in applications to the BBC and the British Council and I forget what else – and presently got a modest bite. The British Council asked if I would like, by way of a trial run, to go for a few weeks in the early summer to Finland, to teach English at a summer school. I jumped at the chance. And so it came about that in May 1948, after a placid journey by boat across the North Sea – somewhere in whose empty expanses we had bobbed about in our dinghy seven years earlier – and on up through the Baltic, I landed at Helsinki and made my way inland to the little town of Hameenlinna, standing among pine forests at the head of a great lake.

The war – our war – had been over for three years, but for the Finns the real war had been that desperate campaign against the Russians in the winter of 1939–40. I was remembering that brave fight as the ship steamed up the Gulf of Finland and into Helsinki's sun-bright harbour. And there was something else in my mind as well, a distant recollection of blue eyes smiling shyly at me under corn-coloured hair on a river bank in France a few weeks before the outbreak of war. It was foolish, I told myself, to hang on to sentimental bric-a-brac like this. It would be absurd to imagine that a pretty girl would remember, after most of a decade in which the whole world had been turned upside down, the endearments I had whispered to her in Madame Taunay's orchard under the full moon. All the same, I might just see if I could trace her and find out – just for interest's sake – whether she had any recollection of the episode, and how things had turned out for her . . .

It was late when I got to Hameenlinna, but in the long northern twilight the lake was still tinged with the after-glow of the sunset. I made myself known, met some of my colleagues, took a stroll down by the water's edge and turned in with the feeling that I was going to enjoy myself.

Next morning I asked the young Finn who was acting as secretary to the course if he could help me to trace an old friend who had lived before the war in a little town on the Baltic coast. He promised to make some enquiries and to let me know in a day or two – so that I was surprised to find him looking for me the same evening. He hadn't been able to trace my friend, he said, but there was a telegram for me, and he put it into my hand. Opening it, I read: 'Welcome to Finland. Shall arrive Saturday. Love.'

'News travels fast in Finland,' I remarked.

He smiled. 'It's a small country,' he said, 'perhaps she has been expecting you?' And he looked at me quizzically.

When she arrived the following afternoon, we shook hands and laughed and told each other that neither of us had changed at all since we had parted on the railway station at Tours in August 1939. But it wasn't true. In all sorts of ways, things were different for us both. It was only later, when we went for a walk along the shore of the lake, whose surface was silver-grey in the evening light, that I understood how different.

In that autumn of 1939, she had gone home to Finland with the threat of war like a thunder cloud on the horizon. Within a month Germany had invaded Poland and then, at the end of November, the Russians had attacked Finland and there had followed that epic resistance, which the Finns maintained for three months before they had to acknowledge defeat. After that, there were five long years in which the Finns were cut off from the continent by a war whose outcome promised no good to them, whichever side might emerge victorious.

It must have been a sombre time for them; but as she described it to me, I had the impression all the time that there was something else, something quite different from the gloom and hardship, that she was trying to communicate to me. In the end she brought it out with a simplicity that both touched and humbled me.

Soon after the end of the war with the Russians, when she was still only eighteen, a childhood friend had proposed to her. She had asked him to wait until life had settled down on a more even keel. When he proposed again six months later, she told him she could not give him an answer until the war in Europe was over. It was then towards the end of 1940 and it was anybody's guess how long the war would last. He asked her why he must wait. Then she told him frankly that while she liked and respected him, she could not pretend to be in love with him; and that meanwhile she was 'in love with a dream', and she would not know until after the war whether it would come true. When the war eventually did come to an end, she asked this patient lover for another six months, to enable her to judge, as she told him, whether the dream . . . was just a dream. And when the six months were over – she married him and their daughter was born a little less than a year later.

I went very pensively to bed that night.

Among my colleagues at the summer school was a talented Englishman who was teaching at the university in Helsinki. His name was James Bramwell and he was deeply versed in Finnish literature and in the sagas which provided the inspiration for so much of the music of Sibelius. It was he who arranged for me, when the summer school was over, to spend another month in Finland acting as a private tutor to Oiva Soini, the director of the opera house in Helsinki.

Professor Soini was a man of about sixty, distinguished in appearance, deeply musical and fanatical in his pursuit of some kind of mystical self-fulfilment through a combination of spiritual and physical endeavour. He lived alone, apart from a housekeeper who prepared his meals and tidied up after him, in a beautiful wooden house, white-painted and gabled, deep in the forest overlooking another of Finland's innumerable lakes. My duties were minimal: he already spoke adequate English and only wanted a sharpening stone for his grammar. More taxing were the physical challenges he loved to set us both – in the manner of an overgrown schoolboy – and which he, with a handicap of more than thirty years, generally met more easily than I.

When I woke up in the morning, I would hear him preparing the sauna for our daily use, splitting logs and stacking them, cutting birch branches, arranging the stones in the oven. We would meet for breakfast and then he would be off again to see how the fire was coming along, returning at intervals to tell me exultingly that another hour, or half-hour, or ten minutes should see it ready for our use. Meanwhile, he would suggest, we might race each other ten times round the house, or play a couple of sets of tennis, or see which of us could get furthest in the hop, skip and a jump.

By the time the sauna was ready, down in its little wooden shed on the lake shore, I was glad of the chance to sit peacefully beside him in its dry heat, the sweat pouring off us both (carrying with it, he assured me, all the acids and impurities we needed to get rid of), until we could stand it no longer and would emerge on to a little platform built over the water, take a grateful look round at the silent ranks of pines and silver birches, and plunge into the water. For a minute or two, we had the illusion that the water was warm. Then, as our bodies adjusted to the drop of thirty to forty degrees in temperature, we would thrash about in the exhilarating coolness until we were ready to repeat the whole process, baking ourselves once more in the oven of the sauna, throwing fresh water on the hot stones, subsiding into a kind of heat-filled daze until we were ready for the next cool plunge.

The professor ate sparingly and his regime of home-made bread and yoghurt, of eggs and fruit and huge glasses of milk, suited me admirably. I have never felt better in my life. How much of this was due to the diet and how much to the daily visits to the sauna, or to all that tennis and long-jumping, I had no way of knowing, but I found the whole pattern refreshing and delightful. I even began to feel that I was on the brink of entering into that mystery compounded of sun and water and the long northern twilight and the loneliness and silence of the unending forest which is so impenetrable to the outsider . . .

In short, I was briefly captivated by this queer northern life, of which Professor Soini, with his energy and his enthusiasm and his talk of music (he took me one afternoon to visit Sibelius but to my lasting regret the old giant was too unwell to see us), gave me such an agreeable taste. If someone had offered me an interesting job, I might well have taken it and made my life there: an intriguing thought since the direction my life eventually took was so very different. As it was, there was a curious irony in the fact that I stayed in Finland just long enough to remain in ignorance of events far away, which were to concern me very closely when I became aware of them later on. For during these two months of May and June 1948, when I was buried deep in an environment where I was as completely out of touch with the outside world as could be – where I could not understand a word of what I read in the newspapers or heard on the radio – Arabs and Israelis were fighting each other in Palestine, and I knew nothing whatever about it.

Even if I had known, there was much else to distract our attention that summer, for it was in 1948 that the iron curtain became a reality. When I returned to England, sailing through that same eerie twilight (at midsummer there is no real darkness in these northern waters), past the ghostly Aaland Islands and so by degrees back into the world I knew, the Russians had just imposed the Berlin blockade, and the US Air Force and the RAF had embarked on the dangerous and ultimately successful routine of flying food and supplies into the beleaguered western half of the city.

So there was plenty to occupy our thoughts at that turning point in the history of post-war Europe. And on top of it all, I got back just as the Olympic Games opened in London. I don't remember much about them now, but I do remember that London in 1948 was inescapably drab and dirty. Essentially, except where it was scarred by ruined churches and derelict bomb sites, it was still the old pre-war London, but sadly in need of a good scrub. Where its old face did survive uninjured, it was thick with soot and the residue of the yellow fogs which still enveloped the city in winter. On the other hand, you could stand on Waterloo Bridge and look across to St Paul's with no slabs of modern ugliness to break the skyline; and where Wren's old spires had not been destroyed by the bombing they still stood up to delight the eye, instead of being lost in a busy and impersonal wasteland.

Like it or not (and on the whole I did), London was to become my base for the next few years. For now, suddenly and unexpectedly, two of my ships came home on the same tide. The BBC offered me a post as a scriptwriter in the European Service and simultaneously the British Council invited me to go as a junior lecturer to the University of Padua.

An agonizing choice indeed. Italy beckoned with a romantic appeal which the BBC could not rival. But the BBC, if it was not – quite – journalism, was as near to it as I could hope to get for the moment. I signalled my acceptance. But as I made my way with a light heart to Bush House one morning early in September, I could not help wondering, as I have wondered ever since, what might have been if I had gone to Padua . . . A quieter life, of that I can be pretty sure. One that promised more fulfilment? Who knows? Either way and inevitably, as T.S. Eliot was to remind me long afterwards:

Footfalls echo in the memory
Down the passage which we did not take
Towards the door we never opened
Into the rose-garden . . .

13

Bush House was in 1948, as it is today, the home of the overseas services of the BBC, which had done so much during the war to keep alive the spirit of resistance in occupied Europe. Now that the watchword was not resistance but reconstruction, the BBC had a similar role to play in the campaign to put Europe back on its feet.

The prospects for such a campaign looked promising. President Truman had just launched the Marshall Plan, through which American capital and technical skill were to underwrite a vast programme for the renewal and modernization of Europe's shattered economies. It seemed a striking expression of the old American instinct for practical idealism and the idea of playing an insignificant part on the fringes of an endeavour so generous and so constructive appealed to me. I knew very little of the problems involved, but I felt exhilarated by the prospect of becoming at least a skirmisher on the frontiers of progress.

Any such romantic view of my new role proved difficult to sustain. Towards lunchtime on my first day at Bush House, after I had been allotted a room and had shuffled a few papers, there drifted into my room an unexpected figure. Portly and dishevelled, wearing an old tweed jacket and a pair of uncreased trousers tied at the waist with string, he introduced himself as one of my fellow scriptwriters and suggested that we go in search of refreshment. Glad of some company, I followed him downstairs and out into the Aldwych.

On the way to the pub we called at a bookshop, where he exchanged an armful of books (they were review copies) for a sum of money sufficient to keep us in wine and sandwiches – and more wine – until closing time. As we ate and drank, he talked endlessly and amusingly, and with no apparent thought for our empty desks across the road, about everything in the world except Bush House and scriptwriting. I wondered anxiously whether I should ever be able to match the company into which I had fallen.

I need not have worried. It was he and not I who was out of his element. For this, in the seedy autumn of his life, was John Davenport, reputedly the most brilliant undergraduate of his day twenty years earlier, poet and littérateur, friend of Augustus John and every writer and artist of note in the thirties, and above all talker: a kind of Sydney Smith character, in that everyone remembered his wit and his shining talents, but no one could quite recall how he had expressed them. The fact is that he was lazy and self-indulgent and the talents which had seemed so exceptional when he was young were too often wasted in throw-away journalism or in writing film scripts for Hollywood. He was cynical and dismissive about the work we were supposed to be doing at Bush House; but if he disconcerted me at first, I was to benefit as others had done not only from his conversation but also from the unfailing consideration he showed to anyone in need of encouragement, specially aspiring writers. It is difficult nowadays to find anything that he wrote himself, but in half the novels and memoirs of the 1930s there is a friendly recollection or a grateful dedication to John Davenport, and that's a form of epitaph that any man might envy.

The other scriptwriters – there were half a dozen of us in the department – were less talented than John but not much less cynical about what we were doing. It provided their bread and butter, but they spent the greater part of their time writing novels (pushing the guilty manuscript under a blotter when their superiors paid them a visit) or planning more rewarding literary ventures. Few of these came to anything and the only one I remember that did was hardly the most ambitious. It was at one of those desks in Bush House that the girls of St Trinian's were brought to hideous life by Geoffrey Willans, in collaboration with the youthful Ronald Searle – and I dare say they did the world as much good as most of the rest of our output.

I don't want to suggest that none of us ever did any serious work. Even in the BBC that would have been a difficult ideal to achieve, although it was made easier there than in most walks of life. But we turned out our scripts more often than not – like the essays I had been writing at Oxford not long before – in a last-minute access of guilty energy; and since I cannot remember that I ever met anyone who had heard one of them, it would be difficult to claim that in writing them we were playing an important part in the betterment of the world. From my own point of view, though, the experience was a useful one, since it forced me to write clearly and concisely and it taught me something about the contemporary world.

Our main effort in my time went into the preparation of a weekly series of programmes under the title of 'The Road to Recovery' which charted the progress of Europe's reconstruction. The great attraction of this series – and it was this more than anything that made me relish the job – was that we were sent out and about in search of our raw material, which meant that during the three years I spent with the BBC I had the opportunity to travel widely through western Europe and I made the most of it.

It was certainly, in the autumn of 1948, a ramshackle and topsy-turvy continent, whose atmosphere of demoralization is not easy to conjure up today. It was not just the devastation which the Germans had left behind them, or the dislocation of social life in communities where men (and sometimes women too), had been carried off into slave labour or to the concentration camps. By 1948 there had been time to restore at least the semblance of normality, to put things back as far as possible where they belonged – and people too. But there remained all sorts of far more insidious evils and they were much harder to put right. There was above all the undermining of old loyalties and the resulting divisions between those who, when they were faced with the impossibly difficult choices which occupation imposed, had come down, some on one side of the fence and some on the other; and there were those who stayed uneasily in the middle. For all of them, reconciliation with those who had decided otherwise was difficult. At best there remained between them a deep sense of mistrust, at worst a literally murderous hostility.

This was a problem which afflicted every country which had fallen under German occupation – but not Britain. Perhaps my years as a prisoner made me particularly sensitive to it. Certainly what I saw in Europe during those early days after the war left a lasting impression on me and I began to realize that our own good fortune in escaping foreign occupation had left us with a handicap of which most of us remained unaware. A Frenchman of my generation or a Norwegian, or a Dutchman or an Italian, not to mention a Yugoslav or a Greek, knew what it was to be occupied, to endure foreign domination and to be able to take for granted none of the freedoms which to us were as natural as the air we breathed. Few Englishmen had any conception at all of what this meant. Nor had we any way of knowing how we would have coped with the problem of occupation if we had been faced with it; and because we lacked – and still lack – this element of self-knowledge, we remained insensitive to the feelings of others for whom this dilemma had become a reality.

This was something of which I only became fully aware much later on. At the time, as I travelled about western Europe, I was conscious of it as an essential part of the psychological background against which the Europeans were trying to rebuild their lives. For some of them it outweighed the material dislocation left by the war. When I went to Belgium, for instance, to visit the headquarters of the new Western Union in Brussels, I ate well (much better than one ate in England at the time) and lived in outward comfort, but I found the Belgians deeply divided among themselves. The division stemmed from the part played by King Leopold, an enormously popular figure before the war, when he was faced with the German invasion in 1940 and chose to make a separate peace without consulting the Western allies. In 1948 the controversy which this had stirred was still raging, and three years later Leopold was forced to abdicate, leaving the problem of reconciling it to his son Baudouin.

In neighbouring Holland, on the other hand, whose Queen Wilhelmina had refused to submit and had established a government in exile in London, national unity had suffered little damage; while the destruction wrought by the Germans when they destroyed the North Sea dykes during their retreat in 1944 was still evident. It was in consequence a poorer but a much happier place to visit; and besides, I was able to indulge my own personal *nostalgie de la boue* by revisiting the prison in Amsterdam which had been briefly my home after the Germans had fished me out of the North Sea in 1941.

Denmark, where a conspicuously successful resistance movement had preserved the nation's morale and where the Germans, in their own interests, had kept the dairy industry working at full stretch, seemed to have got the best of both worlds.

At the other end of the scale in every way was Italy, where the Germans in their hard-fought retreat up the peninsula had left a trail of destruction; but far worse was the spiritual and psychological turmoil left behind by Italy's unhappy identification, first with one side in the war and then with the other, and at the end of it all by the restoration of a democratic regime in which the Communists challenged the Christian Democrats for mastery of the new republic.

All the same, the Italians seemed to have got their heads above water quicker than most, perhaps because so few of them had entered with any enthusiasm into the absurd villainies of Fascism or fought more than half-heartedly either for or against it. Whatever the secret, and despite all that they had gone through, the Italians appeared to be in much better shape five years after the war than the French.

It was to France that my work took me most often during those years at the end of the forties and it is astonishing now, in the light of the self-assurance with which the French have since taken the lead over ourselves in almost every aspect of daily life, to recall the frankly contemptuous attitude we had then towards our neighbours across the Channel. Even before the war, France had been riven by internal dissensions, with unstable governments rapidly succeeding each other and semi-Fascist imposters posing in the wings. By the time it ended, after the humiliation of 1940 and the occupation and the years of bitter subservience under Pétain and the Vichy government, the French were demoralized. '*L'état, c'est pourri,*' was the characteristic comment which any attempt at political discussion elicited, and there seemed to be no leader capable of holding together a country and a people in such disarray.

There was de Gaulle, of course, without whose desperate efforts to restore French morale the collapse must have been even more complete. But de Gaulle, who had almost automatically become prime minister after the war, had resigned at the beginning of 1946 and for the next three years weak governments succeeded each other every few months. It was the Socialists who generally provided the prime ministers, but it was the Communists who won the most votes; and it seemed only a matter of time before they would gain control of the new Fourth Republic.

This was the France I visited pretty regularly between 1948 and the end of 1951, and without much understanding of the matter I suppose I shared the general English assumption at the time that a victory for the Communists in France would be a disaster for all of us. Perhaps it would have been; but for the record I have to relate that, apart from the world of the arts, in which Paris very soon became, as it had always been, a source of constant delight with its exhibitions and theatres and *chansonniers*, the only hopeful manifestation of any kind of civic spirit that I can remember came from the Communists – or rather, it came my way as a result of an accidental encounter with one particular Communist who became, with some hesitancy, my friend.

On one of my visits to Paris in connection with 'The Road to Recovery', my masters in Bush House had instructed me to find out all about housing in post-war France. In government offices they had shown me all sorts of statistics to show how many new houses were being built, but there were other and – I guessed – more reliable statistics which told that most of the houses in France had been built before the *First* World War, that they were decrepit and lacked bathrooms and were often barely habitable. But even if they are accurate, you can't make much of a programme out of statistics. What I needed was some first-hand material that would enliven the programme and give it human interest by showing how people were actually living in the Paris of 1950.

An agreeable assignment, you may say – but not as easy as it sounds; not, at any rate, to a diffident young Englishman conscious of his imperfect French. Parisians guard the privacy of their own homes as jealously as anyone and from my first few attempts to intrude on it I gained precious little, while in one or two cases I was made to feel lucky that I had escaped without serious injury. But then I had a stroke of luck. I was in the Rue Gabrielle, not far from the Sacré Coeur, where seedy tenement houses faced each other across a narrow street. It was a glorious afternoon in late April and happening to glance upwards I saw a man in shirt sleeves leaning out of the window of one of the top-floor flats. There was something about the air of contentment with which he was looking out into the distance which attracted me. Without a second thought, I turned into the doorway of the house and began to climb the stairs.

The atmosphere was damp, the stairs were in semi-darkness and from what I could see of the walls they were cracked and discoloured. When at last I reached the top floor and paused to catch my breath, there was a window which gave on to a pile of rubble. It looked as though the house next door had collapsed, and it seemed likely enough. I rang the bell and silently rehearsed my excuses for the *dérangement*. Presently the door opened to reveal a fair-haired man of about thirty-five, squarely built, with his shirt sleeves rolled to the elbows above powerful forearms. I began to explain my errand but he cut me short with an impatient gesture.

'*Entrez, monsieur,*' he said, and stood aside to let me pass.

I found myself in what was in effect a one-room flat, divided in two by a curtain which was drawn back. Where I stood there were two or three straight-backed chairs, a table and a couch, with a kitchen recess. Beyond the curtain was a bed-sitting room, whose two windows looked out over a view which kings might envy. From them the eye travelled out over the shelving roofs of Montmartre to where the city lay in the plain below, steeples and domes rising out of a purple haze, with the river winding among them like a thread of silver. For all this (and the defective sanitation) I learned presently that my host paid a rent of precisely 5,000 francs (£5) a year.

He let me enjoy the view for a minute or two; then he introduced himself as Jean G., foreman of a garage, and asked me for the truth about myself. I began to repeat my well-worn formula about an *enquête* for the BBC, but he cut it short and said that I could be frank with him. I asked what he meant by that, and he shrugged his shoulders.

'You mustn't be offended,' he said. 'I know you're only doing what you have to do. Let's drop the subject. You can tell me the truth later if you like. Meanwhile let's make ourselves comfortable.' And he pulled up a chair for me in front of the window, offered me a Gauloise and, seating himself beside me, began to talk.

I've sometimes been told that I am a good listener. No one ever put the matter to the test like Jean. For the most part, he talked about politics, and my enquiry about housing conditions gave him a convenient short cut on to his home ground. He was a Communist and an ardent member of the CGT, the Communist trade union. But politics for Jean included pretty well everything under the sun, and his conversation ranged happily over the whole field of human activity, bubbling with humour, caustic, flamboyant and malicious. His wife sat beside him knitting. Occasionally, as he approached the climax of some broad sweep of rhetoric, she would raise her eyes to mine . . . and wink. To her it was a routine performance. From the outset he was convinced (or pretended to be) that I was a spy, an *agent provocateur*, a secret-service emissary – I never gathered exactly what. Nothing I could say would alter his conviction, so I gave up and let myself be carried away on the whirlwind of his eloquence.

It was through Jean that I heard of Deligny. The two of them worked together in an enterprise of which Deligny was the creator and chief, and which stood out, by its warm-hearted idealism, against the background of cynicism and self-interest which characterized the early post-war years in France. This was '*La Grande Cordée*' and the idea of the '*Cordée*', the climbers' rope, where the safety of each individual depends on the strength and willingness of his fellows, aptly symbolized the spirit of the undertaking.

Briefly the '*Grande Cordée*' was a society for the rescue of young delinquents. At the end of the chain were one or two members who made it their business to attend the magistrates' courts whenever cases of juvenile hooliganism came up for consideration. If a boy was remanded, or was in danger of being sent to a reform school or to prison, they would apply for permission to assume responsibility for him and stand surety for his good behaviour. Then they set about finding out where his interests lay, and giving him whatever they judged he needed most: a home, or a job, or the prospect of one – never charity, but always the chance to make himself useful, and to develop what in most cases he lacked (and whose lack was probably the cause of the trouble), a sense of belonging somewhere, of being a part of the community instead of an unwanted outsider.

The rest of the *Cordée* consisted of a network of ordinary people all over France – they might be shopkeepers, lorry drivers, blacksmiths, farmers – anyone at all who would be willing to find a place for a boy whose energies needed an outlet, and to take him on as an apprentice or at least give him food and shelter and the chance to feel useful. It was a good idea, and like most good ideas a simple one – but it also needed energy and organization if it was to succeed.

When I said so, Jean remarked that any enterprise that had Deligny behind it was bound to succeed. 'You ought to meet him,' he added, but when I said eagerly that I should like to, he switched the course of the conversation abruptly, giving me the impression that his absurd suspicions about me had revived. Instead he went back to politics, insisting vehemently that nothing but a Communist regime could save France; and when I argued with him, he suddenly jumped up and opened an ancient gramophone which stood on the floor in one corner.

'If I can't convince you with words,' he said, 'let's see if music will do the trick. I'm going to put on two records. One contains the spirit of this new world we want to build, a world full of courage and optimism, where a man can *breathe*. The other expresses all the defeatism, the empty, hollow pessimism of the world that's finished and gone. Tell me honestly which you prefer.'

By this time I was beginning to get the pace of the wicket, and I was on my guard. The first record was of a Russian song, full of energy certainly, and beautifully sung by a male choir; but I told him the Germans used to sing well too, when they marched past our prison camp singing the Horst Wessel song. And when he played the second record, I annoyed him by asking him to put it on again; it was of Madeleine François singing 'Les Feuilles Mortes', and it happened to be a particular favourite of mine.

After that we called a truce and Jean's wife got us all some supper and soon I said it was time for me to go. As I went down the damp stairway and out into the moonlight, I had the impression that since midday I had come to some sort of frontier and looked across into unknown territory which it would be fun to explore. I don't mean that I was attracted by Jean's vision of the new Jerusalem, but what had dawned on me as I listened to him was the fact that I knew nothing at all about the real France or about the post-war Europe that was taking shape around me. Somehow I had to find a way of getting closer to the real world if I was going to be able to understand it and write anything less superficial than those radio scripts about 'The Road to Recovery'.

It was that evening with Jean that started somewhere inside me a tiny flicker of restlessness. In its light there began to dance on the walls of my mind all sorts of shadowy recollections of things I had half forgotten; the Russian prisoners I had seen shuffling anxiously through the snow at Luchenwald, the dreams and ambitions that had stirred in me when I lay reading Browning and Emerson on my palliasse of wood shavings at Heydekrug, and that breathless night under the stars on the Lüneberger Heide. There seemed to be some sort of link that I could not put my finger on between all these and the world of which Jean had given me a glimpse, and from then on it was as though there was a fuse burning which must presently cause, perhaps not an explosion, but at least some radical alteration in the pattern of my life.

Meanwhile I went back to Bush House and to the perfectly agreeable life I was leading in London. At last, austerity was on the way out, and both physically and spiritually most of the rubble of wartime had been cleared away. In 1951 the Festival of Britain encouraged Londoners to engage in a slightly self-conscious access of gaiety. When it was over and the temporary pavilions and pleasure domes had been dismantled, we were left with the Royal Festival Hall, which at last filled the gap left by the bombing of the old Queen's Hall during the war. Now it was possible again to hear good music in London, and in a hall which could hold its own with anything in Europe. I went to hear Claudio Arrau, from whose lightning hands at the piano the music seemed to fly off like a shower of icicles; and Segovia, a middle-aged man in an ill-fitting dinner jacket, who took his place modestly on a stool in the middle of an empty stage and at once begun to fill the hall with magic.

We had a good few years to wait yet before the National Theatre rose alongside it, but meanwhile London's older theatres were enjoying a splendid renaissance. Gielgud and Ralph Richardson and Laurence Olivier were in their prime, and Edith Evans and Peggy Ashcroft as well. Of the rising generation Paul Scofield and Claire Bloom charmed us all in plays by Anouilh and Christopher Fry, while in *The Living Room* Graham Greene wrote the most depressing play I ever saw, but provided the occasion for Dorothy Tutin, not yet twenty, to make her triumphant debut.

Bernard Shaw was still alive when I went to live in London. With his beard and his hobby-horses and with a string of fifty plays behind him, he was a part of the fabric of English life (the fact that he was Irish seemed just another of his eccentricities). It was more than half a century since his first play, *Widowers' Houses*, had appeared (in 1892); but shortly before he died in 1950 at the age of ninety-four he had overcome his aversion to the cinema, and after years of stubborn resistance had allowed Gabriel Pascal to make a film of his *Caesar and Cleopatra*.

Its success delighted the old man and the novelty of it was typical of a period which enabled the cinema to enjoy a kind of Indian summer, before television and the wide screen changed all the rules of the game. Films which today are affectionate museum pieces were then new and fresh: the Ealing comedies – *Passport to Pimlico* and *The Man in the White Suit, Kind Hearts and Coronets* and *The Lavender Hill Mob* – imagine seeing them for the first time, with Alec Guinness a rising star and Smiley still unborn!

Life in this resurgent London was pleasant enough – and yet . . . that fuse was burning away and my feeling of restlessness grew. I couldn't account for it and goodness knows I had nothing to complain about, but that encounter with Jean in Paris had reinforced the sense that it was all too limited, too unadventurous, too secure. To travel as I did with the comfortable weight of the BBC behind me, with someone to arrange my tickets and book my hotel room at the other end – this was not what I had pictured back there in Germany, when from inside the barbed wire I let my imagination roam with Flecker's pilgrims:

> . . . who go
> Always a little further. It may be, beyond
> That last blue mountain barred with snow,
> Across that angry or that glittering sea,
> There dwells a prophet who can tell why men
>   were born . . .

'The Road to Recovery' might be interesting, but it was not the *Golden Journey to Samarkand*, not by a long chalk. And if I wanted to put the matter in less romantic terms, I felt like the fish in Rupert Brooke's 'Heaven' who mused:

> . . . we have our stream and pond
> But is there anything *beyond*?

In short, I felt the time had come to extend my range. But how?

What brought things to a head was a journey I made – my last for the BBC, as it turned out – to Turkey. It was in the autumn of 1951, when the cold war seemed to be warming up. The Russians had exploded their first atomic bomb, the Western nations had signed the North Atlantic Treaty and the Korean war was under way, marking the first open confrontation between East and West. Turkey was closely involved in all this, and sent a contingent to Korea which was to prove itself in the hard fighting which followed. One of my clearest memories of that first visit of mine is of seeing the Turkish contingent on the move southwards through the Taurus mountains on the way to Iskenderun, where these conscripts from the Anatolian plateau were to embark for a country of which they knew nothing and in a cause which can have meant little more to them.

In Turkey, for the first time, i found myself in what we still called the underdeveloped world. As I journeyed hurriedly about its vast distances between the Mediterranean and the Black Sea, I was fascinated by the landscape and the history and the sombre and compelling personality of Kemal Ataturk which brooded over it – and I decided that it was time to have done with this helter-skelter scratching of the surface of the world. This was not the way to travel. If I understood little of Europe as I went from one capital city to another, what could I make in this random fashion of a country like Turkey, where everything was so alien and where my few points of contact were so superficial?

By the time I got back to London the germ of an idea had planted itself in my mind. It was very indefinite and at first sight quite impractical, and it had its origin in several different impulses. There was first of all this impatience with the idea of scurrying around the world seeing so much and understanding so little. I wanted to go on travelling, but to stay in one place long enough to get the hang of it, to learn one or two languages properly, to go on asking questions, but to have time to digest the answers – perhaps even, in time, to be able to frame my own answers instead of regurgitating those of others. There was also, to be honest, a strong element of self-indulgence about the idea. I wanted to write my own ticket, to go where I wanted and do what I liked and try to make of it all something that had my own stamp on it, something that would equip me for . . . whatever challenge might lie ahead.

And there was one other element in this imprecise pattern. It must have been stirring in my subconscious, and it came to the surface when the head of my department at the BBC asked me one day what plans I had for my future career. I was quite unprepared for the question and my answer surprised us both. Without hesitation and as though it had been waiting for the opportunity, a voice over which I had no control told him that I wanted to go and live abroad for a year, without any commitments, and to see what happened.

Why, he asked, very reasonably. I replied that during the war I had got into the way of living on very little and without much thought for the morrow, and I wanted to make sure I had not lost the knack of it. I don't suppose he found it a very convincing reason: and yet it was not unreasonable. Browning had put the matter well when he wrote in one of his letters that 'for my own future way in the world I have always refused to care – anyone who can live a couple of years and more on bread and potatoes as I did once on a time need not very much concern himself beyond considering the lilies how they grow'.

The upshot was that when I went home that night I had committed myself to leaving the BBC at the end of the year and to staying abroad for twelve months. I would take the £30 which was all the government allowed British tourists to take out of the country, but beyond that I would follow the example of the lilies of the field.

When I was at Oxford, I had been surprised one day to find that I had been awarded a minor exhibition for which I had not applied. When I asked the authorities how this had come about, I was told that the exhibition had been endowed by the Dr Fell of whom one of his colleagues had said 'I do not love thee, Dr Fell, the reason why I cannot tell', and that the unlovable doctor had ordained that his money should be given to a student who was judged to be 'indigent and ingenious'. With £30 as my total budget for the year, I should certainly be indigent. To survive, I should need to be ingenious as well. It seemed an interesting experiment.

PART FIVE

Snakes in the Ocean
(1952)

14

On New Year's Eve, carrying a suitcase and an old-fashioned bed-roll, I caught the night ferry to Dunkirk on my way to Paris – and freedom. I had chosen this route because it meant that the turn of the year would find me poised halfway between the old life and the new – and because it was cheap. Comfort and security were behind me. Ahead lay what seemed to me the luxury of knowing next to nothing about the future.

I had decided to go to Paris first because it was the only place where I could speak the language and because a chance acquaintance in London, a Frenchman who was going to be out of the country for a few weeks, offered me his tiny flat until I found myself somewhere to live. At first I turned it down, thinking this hardly suited my new style; but he put my mind at rest. 'Don't worry,' he said, 'it's only two rooms, no bathroom and it's in a slum.' Reassured, I accepted his offer and awaited the outcome with curiosity.

At midnight I saw the new year in with a Frenchman, who asked what my business would be in Paris. Foreseeing some difficulty in explaining it, I said I was going there to improve my French. And where would I be living, he asked. 'Belleville,' I replied, and to my surprise he burst into peals of laughter, and called his friends to share the joke. 'You'll learn to speak French there all right,' said one of them, wiping the tears from his eyes. 'Better not use it outside Belleville though,' said another; and they all doubled themselves up with laughter again. They wouldn't tell me anything more about the place, but when we parted the first man slapped me on the back and roared '*merde*'! I suppose I looked a bit startled, for he went on to explain: '*Chez nous, ça veut dire "bonne chance"* ' – and with that I had to rest content.

In Paris the sun was shining and as I made my way across the city, with that equivocal benediction ringing in my ears, I felt that the year had got off to a good start. There was clearly something . . . distinctive about Belleville, and whatever it was, I had the feeling that it was going to suit my purpose admirably. And when I got there to find a fair in full swing outside the Metro station on what I came to think of as the frontier between Belleville and the rest of Paris, I knew I was right.

It was less than fair to call it a slum. On an ordinary weekday, when the roundabouts and the hurdy-gurdys had been replaced by a street market, Belleville revealed itself as a run-down working-class district with no pretentions to be anything else, and with a boisterous life of its own. One day in a little restaurant round the corner where I took to having my one serious meal of the day, I asked a neighbour – there was no nonsense about separate tables in the Maison Claude, which suited me well since I could not help getting into conversation with those around me – how he would describe his neighbours. He looked round at the rowdy assembly of porters from the nearby meat market, charladies, factory workers and black marketeers – what in the England of those days we called spivs – and gave a wide grin.

'*Eh bien, M'sieu,*' he said, '*les gens du quartier, ce ne sont pas des vieilles contesses du seizième.*' Which I suppose you might translate by saying 'Well, the people round here – they're not a set of old Kensington dowagers!'

Among them I soon lost my shyness and they made me surprisingly welcome. At the Maison Claude, after some initial suspicion, they took me pretty much for granted and the tide of their conversation, raucous and vulgar and vivid, flowed unconcernedly about me. I saw the point of that exchange in the bar of the night ferry: it was not just the ideas they expressed but the language in which they expressed them that were their own, and it took me some time to get used to them both. Once I had done so, I had to be careful, when I crossed the invisible frontier with the rest of Paris, not to use some of the terms which were common currency in the Maison Claude and in the street market below. As for the ideas, they were mostly picked up from *L'Humanité*, which was passed from hand to hand in the Maison Claude, for he would have been a bold individualist in the Belleville of 1952 who admitted to voting for anyone but the Communists. I soon learned to use my ears more than my tongue when the conversation turned to politics.

Badly housed and underpaid as most of them were in a France still struggling back from the degradation of the 1940s, with governments still tumbling every few months and the shadow of defeat looming in Indo-China, it was not surprising that they gave their allegiance to the only party not associated with their past or present discontents. But their Communism, from what I could gather, represented a protest rather than positive sympathy: a protest against corruption and manipulation, which they summed up by saying '*l'état, c'est pourri*', and you could hardly blame them if they looked with enthusiasm towards something as different as possible from what had gone before. Their views were one-sided and often bitter, but they argued with a clarity and a respect for logic which their counterparts in England would seldom match; and they brought to every discussion, whether about politics or about anything else, such racy good humour and so much wit that these encounters in the Maison Claude or over a coffee and a cognac in the Café au Point du Jour opposite were for me both an education and a delight.

But I had more to do than listen and observe; I had to try to earn a living. Even in Belleville, where a three-course meal cost me a couple of shillings, my £30 would not last indefinitely and before long I should have to pay for my lodging. I set about looking for employment, and found it harder to come by than I had expected. With George Orwell's *Down and Out in Paris and London* in mind, my intention had been to find work as a waiter, or perhaps a chauffeur, and I presented myself at all sorts of hotels and restaurants and even night clubs where I suggested that an able-bodied young Englishman with adequate French and a little Italian and a smattering of Swedish might be useful with the foreign clientele. But I found that times had changed since Orwell's day and that there stood in the way of my modest ambitions an obstacle which I had not foreseen and which it was almost impossible to circumvent: the trade unions. I was pleasantly received, as a rule, but it was soon clear that there was nothing doing in this line of business and I was forced to revise my ideas. Perhaps it was as well, for in falling back on to more familiar ground I found opportunities opening up which promised more in the way of that education, in the broadest sense, which I was hoping to acquire.

One day a friend of a friend asked if I would give him lessons in colloquial English. It was money for jam, for all he required of me (like Oiva Soini in Finland a few years earlier) was that I should spend an hour speaking English with him once or twice a week. For this he would pay me 500 francs – ten shillings – an hour, which would keep me going for a couple of days in Belleville. And when presently I picked up another customer – who beat me down to 400 – and found that, like the first, he liked nothing better than to talk politics, I quickly realized that I was on to a good thing. For the beauty of it was that the two of them had diametrically opposed views, especially about the state of the French nation and the reasons for it. Between them and with the Maison Claude as a constant background, I began to feel that I could dispel the ignorance of which I had been made aware on that last visit to Paris for the BBC a few months earlier and which had planted in my mind the idea of this year of wandering.

My two pupils formed a marvellous contrast with each other. Monsieur Barcelot was a businessman in his forties, a conservative, who felt – or rather, *knew* – that what was wrong with France was a lack of discipline. And the reason for the lack of discipline, and so for the whole breakdown of the traditional pattern of organized French society, was *la résistance*: the refusal, after the catastrophe of 1940, to accept and abide by the terms of France's capitulation. Whether one had in mind de Gaulle or the partisans of the resistance or the Communists, for M. Barcelot all these were the agents of decline, who had undermined respect for the institutions of the state and brought France to its present pass.

When I went on to meet André Guyot, a young army officer who had escaped to England in 1941 and served with de Gaulle, I would hear of the iniquities of the Vichy government, of the humiliation which Pétain and Laval and their whole *galère* of collaborationists had brought on France, and of the pressing need to make a clean sweep of them all (for they survived and were entrenched, Guyot insisted, in every department of French life) if the country was ever to raise its head again.

Opposed in politics, these two differed in everything else as well. Barcelot, the *homme d'affaires*, with a well-appointed flat in Auteuil, was the complete French *bourgeois*, for whom appearances were all-important and good food a serious ideal (he was a busy man and sometimes asked if I would give him his 'lesson' over dinner at his house, which greatly increased his value to me). His world had a number of fixed points and he liked everything in between to keep to its appointed place. He was well-mannered, well-educated, dependable and unimaginative, and I put on a collar and tie for our lessons – for which he always paid me on the dot. Guyot, by contrast, was like a caricature of the romantic Frenchman, small-boned and dapper in appearance, hot-tempered, impulsive, unreliable in such matters as punctuality and unfailingly entertaining. He would pick me up in his tiny car and take me darting through the traffic in the centre of Paris, talking all the time except when he broke off to whistle at a pretty girl or swear at another driver as undisciplined as himself. And he always forgot to pay me unless I reminded him.

It would have been interesting to bring the two of them together and to sit on the sidelines. Barcelot would have been urbane, icy, contemptuous – unless Guyot's charm won him over. But Guyot, I fancy, would have hit him before they had been talking for ten minutes.

There was just one thing, though, on which they would have agreed with each other and with my friends in the Maison Claude in Belleville: that *l'état, c'est pourri* – although each of them would have given quite different reasons for the judgement.

If this suggests a sombre undertone to my life in Paris, the impression is misleading. For one thing, in the discussions I had with all sorts of people we didn't always talk about serious things. Much of the time we did, for I was eager to learn; but whether we talked about politics or the state of the nation or the Americans (a particular *bête noire* in Belleville), or about rugby football or about anything else under the sun, what emerges from the diary I kept in Paris is the delight I took in every encounter with people more consistently lively and stimulating and entertaining that any I had met in my life. In my two bare rooms in the Rue Vincent, with their stone floors and no hot water – and no heating either until I borrowed a little electric fire (and blew all the fuses) – there was little to detain me. Now and then I sat myself down to write an article or a few letters, wearing all my warmest clothes and with a pile of old newspapers under my feet. But for the most part I went out and about, mainly on foot, all over the city, looking for work (apart from the English lessons I picked up some work as a translator and one or two commissions from more established journalists) and falling into conversation with an extraordinary variety of people.

I went back of course to see Jean Godignon in his top-floor flat near the Sacré Coeur, where this whole venture had had its starting point, and found him as talkative as ever and a little less suspicious of me, now that I was living in Belleville instead of a hotel off the Rue Royale. At all events, he consented at last to put me in touch with his hero, Deligny, of whom he had sketched for me such a glowing portrait at our first meeting.

One afternoon in January I set out to meet the great man. The address Jean had given me was in Montmartre, not far from the Moulin Rouge, and as I found my way along a dingy back street and climbed a rickety staircase to the third floor of a damp, cold house, I wondered whether Jean was having a joke at my expense. Or was he just sending me to listen to another Communist tub-thumper? But then I remembered the outline he had given me of the *Grande Cordée* and how his manner had altered when he spoke of it and of Deligny, its creator and anchorman . . .

From the landing I entered a large, cheerless room, in which two girls sat typing, both muffled up against the cold. My footsteps echoed on the bare boards as I walked across to them and asked to see M.

Deligny. I had to wait a few minutes, and as I turned over the pages of
flyblown copies of *Paris Match* one or two shabby individuals came
and went, glancing incuriously at me in my corduroys and old raincoat.
Outside, the half-light of the winter afternoon was fading; there was a
grey gloom over everything and I cursed myself for being so
impressionable as to let Jean send me on this wild-goose chase. Then
one of the girls pushed back her chair and beckoned me to follow her
into an inner room.

Here too there seemed to be no heating and only the barest essentials
in the way of furniture: a filing cabinet, a couple of tables, a shelf full of
pamphlets – but in a moment I had forgotten the bleakness and the
cold, forgotten my doubts and everything but the personality of the
man who rose to greet me. The impression he made was the stronger
because he so obviously did not care whether he made an impression at
all. He was unshaven and untidy, dressed in slacks and a corduroy
jacket, with an old woollen scarf round his throat; but his face was lean
and sensitive and a pair of burning eyes spelled the character of the
man. When he talked to me across the table, quietly and with no
gestures (he could not have been more different from his apostle, Jean),
even his hands, which lay motionless on the papers in front of him,
conveyed a powerful sense of confidence and control.

I suppose he was a Communist, for otherwise even his magnetism
would have found it difficult to break through the defences which Jean
had built round his own mind. Certainly he was a rebel in the wider
sense, for whom authority and tradition and experience – the
experience of others – had no validity until they had been weighed in his
own personal balance and had stood the test. But whether he was a
Communist or not, he was someone in whom the yeast of idealism had
for once leavened the whole man. Politics, so far as I could tell, had
nothing to do with the task he had set himself or the single-mindedness
with which he pursued it.

There was no capital behind the *Grande Cordée*, only his own driving
energy and, as Jean had made clear to me, the enthusiasm with which
he inspired others. Deligny was a trained psychologist, and this had
helped him to win the trust of magistrates and probation officers; but
his own profession, I gathered, regarded him as a renegade, treating his
unorthodox approach with the hostility which the professional will
always feel for someone who does his own job better than he can – and
by using the 'wrong' methods.

Jean had told me how the *Cordée* worked; what I had not
understood was how it could provide sufficient scope for the ambition

of a man whom Jean had represented as being so outstanding. Now that I had met Deligny and heard him explain, in a quiet voice and with no hint of complacency, how he had conceived the idea and pursued it with all the insistence of a guerrilla leader against the forces of apathy and cynicism, there was no longer any mystery. There is more than one way of measuring ambition and Deligny's was not the world's way. It had nothing to do with power or worldly influence; above all, it had nothing to do with *self*. But he was ambitious all right, and he knew the secret of success, as Browning knew it:

> Let a man contend to the uttermost
> For his life's set prize, be it what it will!

I don't know how long I stayed there: perhaps an hour, perhaps less – and I never saw Deligny again. If it seems strange, even to myself, that he could have made such a lasting impression on me, I can only quote what I wrote soon after that meeting: that 'there in that cold, bare office, through the unlikely agency of Jean, the garage foreman, I met one of the few great men I have known'. And there was another thing. Deligny was one Frenchman who did not tell me that France was *pourri*; and if he thought it was, then at least he was doing something about it. Perhaps that's why I've never forgotten him.

January, cold and bright, with early-morning mists along the Seine, gave way to a wet February and I couldn't pretend I was altogether sorry when the time came for me to leave the Rue Vincent and find another home. I came on one through the accident of meeting an old Egyptian Jew with the charming name of Ebenezer Aladjem, who had once worked for my father in Cairo and was now eking out a small pension in a back street in the Latin Quarter. When I called on him one day at my father's request, he received me with exquisite courtesy, serving me tea (which we drank muffled up in our overcoats against the cold) and discoursing to me in a French so elegantly rounded that his garret took on the air of an eighteenth-century salon. And when I left him and walked round the corner into the Rue Monsieur le Prince, I liked the name so much (and the warmth of Ebenezer Aladjem's welcome had left me in such a sunny mood) that I found myself a room there on the spot and said I would move in at the end of the week. It cost 350 francs a day (seven shillings) and in addition to a bed and a cupboard for my few clothes, it had a table where I could write and a washbasin with hot and cold running water; and as if this were not luxury enough, it was heated by a huge old-fashioned radiator which gurgled encouragingly, as though to make sure you knew you were warm.

It cost me a pang to leave Belleville and I still used to go out there often to have lunch with my friends at the Maison Claude. For most of my purposes, through the Rue M. le Prince was much more convenient. I could walk almost everywhere and the Latin Quarter had its own attractions. By now, too, the pattern of my life was changing as the result of a stroke of good fortune. Meeting one day an Arab journalist whose status was hardly more established than my own, I found that he had a press card which opened all sorts of doors closed to me. I asked the press attaché at the British Embassy if he could help me to acquire a similar talisman, but he cautiously excused himself; so I decided to make a frontal assault on my own. Finding the appropriate office in the Présidence du Conseil, I marched in carrying a copy of *Time & Tide*, an obscure political journal, in which had appeared an article I had written about my trip for the BBC to Turkey. When I showed it to a bored official, I saw no point in explaining that it was in fact the only article I had written that had ever been published anywhere; but he seemed to sense it for himself and was on the point of refusing when his eye fell on the 'Notes on Contributors', where it was stated that 'Michael Adams was educated at Sedbergh, Oxford and Stalag Luft III'.

'*Vous étiez prisonnier de guerre?*' he asked, and at once we were off on a flood tide of reminiscence. When at last he returned to the matter in hand, the official's manner was quite altered. What was it I needed? Ah, yes, a press card, he said, reaching into a drawer, '*Rien de plus facile*'. And in five minutes the thing was done.

Armed with this magic piece of cardboard, I found my horizon marvellously extended. At the Théatre Marigny, where Jean-Louis Barrault was playing in Sartre's *Bacchus*, it was not a question of whether I could get in but of how many seats I wanted. When a friend drove me out to the Stade Colombe, it needed only a tiny bit of sleight of hand to find us two places in the press box for the rugby international between France and Ireland. Galleries, dress shows, exhibitions, all were suddenly open to this renegade from Belleville, and all for no more than it cost me to enjoy the fun fair in the *place* outside the Maison Claude on a *jour de fête*. I felt myself a positive *boulevardier*.

And so it might have gone on for ever; but I recalled that I had other plans. I was into my third month of freedom and it would soon be time for pastures new. Besides, the south beckoned me and the sun. I began to look about me for the next move.

A friend I had encountered on 'The Road to Recovery' left a message for me one day to say that an American from the Marshall Plan mission in Greece was in Paris looking for a scriptwriter. He didn't know where the man was staying . . . and he was there only for a couple of days; if I was interested . . . I was up early the next morning and on the trail of that American all over Paris. At last I ran him to ground in his hotel and summoned all my resources to convince him that not only was I a scriptwriter, but that with my background and talents and varied experience (here I used the broad sweep, without too much attention to detail), not to mention my facility for languages (the fact that Greek was not among them could easily be remedied), I was almost supernaturally endowed to be his man. The American had had a hard day; he had little liking for Englishmen; he seemed unresponsive to my message. But he promised he would think it over and let me know when he got back to Athens.

For a week, as I went about my varied errands, I wondered and dreamed and doubted whether my luck could run so smooth; and then came a telegram clinching the matter and I went out with a friend to celebrate. We had dinner in a tiny restaurant run by White Russians, where *bortsch* and *boeuf stroganov* cost a couple of hundred francs, with a glass of vodka thrown in if little Maroushka was in a good mood, as she generally was, and then we went for a drink to a *cave* on the Rue de l'Abbaye, where a negro in a white silk shirt was playing the guitar and singing a song called 'Wandering'. It sounded the right theme song for me and I scribbled the words on the back of an envelope.

It took a couple of weeks to complete the arrangements for my departure, during which I walked nostalgically about a Paris on the threshold of spring and ate a last lunch at the Maison Claude and signed off my pupils and said goodbye to friends high and low. And then, exhausted and exhilarated at the same time, I went to the Gare de Lyon to catch the Orient Express to Athens. As I walked along the platform past the blue *wagon-lit* coaches, I tried to look as though this was the way I always travelled; but under my breath I was rolling out to myself, with an excitement that was difficult to control, the splendid battle honours posted on their sides – Milan, Venice, Trieste, Belgrade, Salonika – until I took my place in the single carriage labelled Athens.

I went in search of something to eat – not much, for my farewells had left me with what the French melodramatically call a *crise de foie* (the English just say mildly that they are 'upset') – and when I got back I found the compartment transformed into a snug little cabin. The train was driving purposefully into the night, as though it too was impatient for the warm south, and I drifted off to sleep, my mind full of jumbled recollections of other journeys in different circumstances: of the delousing expedition . . . of climbing up in the cattle truck to look out through the tiny grille at Tilsit and the river Niemen . . . of the dinghy. And through them all came the voice of the negro in the Rue de l'Abbaye, humorous and insistent:

Snakes in the ocean, eels in the sea,
A red-headed woman made a fool out of me;
And it don't look like I'm ever going to cease my wandering,
It don't look like I'm ever going to get me home.

15

The train took three days to get to Athens and on the first of them, as we ran down out of the Alps and raced across the north Italian countryside, past Verona and Padua to Venice, I was happy to sit quietly and adjust my sights to a new perspective. Next day, abruptly, the mood of the journey changed. The train seemed to lose its assurance and as it dragged its slow way down through Yugoslavia it reminded me of Matthew Arnold's description, in 'Sohrab and Rustum', of how:

> The shorn and parcell'd Oxus strains along,
> Forgetting the bright speed he had
> In his high mountain cradle in Pamir.

An Edwardian antique had been substituted for yesterday's luxurious French dining car and in it, while a middle-aged Greek lectured me about Cyprus, we ate mysterious dishes and drank *slivovitz*. Outside, instead of the sunlit Italian landscape, were bare hillsides and a succession of dilapidated villages separated by patches of melting snow.

Already Paris seemed very far away – and when I awoke on the third morning I was in a new world, the world of the Aegean, with the tumbled houses of old Salonika scattered across a hillside and islands out in the bay, and presently the bulk of Mount Olympus reaching up into the sky, its crest shielded from mortal view by the only cloud to be seen.

Even the most imaginative among us can hardly set foot in Greece without feeling that in some sense he is coming home. The Olympic Games, Byron dying at Missolonghi, those other Englishmen who fought and died more recently on Crete, the Parthenon which inspired our nineteeth-century architects to so many unsuccessful imitations – all those remind us that without Greece we should not be what we are.

Preconceived ideas, though, can be wonderfully misleading. I once knew an English girl who was disappointed by the Pyramids; she said she had expected them to be . . . bigger. I remembered her when I came out into the sunshine of my first morning in Athens and gazed expectantly about me for the embodiment of my dreams – to find myself instead looking up a long, dull, straight street of concrete façades. At the sight of them I felt my heart sinking – until in the far distance, crowning a little hill and seeming to float like a figment of the imagination over the second-rate architectural clichés below, my eye lighted on the Parthenon.

Athens was to be my home for three months and I found it always stimulating, at times exhilarating, at others infuriating. Above all, it never ceased to surprise me by the violence of the contrast between the legend and the reality. Apart from the Parthenon and a few little jewelled Byzantine churches, there seemed to be no echo of classicism or romance about this ugly, noisy city. As for the Athenians themselves, those carriers of the torch of civilization, if I expected to see fulfilled in their bearing the ideal of moderation in all things, I soon found them (and in a way it was a relief) to be quite otherwise.

As I became familiar with the life of the city, what distinguished it above all, it seemed to me, was its restlessness. Under that blinding sun, in whose light every outline was a razor-edge, a ceaseless murmur of excitement, of intrigue, of passionate controversy and burning resentment filled the clear air. Every café was a centre of faction, from every kiosk the newspaper headlines signalled recrimination and threatened revolt. Waiters and shoeshine boys, clerks and taxi drivers – all were ready to buttonhole any listener with tales of scandal in high places and to hint gloatingly at the judgements in store when the malefactors should be called to account.

It was difficult to know how seriously to take any of this and the first thing I needed to do was to find someone to advise me, to act as my guide and interpreter and steer me through the labyrinth. To obtain advice presents no problem in Greece; any self-respecting Greek is ready to assume the role of the ancient philosophers. Within a few days of my arrival I had been taken in hand by an Athenian who had spent some years in England and so had faced the same problem from the other end. He sat me down with a cup of sweet coffee and looked at me kindly.

'If you want to understand the Greeks,' he said, 'you must make an effort of the imagination. You've come to a new world (although of course it's really a very old one) and you must try to forget the one you've left behind. To start with, you've got to put aside the values you were taught at home – and you won't find that easy.'

He looked at me quizzically and I smiled back in what I hoped was a dashing and cosmopolitan way, indicating that I was ready to kick over the traces at a moment's notice.

'You were brought up to think that the most important thing about a man is that he should be honest and reliable: an Englishman's word is his bond and all that. And I'm not saying it isn't an admirable point of view – but it's not ours. The sort of man we admire is one who is clever (you don't like that, do you?) or, better still, cunning (and that's worse). The fact is, you haven't got a word in English for the quality I mean, so you'll have to learn the Greek one: exypnos. It is impossible to translate, because it carries all sorts of overtones; but literally it means 'out of sleep', and so 'wide awake', what the Americans call 'on the ball'.

'A man who is exypnos is a man who knows how to look after himself, whether he is haggling over the price of a pound of tomatoes or manoeuvring for a place in the government. By your standards, he may not be very nice to know; in fact, you would probably call him a 'slippery customer', because he's not always too particular about the methods he uses.

'Try reading the *Odyssey* – I don't suppose you've read it since you were at school – and you'll see what I mean. Odysseus was Homer's ideal type of man – and he is still the ideal of most Greeks today – not because he was brave and fearless and all the women ran after him, but because he was wily and resourceful, the sort of man who could get round anything and anybody. Remember how he dealt with the Cyclops? That was really exypnos.'

The point my instructor was making with such agreeable irony was a useful one. Unless he can shed his insularity and open up his mind in a way that few of us find easy, an Englishman will always find the Greeks baffling and a little disreputable; just as they find him pretentious and hypocritical. Before there can be a profitable encounter between the two, there has to be an armistice in which each agrees to suspend, for the time being, his conviction that his way is best. And since in Greece it is the Greek pattern that will prevail, the Englishman who travels there may as well adapt himself to it as best he can.

In trying to make this adjustment, I took help wherever I could find it. I rented a small room with a large balcony at the foot of the hill called Lycabettos (by leaning dangerously far out I could catch a glimpse of the Parthenon) and from my landlady, Mrs Xenophon, the impoverished widow of a shipowner, I absorbed much instructive gossip about Athenian society. For my initiation into the language I turned to Mrs Prevelaki, who looked, with her hair drawn back from a wide brow and fastened at the back in the classic style, as though she had just stepped out of the frieze round some ancient temple. When I mangled the liquid Greek vowels, she would turn her dark eyes on me in soft reproach; and when I composed my first heartfelt sentence ('the teacher is beautiful and the pupil is glad') a smile twitched at the corners of her mouth as she gravely corrected my syntax. And of the others who helped me through my apprenticeship in things Greek, I must single out Shan Sedgwick, the elegant and engaging correspondent in Athens of the *New York Times*.

Sedgwick was a foreign correspondent of the old school. Meeting him for the first time, with his Homburg hat and his gold-topped cane, it would have been easy to mistake him for a dilettante of charm in whom some stray impulse had awakened a passing interest in Greece and the Greeks. It would only be by dint of persistent questioning that you would learn that he had lived in Greece for twenty years (he was married to a talented and charming Greek wife) and that his grasp of the character and history, the political life and the social problems of modern Greece, was shrewd and extensive.

It was from Sedgwick that I began to learn how to distinguish what was serious in the passing scene from what was merely a part of the charade, sometimes frivolous and sometimes melodramatic, with which the Greeks enlivened their political life. One day, for instance, when I had been in Greece for a month or so, his warm voice hailed me across the street and we fell into conversation in the shade of the awning over a fruiterer's shop. He asked me what I thought of the political situation and listened gravely to my reply, as though expecting to learn something of use and interest to himself. When I had done, he mentioned diffidently that he had spent the previous evening in the press gallery of the National Assembly. He realized as clearly as I did, he said (this was the first I had heard of it), that the debate in progress was a crucial one, and he suggested that we might go along together that evening. There might be a division; and even without it the session was likely to be a lively one.

The debate was about the outcome of a trial which had been dominating the headlines ever since my arrival and in which six Communists were accused (and eventually convicted) of espionage. The case was a melodramatic one, which embraced all the classic elements of Greek political life at the time: there were disguises and a clandestine radio station and Bulgarian agents and of course the CIA. A number of prominent reputations were at stake, and all the political parties were trying to use the trial for their own ends, to blacken the faces of their opponents and represent themselves as the only true guardians of the timeless values of Hellenism – and a lot more along the same lines. And now that the verdict had been handed down, the battle was being fought out all over again in the assembly.

At first, when we arrived in the chamber, I thought that Shan had misjudged the occasion. The debate seemed to be proceeding with something like decorum, in the manner of the House of Commons on one of its noisier nights. But when the speaker left the rostrum, a buzz of anticipation greeted his successor, a square-built man in middle age – he was a cabinet minister, Shan told me, who had been under fire in the press after making a public speech about the spy trial – and it didn't take him long to transform the atmosphere in the assembly.

At first he provoked only grunts and an occasional growl of dissent from his opponents. Then a young deputy from the KKE, the party of the extreme left, jumped up to make a point of order. As soon as the interruption was over, the minister replied with what was obviously a sarcastic reference to the KKE – and in a flash pandemonium broke loose. The young deputy was on his feet again and shouting at the top of his voice. The minister was shaking his fist and shouting back. The president of the assembly was banging his desk with a gavel and all over the chamber men were jumping up and down to exchange insults with the minister or with each other, or to appeal to the president to restore order. The only result was to add to the din, for the president's reaction was to summon up his reserves by setting off a buzzer: the kind of buzzer that announces the lunch hour in a factory and which is designed to be clearly heard over a large area.

Eventually some semblance of order was restored. It was the buzzer that did it, for it completely drowned out every other sound and set our eardrums throbbing. The minister caved in before it, and even the young man from the KKE, although he outlasted everyone else, bobbing and gesticulating like a figure in an early silent film, at last subsided into his seat to mop his brow and quiver spasmodically with rage and frustration.

The rest of the evening had its moments, but it never recaptured that first fine careless rapture. Considered as the prelude to legislation, the performance had its shortcomings; but as ballet I found it invigorating and I was surprised when Shan apologized as we made our way out. 'Disappointing', he said, 'I thought we were in for a lively evening.'

All the same, it would have been a mistake, as I was soon to discover, to discount these emotions altogether. Not long afterwards I heard a tragic echo of that debate and of the trial that had prompted it and which resulted in the execution of several of the defendants. I was on the island of Hydra, walking one evening with a Greek friend along the shore under a half moon, when a voice from the balcony hailed my companion and together we climbed the outside stairway of a little cottage perched over the water's edge. It was attractively furnished and there were shelves full of books in three or four languages. I had no idea who our hostess was when presently she led me out on to the balcony, from which there was an enchanting view over an inlet to a line of mountains all splashed with crimson from the setting sun. I said that anyone must envy such a view.

'Oh yes, it's beautiful,' she said, 'but I can't wait to get away.'

I was startled by the bitterness of her tone; but she went on: 'My husband and I were always happiest here. There's no point in staying on alone and making myself unhappy with memories. As soon as I can sell it, I'll go back to Athens and start again.'

In Greece you soon forget to be shy about asking questions and I scarcely hesitated before asking what had happened to her husband.

'Oh, didn't you know?' she said carelessly, and there was a pause while she looked out across the strip of water to the mountains, dark now against the night sky. And then she added in a flat, contemptuous tone: 'They shot him last month.'

You can't escape politics in Greece – but they were not my concern. My job with the Americans was to see what they were up to with their Marshall Plan and to write scripts about it for the radio. The assignment was tailor-made for me, for it required me to travel about the country, mostly to remote places where they were building a dam or there was a land-reclamation project or a scheme for a new road to link outlying villages to the mainstream of Greek life. My contract was for three months and in that time I was determined to see as much as I could of the country – and to save enough money for a long slow trip through the Greek islands at the end of it.

To explore Greece in springtime: it was not an onerous assignment and I still recall my sense of disbelief at my own good fortune. Finding that no one had thought out in advance how my work was to be organized, I set about organizing it myself, on lines that could hardly have been simpler. Taking a large-scale map, I would decide where I wanted to go next, find out what projects there were in the area, and then set off to see what I could see and write about. Back in Athens a week or so later, I would write my script – it might take me two or three days – then get the map out again and start to plan my next expedition.

If it was not exactly the Golden Journey, it was as near to it as most of us are likely to get.

April saw me in Macedonia, driving westwards from Salonika in a jeep, first over a new road which the Americans had built, which climbed steeply into the mountains and on into country only now recovering from the civil war that had ended three years earlier. Over the Khandova Pass at something above 4,000 feet we drove down into the valley of the Aliakhmon river and took to country roads and then to tracks where the mud was rutted by mule carts, and finally on to the open plateau to follow the paths of shepherds from one lonely village to another. Most of them had been destroyed, from some the inhabitants had been driven away or had fled, and in each the villagers were trying now, with courage and an almost total lack of every sort of equipment, to rebuild their lives.

Their poverty was such as few Europeans can even imagine. The children were barefoot, their parents wore strips of uncured hide tied across the instep with string. They were dressed in rags, or in scraps of the uniform of half a dozen armies – war booty, reparations, relief, God knows what it was, or where it had come from. Their existence was precarious and they lived under the recurring threats of hunger and disease, or of invasion from across the nearby frontier of Albania. But their spirit was astonishing, and their toughness, and the tenacity with which they clung to their barren fields and ruined houses.

In the eyes of the villagers my companions and I presented a welcome diversion, and the elders would place stools for us in some ramshackle shelter while the children scampered about our feet and fingered our clothes. But beyond this there attached to us – or rather, to the engineers whom I was accompanying – a particular aura; for they brought with them the magic of technology. They knew how to mend a pump or survey a difficult stretch of road-building, and in one delighted village they coaxed into life the only wireless set in the place, which had long been defunct. The villagers there saw us off as though we were a patrol from an army of liberation; and so in a sense we were, and I almost forget that I was only a camp follower.

It was the warmth of their welcome that transformed what could otherwise have been a sombre expedition; that and the beauty of their surroundings. All the way we wound in and out of the mountains, bare and austere, their colours changing throughout the day. And at the end of it all, dusty and tired and sore from jolting over those uneven tracks, we had our reward.

The furthest point of our journey was the town of Kastoria, which stands 2,500 feet up at the head of a mountain lake near the point where the frontiers of Greece, Albania and Yugoslavia meet. When we had refreshed ourselves as best we could in a country inn, we drove out along the lake shore as the sun set and the mountain beyond it took on a theatrical shade of purple, which was reflected in the still surface of the lake. As the shadows deepened, we left the jeep and walked along the shore, the water lapping at our feet and the rocky shoulder opposite glowing brighter than ever against the fading sky. And then, just as it seemed that such perfection of colour and stillness and beauty were all that one could ask of life, the full moon rose, paused for a moment on the very tip of the mountain and then floated up into the sky to mingle with the last traces of the sunset. And a bar of silver ran towards us across the surface of the lake.

After Kastoria and those desolate uplands, Athens seemed noisier than ever, but Easter was upon us and when friends invited me to join them in a visit to Yannina deep in the mountains of the Epirus I accepted with alacrity.

As the crow flies, Yannina is only a couple of hundred miles north-west of Athens, but between them is the wild, high range of the Pindus, running from north to south and cutting Greece in two. So we set out westwards, past Salamis and along the northern shore of the Pelop-onnese, to Patras, where we crossed the mouth of the Gulf of Corinth by ferry and drove north past Missolonghi, among orange groves and over a hump-backed Turkish bridge and through villages where there were storks nesting in every chimney and owls sitting sagely in the eaves of cottages. Then we were climbing, at first up the delicious valley of the Louro (the first river I had seen in Greece that had any water in it) and then higher and higher until we crossed a last ridge and ran down into a fertile plain where, under the mountains at the edge of a lake, lay Yannina, the capital of this remote province.

We arrived late on Good Friday and on the Saturday there was an extraordinary air of tension and expectancy as the climax of the Easter celebrations approached. Late in the evening we took candles and squeezed ourselves into the Mitropolis, the cathedral of Yannina, already packed with a crowd of worshippers. The air was heavy with incense and as midnight approached the choir chanted unceasingly, while the crowd stirred and murmured in anticipation, every eye on the bishop where he stood bearded and in his robes and mitre in front of the ikonostasis.

Suddenly, on the stroke of midnight, all the lights went out. There was a moment's pause, and silence, heavily charged. Then a single high-pitched voice called out of the darkness, '*Christos Anesti*' – and with a great roar that was like the release of a tidal wave the congregation took up the cry, as the bishop emerged from the shadows carrying an enormous lighted candle. Those nearest rushed upon him, holding out their own smaller candles to catch the flame from him. For a moment, catastrophe seemed to threaten; but the bishop stood his ground, the candle at arm's length for as many as could reach it; and these in turn passed on the flame to those behind them so that it spread like lightning all through the church. Then the bishop shouldered his way through the congregation and out by the main door to where a great crowd jostled and cried out as they too strove to light their candles, while inside the chanting began again and the congregation swayed and shifted excitedly, the smoke from their candles curling up into the shadows of the domed roof.

Anyone who gets the holy fire from the fountainhead and can reach home safely without letting it go out is assured of prosperity for the coming year. When we left the cathedral and made our way back in that first hour of Easter day, the streets of the old town were full of slow-moving figures, each shielding a tiny flame against the night air. The tension was gone, the time for rejoicing had come. Everyone was chattering and laughing and overhead fireworks scattered stars among the storks' nests, as from every church in Yannina the bells rang out the glad news: *Christos Anesti*, Christ is risen.

How pallid and inhibited must seem the rites of the Anglican Church to people who bring to their own devotions such an intensity of feeling! Try to picture such a scene in the Close at Salisbury or outside York Minster, or where the dark mass of Durham Cathedral stands on its ridge high over the River Wear – and you sense the gulf that divides us from the Greeks and their dramatic approach to every aspect of life, and to religion perhaps most of all. And if that Easter celebration at Yannina stays in my mind as a vivid illustration of that approach, you find it too in the monasteries, large and small, where all over Greece monks and devotees seek not just the refuge of some modest cloister but a hermitage so exaggeratedly remote as to leave them suspended halfway between earth and heaven.

There are mysteries here than we cannot penetrate, we of the cold and rational north. Even Mrs Xenophon, when I got back to Athens, would listen with tolerance and a touch of scepticism to my traveller's tales. Cosmopolitan to the last, she much preferred to talk of Paris and

London, where she felt at home. Macedonia and the Epirus were for her wild, outlandish places, peopled in her imagination with brigands and wolves, almost as foreign and forbidding as Turkey. She was happier, as spring slipped into summer, when I told her of expeditions to Delphi and Mycenae, and pleased when I brought back an enormous *barbounia*, which a fisherman had insisted on giving me near Corinth; for these were places whose names were familiar, though I'm not sure she had ever visited them herself. She had no feeling for the romance of the Greek countryside or the legends which came so insistently to life around me as I travelled between the mountains and the sea, with the scent of wild thyme in my nostrils. When I talked to her of Marathon, she was interested to hear that the Americans were building a dam there (even the dam was made of marble) to relieve the water shortage in Athens; but she was unmoved when I reminded her of how, when the Persians threatened, Pheidippides had run for two days and nights to get help from the Spartans and had asked, when the Spartans refused:

> . . . but Athens, shall Athens sink,
> Drop into dust and die – the flower of Hellas utterly die,
> Die, with the wide world spitting at Sparta, the stupid,
>   the stander-by?

Perhaps Mrs Xenophon was right to be sceptical. Perhaps the Athenians had embellished the story, had even made the whole thing up. They were certainly capable of it – and that was half the fun. For of all the engaging diversions of the Greeks, to me the most enjoyable was their habit of creating and remembering and *believing* a story to explain everything. I stepped ashore once in the island of Tinos to fight my way across a little square to the door of the hotel in the face of a wind so powerful that it was all I could do to keep my feet. Once inside, I straightened myself and asked a man who came forward to meet me whether Tinos often experienced a wind like this.

'Nearly always,' he replied in a matter-of-fact tone. 'You remember, it was here that Aeolus came with the winds in a bag and accidentally released them.'

Today, with package tours shuttling to and fro through the Greek islands, I hope the legends survive. When I sailed among them in 1952, tourism hadn't reached the Aegean and the islands were as I had pictured them in my imagination: wonderfully simple and still and lonely. In Mykonos, where I stayed for a week in June, I met one other foreigner, a young Belgian, with whom I went on to Patmos. There, as we climbed the long flight of shallow steps to the monastery of St John or walked round the shore to find new places to swim, there was nobody about except the fishermen who invited us to share their catch and cottagers who would press fruit on us, figs and apricots, or ask us in for a cup of coffee and an exchange of gossip. To get from one island to the next, if there wasn't a steamer for a week it was easy enough to find a place on one of the caiques trading between the island ports; and at the end of the voyage – often a rough one in the teeth of that fearsome north wind, the *meltemmia*, which blows through the Aegean in summer – there would always be someone on the quay to lead me to another room in a whitewashed cottage, with carnations in the window and cool water from the well in the garden, and the friendliest of welcomes when I came home at the end of long days of idle exploration. It was a simple life, as I wrote to my father from one such haven at the southern tip of Euboea:

I eat and sleep and walk and swim, and for an hour or two I read the *Odyssey* in the shade of an olive tree or on a rock on the shore – it's fun to read it here, with the 'wine-dark sea' in front of me and the place names familiar from my own wanderings. The weather is warm but there's always a breeze (and today a strong wind ruffling the water out in the bay) and whatever happens the sun shines for fifteen hours a day and then the soft, cool evening air spreads over sea and shore and the stars come out and the sound of the sea drops to a tiny murmur and the wind dies away until the next morning.

For a month that was the life I led – and the spirit of Greece and the warm south must have penetrated deep into my being, for I felt no northern qualms of conscience about such self-indulgence. It was, after all, part of the whole imprecise plan which embraced Belleville and the Maison Claude and the Orient Express, and which had its remote origin in the dreams I had dreamed in a prison camp far away in the cold discomfort of East Prussia.

Presently, though, it was time to take stock. Life in the islands was absurdly cheap, but even so, the money I had saved was trickling away. Besides, more than half the year was gone and I wanted to spend a part of what remained in Italy; but Italy was on the way home and it seemed a pity not to go first a little farther afield. Turkey had stirred my imagination on that first brief visit a year earlier, and now it lay just across the water. When I got back to Athens and floated the idea of spending two or three months there, Mrs Xenophon was horrified, foreseeing untold calamities and hinting that she would feel it disloyal if I strayed on to such alien ground. I was inclined to defy her; and my

resolve was strengthened when I heard the unexpected end of a story
that had begun for me three months before.

It was on a Sunday afternoon in April that I had set out on foot to
climb out of the dusty heat of Athens on to the flank of Mount
Hymettus. I was in search of a little monastery whose name I forget but
which had been much praised by Osbert Lancaster in his engaging
Classical Landscape with Figures. The directions he gave were confusing
and I lost my way, stopping eventually by an outcrop of rock to rest
and look contentedly out over the city to Salamis and the blue width of
the Saronic Gulf. The air was fresh, the ground carpeted with wild
flowers. There was no one about and nothing could have been more
tranquil, until suddenly the stillness was broken by the sound of voices
raised, it seemed, in angry altercation.

When I went to investigate, I found that I was almost on top of the
monastery, whose tiled dome nestled under a group of cypress trees in a
fold of the hillside. In front of it, on a patch of thin grass, linked by the
bond of some unexplained enmity, two curiously diverse figures were
engaged in what looked like an impromptu ballet.

Given the Greek temperament, there was nothing remarkable about
the scene and I should have turned away had I not realized that the
leading figure in the dance was an Englishman, elderly, hot, and plainly
out of temper. He had a wooden leg and he was lunging awkwardly
with his walking stick at an urchin who kept darting in and out of range
saying, 'spik English'. I went to his assistance and when I had chased
off the boy, the Englishman and I fell into conversation – to find that
with all the differences between us, we were serving, so to speak, under
the same banner.

He had enjoyed a classical education and for half a century he had
been meaning to come out and see for himself the places he knew only
through the pages of Homer and Xenophon. 'But first I had to get a
job, and soon afterwards I got married, and then came the war (the
1914 war, I mean), which left me this' – tapping his wooden leg with his
stick – 'and a family business to put back on its feet. Somehow the time
slipped by, and I never got any nearer to Greece; it was always just over
the horizon, one of those things you go on thinking about and putting
off, until suddenly you realize it was only a dream.'

We were driving back to Athens by now, in the taxi which had
brought him out, and he broke off what he was saying to watch two
small boys who were standing in the middle of the road in exaggerated
poses of defiance, daring us to run them over. The taxi driver drove on
unswervingly and at the last moment they sprang out of the way with

shrill screams of protest and started throwing stones at the back of the car.

'A couple of years ago,' the old man went on, 'I retired, and almost immediately my wife died. My sons were both married, and there didn't seem to be much left for me but to settle down to a bit of gardening and some reading, with an odd game of bridge – until it struck me that for years I had been saying I wanted to go to Greece and imagining it and reading about it; and now there was nothing stopping me. Nothing except laziness, that is. You don't know what it's like to feel yourself growing old; there's a kind of inertia you have to overcome – and then everyone's always telling you to take care of yourself and not overdo things, as if there were any point in sitting quietly in an armchair with your slippers on, instead of making use of what little time you have left.'

He looked at me doubtfully, wondering whether he had bridged the gap of years that separated us. But I was thinking only how little age had to do with it. The obstacles to happiness change, but the arguments that hold us back from achieving it are the same: security, safety first, being 'realistic' – 'as though to breathe were life'.

'I was all set to come last year,' he said 'and then I was very ill. After that they told me it was out of the question. But I spent the winter making my plans and a week ago I just slipped off – and here I am!'

We had supper together in a taverna and then went back to my balcony to sit under the stars comparing our plans and our reasons for embarking on them. There was one big difference between us. With little time to spare, he had everything carefully worked out. He had been to Olympia and Marathon and Mycenae and he had still to see Delphi and one or two other places on the mainland. Then he was going to Istanbul and down the Aegean coast of Turkey to Ephesus and Pergamum, which shone bright in his mind's eye, although he had never seen them: and finally across to Cyprus, where he had chosen to end his pilgrimage. After that and another few days in Athens on the way home, he would be satisfied.

It was late and the stars were brilliant when I walked back with him to the British School of Archaeology where he was staying. There I left him, wishing him well with his plans and with little thought that I should hear of him again. But a few weeks later, when I got back to Athens from my own journey through the islands, a friend told me the rest of his story. He had gone to Delphi, and then on to Istanbul, this elderly, boyish figure, with his game leg and the crusty manner which almost disguised his youthful longings, and had written with excitement of seeing the Bosphorus and looking across from Seraglio Point to the low shore of Asia. At last he had reached Cyprus, the goal of all his wandering, the sunlit island of his imagination where beauty herself was born – and there, suddenly and without fuss, he had died.

For a moment I was shocked: not at the death of an old man whose life had run its span, but at the thought that such zest for life had suddenly been stilled. And then I saw that here, for once, was the right ending. Not for him that reproach of Browning's which so few of us can escape:

> . . . the sin I impute to each frustrate ghost
>
> Is, the unlit lamp and the ungirt loin . . .

His lamp was alight to the very last; and soon after I heard of his death I was off in his tracks.

16

Whether you think of it as Istanbul or Constantinople or Byzantium, there is no mistaking the fact that the old capital down on the Bosphorus is a city by any standard. Coming to it from six weeks of lotus-eating in the islands, I felt, as I watched the traffic streaming over the Galata bridge and the ferryboats darting between Europe and Asia, like a peasant thrown in at the deep end of the world.

For the moment I had no time to stand and stare. The islands had refreshed my soul, but they had left me almost penniless and I was glad to find that an arrow I had shot into the air had found its mark. The Americans of the Marshall Plan, who had employed me in Greece – much to my advantage, it seemed to me – had an office in Turkey as well, to which I had sent a cable offering my services. Without waiting for an answer, I followed it up and was relieved to find that I was expected. After a quick look at the mosques and museums of Istanbul, I took one of those ferryboats across the Bosphorus to catch the night express to Ankara.

Behind me, as we neared the Asian shore, Seraglio Point was warm in the light of the setting sun. There, among the minarets of Aya Sophia and the Blue Mosque, was the old Turkey, out on the margin of history now, the Turkey of sultans and scimitars and the jewelled crowns I had seen in the Topkapi Serai; and before that of the imperial court of Byzantium, so confident in its splendour and sophistication that the crusaders from France and England, when they came here on their way to Palestine, had been disconcerted to find themselves treated – and rightly – as crude provincials. As I climbed gratefully into my compartment in the Anatolian Express, my head full of these jumbled visions, I was only half prepared for the violent contrast that awaited me.

From Istanbul and the soft half-tones of the Golden Horn and the old country houses and vineyards along the Bosphorus, the night train wound and groaned its way into the foothills and up through the darkness for two thousand feet, to clamber at last over the rim of the Anatolian plateau. And there I emerged at daybreak into another world. Gone were the sea and the pinewoods and the soft Mediterranean air; in their place was the great broad back of Turkey, still and harsh and lonely under a limitless sky.

When I got used to it, I came to love the atmosphere of Anatolia, loved its loneliness and the way that undulating pattern of steppes seemed to sweep and roll away, like the waves of an immense ocean, towards unimaginably far horizons. At first, though, after the vibrant Mediterranean world of which Istanbul was still a part, Anatolia had a daunting aspect; and Ankara itself, up there on the windy plateau hundreds of miles from anywhere, had never quite shaken off the look and feel of a frontier town. I wondered how the Turks could have brought themselves to snatch the crown from the wise old capital on the Bosphorus and confer it instead on this provincial outpost in the windswept wilds of Anatolia.

Ankara was to be my home for the next three months; or rather (for my work followed the same agreeable pattern as in Greece) the base from which I travelled about the country, tracing the activities of the Marshall Plan and learning what I could about Turkey in the process. And one of the first things I learned was that the transfer of the capital had been a fundamental part of the revolution forced on Turkey by one of the most remarkable figures of the twentieth century.

Mustafa Kemal, known to history as Ataturk, had died in 1938; but everywhere I went I found that even from the grave his influence outshone that of any man alive in the Turkey of 1952. He had made his name as the defender of Gallipoli against the British in 1915 and as a result he was almost the only man to emerge with credit three years later, when the Ottoman Empire collapsed in the wake of a defeat from which recovery seemed out of the question.

And so it might have been; for the victorious allies, not content with stripping Turkey of its subject provinces, seemed bent on dismembering Turkey itself. The British were in occupation of Constantinople, the Italians of a stretch of the Mediterranean coast, and in May 1919 the Greeks landed an army in Smyrna (the modern Izmir), with the intention of carving for themselves a colony in western Anatolia. It was now that Mustafa Kemal earned his soubriquet of Ataturk – it means 'Father of the Turks' – by engineering a miracle.

The day after the Greek landing at Smyrna, he slipped out of Constantinople and set about organizing a resistance movement in the interior, travelling in secret from place to place rallying support and putting new heart into the leaderless peasant population. When he felt the time was ripe to establish a rival government to the puppet regime in the capital, he looked about for a home for it and his eye fell on a little town – it was hardly more than a village – three hundred miles away across that shelving plateau. It was called (though few had ever heard of it) Angora.

In Angora, which he renamed Ankara, Ataturk installed a provisional government and then went off himself, with his ragged levies, to confront the Greeks advancing eastwards into Anatolia. In the summer of 1921, on the Sakarya river west of Ankara, his peasant army checked the Greek advance. For a year his men held the line, while Ataturk scoured the countryside for arms and recruits, using his own extraordinary blend of charm and menace to build an army and a nation out of the flotsam of a defeated empire. Then, on 26 August 1922, he struck. The Greek forces wavered, faltered, fled – and a fortnight later and nearly three hundred miles to the west the last of them were driven into the sea at Smyrna and the Turkish flag was raised again on the shore of the Aegean.

This much I knew of the story when, by a curious chance, I was sent to Izmir and there heard a first-hand account of these events, just thirty years after they had occurred. For it was early in the morning of 27 August 1952 that I flew down from Ankara, west and south across the Sakarya river and on over the empty uplands to the sea. I tried to imagine the line of fugitives on the plain below, the smoke from the burning villages (for the Greeks destroyed everything in their retreat), all the tragic debris of an adventure which had miscarried. And the day after my arrival in Izmir, when a light breeze tempered the damp heat of the evening, I found myself dining in the harbour where that terrible story reached its climax.

My companion was a Turk in his middle forties named Hakki. The annual international fair was about to open and Hakki and I were responsible for arranging the American pavilion. When the day's work was over, we went together to a restaurant on the waterfront; and it was there, with the harbour lights shimmering across the bay, that we fell to talking about the battle of the Sakarya and Ataturk's pursuit of the Greeks that had ended within sight of where we sat. To my astonishment, Hakki told me that he had taken part in it.

'I was just sixteen,' he said, 'and I had been with Ataturk's army for a year, since just after the battle on the Sakarya. At that time, anyone who could carry a gun was a soldier. Ataturk could have made an army out of anything. You couldn't despair in his company; you just took his word for it that you would win because you had to.'

He told me of that frantic rout from Eşkisehir to the sea. It sounded incredible – that an army without transport except oxcarts could cover nearly three hundred miles in a fortnight. Yet they did, and the first Turkish soldiers entered Smyrna on 9 September, slaughtering the Greeks as they overtook them. It was not a pretty story, for the Greeks had spared nothing and no one in their path and the Turks in their turn, when they reached Smyrna, had butchered whatever Greeks they could find. Finally someone – it has never been established who – set the city on fire, so that the final act of the drama was played out in a maelstrom of smoke and flames.

'I was thinking of it a moment ago,' said Hakki, 'when you remarked how peaceful it all looked. I was remembering the first time I saw this harbour thirty years ago. There were lights reflected in the water then, but they were from the fires that were burning all along this waterfront. The harbour was full of corpses and in the light of the flames were men running this way and that and the sound of rifle fire and shouts . . .'

The Greek army of occupation was totally destroyed, and its destruction undermined the position of the allies who had encouraged it. They found themselves face to face with a paradox: in trying to dismember the old Turkey, they had helped Ataturk to raise against them a new Turkey which they could not control. Within a year the last foreign troops – they were British – had left Constantinople, Lloyd George's government had fallen and the allies had accepted the Treaty of Lausanne, which drew the boundaries of this new Turkey. On 23 October 1923 the Turkish Republic was proclaimed and Ataturk's victory was complete.

That, you might think, was enough for one man; but Ataturk's work was only half done. In 1923 he was forty-two years old, and in the fifteen years that were left to him he set out to overturn the whole creaking structure of the empire: its laws and customs, its political system, its pattern of social organization, even the very alphabet – and to raise in their place the framework of a modern state, modelled on the Western democracies and looking to them for its social and political inspiration.

When I travelled about Turkey in 1952, fourteen years after his death, there were still men and women who had worked for Ataturk, served under him, occasionally even argued with him – although that required exceptional courage – and from them I gained an idea of his personality, in which were blended the most diverse and often contradictory characteristics. He was a dictator with a passionate devotion to liberty, an ardent believer in women's emancipation who held his own exceptionally able wife in subjection. He inspired in both men and women a loyalty that was unquestioning, and if there was any single key to this man and to his phenomenal achievements it seemed to me to be this: that no task was too great for him and none too small – and that to both he brought the same superhuman strength of purpose.

Of all the stories I heard about him, one of the most vivid was told to me by his godson as we drove together one October day over the great calm sea of the Anatolian plateau from Ankara south-east to Kayseri. His name was Tanju and he was thirty-five, completely Westernized in outlook, a bit of a cynic, excellent company, perfectly aware of the shortcomings of modern Turkey but fiercely patriotic if anyone else criticized them. As a child he had been often in the company of his godfather, who was fond of children – it was another unexpected aspect of the personality of this most undomesticated of men – and had a way with them.

Tanju said he was about eleven at the time and going to one of the new schools that had been opened in Ankara (this was only three or four years after Ankara had become the capital). One morning in early summer he decided to play truant. Instead of going to school, he ran off and climbed the hill to the south of the town and sat there in the sunshine feeling very pleased with himself. Presently he noticed a lone figure climbing the hill and making straight for the place where he was sitting – and as he watched the man, his heart sank; it was his godfather. Ataturk stopped beside him and stood looking down at him in some surprise. Finally he asked Tanju why he wasn't at school and Tanju was wise enough to tell him the truth. Ataturk was silent for a moment, staring out over the hillside. Then he asked Tanju what lessons they were having in school that morning; and when Tanju told him that among them was Turkish history, Ataturk looked at him, a long, penetrating look out of those grey eyes which no one who met Ataturk ever forgot. Then he sat down on the grass and began to talk.

'Although this was twenty-five years ago,' Tanju told me, 'I can still hear that quiet voice in my ear and remember what he said to me. He told me that the Turks were a fine race who had ruled a great empire in the past; but then their rulers had grown slack and the country had fallen into decay. He said that in the new Turkey everyone would have work to do and enough to eat, there would be schools and hospitals and factories, the government would be honest and the people healthy and hard-working, so that others would admire them and the Turks themselves might feel proud of being Turkish.

'It would be a long time, Ataturk said, before all this came true and in the meantime the people who could help most were the ones who were educated and could teach others to read and show them how to cure diseases and to make use of new and sensible ideas.

'And then,' said Tanju, 'he fastened those tremendous eyes on me again. "It's the young people who will have to do the work," he said, "and especially the young people like you who have the chance to go to school and to learn about your country, so that when you go out into the world you can tell others what needs to be done to make Turkey great again. Now do you see why it's worth while spending a sunny morning in a classroom learning about Turkish history?" And then I ran off down the hill and back to school as fast as I could.'

It was thirty years ago that Tanju told me that story and since then things haven't always gone smoothly with Ataturk's vision. I was in Istanbul to witness the trial of strength that came in 1960, when some of the friends I had made on that earlier visit were involved in the overthrow of Adnan Menderes, because they thought he was deflecting Turkey from the course that Ataturk had charted. And I was in Ankara again in 1970, and saw rival factions fighting each other on Ataturk Boulevard at the start of the unrest which has plagued Turkey ever since. Looking back with the advantage of hindsight, it is easy to see that the roots of discord were already there in 1952. Despite all his efforts to involve the whole nation in his ideas, the new Turkey which Ataturk left behind him was almost entirely confined to Ankara and Istanbul, to the journalists and intellectuals who embraced his gospel of modernization and to the technocrats who put into effect his blueprint. But the old Turkey consisted of the peasants living in 20,000 backward and isolated villages scattered across the wide face of Anatolia. To them the avalanche of new ideas, theories, customs – the whole pattern of a secular, modern, Westernized society – was barely comprehensible; and when they did understand it, it aroused their deepest misgivings.

You could not fail to notice the contrast, although few people seemed aware then of its dangerous implications. The memory of Ataturk's presence was still fresh and there was a marvellous sense of unity and purpose about the country, so that you felt caught up, even as an outsider, in the resolve of a brave people to make a new start. That was how it seemed to me – and not just among the friends I made in Ankara, the Tanjus and Hakkis who shared so much of my own outlook on life, but also whenever I was able to burrow beneath the surface of that other, older, inarticulate and almost impenetrable Turkey of the countryside.

One glimpse of that world I shall never forget. It was the thirtieth anniversary of Turkish independence day (which was also the day, 23 October 1952, when the first British atomic bomb was exploded), and I had taken advantage of a long national holiday to travel south to Antalya on the Mediterranean coast. In my pocket I had a sketch-map of an area in the hinterland where there was a ring of Hellenistic cities to be discovered. Nowadays they are reasonably accessible and have been partly excavated; but in 1952 the few roads in the area were unsurfaced and there were no accurate maps to lead me to my goal. As for transport, even in Antalya itself, which was the seat of the Vali, the provincial governor, there wasn't much of it apart from the horse buses in the streets, charmingly painted and with lace curtains, making their way as best they could among the camel trains. Even if I had possessed more money, I should not have found it easy to travel far.

As things turned out, money was the last thing I needed. After a long day's travelling from Ankara and a good night's sleep, I sought out a school teacher whose name someone had given me; he spoke a little French and he was supposed to know all about these Greek cities. How was I to reach them, I asked, and after a moment's thought he replied that I should call on the Vali and 'the Vali will make proposals'. I didn't see why he should, but I took the advice and the Vali surpassed all expectations. He dispatched messengers, summoned inferiors, gave orders, so that in no time at all I was on my way in a truck belonging to the *kaymakam*, the Vali's subordinate, heading into the mountains behind Antalya.

The *kaymakam* had business to transact here and there in the area which interested me and for three days we travelled together through these tangled mountains, alternately climbing to 6,000 feet and then dropping down over rough tracks to some tiny harbour. Wherever possible, the *kaymakam* would make for my benefit a detour in search of one of the old cities, of whose whereabouts no one knew anything and whose jumbled ruins, when we found them, were overgrown with fig trees and dense scrub. It was a marvellous journey and on the last day, when the *kaymakam* had completed his mission and we were homeward bound, we came to what was left of Xanthos, a Lycian city which had flourished in the last millennium before the birth of Christ until it was destroyed by Brutus and his Romans in 43 BC. By the time the *kaymakam* was able to drag me away, the light was fading and almost at once we lost our way in an especially wild piece of country. The *kaymakam* was undismayed. After a rapid conference with a forestry official who had joined us, he turned to me and said there was no problem; we could get back to Antalya in the morning. Meanwhile, he said, 'tonight we shall sleep here'.

Where, I wondered, and so, I presently found, did they. There was no habitation in sight and by now it was dark, but we drove off down a track and after an hour or so a farmhouse appeared in the beam of the headlights. There were no lights showing and not a sign of life. The driver pulled up outside it, put his hand on the horn and kept it there. My toes curled in embarrassment as I wondered what sort of reception we should get.

Presently a light flickered and a figure came running out of the darkness. It was briefly explained to him that there were four of us and that we were hungry and needed somewhere to sleep. He replied equally briefly and went bounding off in the direction of the farmhouse, where more lights now appeared and the whole place came rapidly to life. We climbed out and followed him.

There we were, four uninvited guests arriving an hour after sunset at a lonely farmhouse on the road to nowhere – and there was no doubt about it, they were delighted to see us. 'Allah be praised who has brought guests,' they said, ushering us into a large room on the first floor (the ground floor was occupied by their farm animals). We left our shoes at the threshold, shook a lot of eager hands and sat down on folded mattresses placed round the walls. I could have done with a wash, but first things had to come first. We came after all from the great world outside, from Antalya, with its electricity and paved roads – and horse buses; we must know what was happening there and in Ankara and even beyond. We must talk, by God, we must tell them *everything*. We did our best until the meal arrived, when a small boy poured water over our hands from a tall brass jug and we set to work on three or four courses of eggs and meat and breadfruit and a sweet and yoghurt. Then there was more talk until it was time for bed and the mattresses were unrolled and the family stood round us as we undressed, determined not to miss a moment of conversation. At last someone blew out the lamp and in a moment I was asleep, to wake up at 6.15 and find the others upbraiding each other for sleeping so long.

I wonder if life is still like that up there in the mountains behind Antalya, when at the heart of things the Turks seem to have lost the sense of unity which Ataturk left to them. I expect so, for what I encountered there had nothing to do with politics; it was just the natural decency and hospitality of simple people who had yet to come to grips with all the implications of Ataturk's revolution.

At the time, though, it seemed to me that there was no corner of Turkish life where the influence of Ataturk had not penetrated. At every turn you felt conscious of his shade looking down, from whatever Valhalla he had gone to, urging, exhorting, cajoling, if necessary cursing the Turks into carrying on with the enormous task he had set them. In Zonguldak and among the coal mines of the Black Sea coast; at Iskenderun in the steamy Mediterranean heat; on the quiet banks of the Sakarya river; among the old Seljuk monuments of Konya; and most of all on many crossings, by bus or car or train and sometimes in the friendly cab of a Turkish truck driver, of that great bare expanse of central Anatolia, whose peasant strength carried Ataturk to victory in 1922, you felt yourself always under the spell of his personality.

Before I left Turkey a friend took me to see the place where Ataturk was buried. His body has been moved since then, to a huge pillared mausoleum which they were building in 1952. At that time there was just a simple memorial to mark his grave and as we stood there we were joined by a *hamal*, a porter, bare-footed and dressed in rags. He stood quietly, twisting his cap in his hands, and then he asked us if this was indeed the place where Ataturk was buried. My companion told him it was and the man was silent for a moment. Then he spoke softly, as though to himself, in Turkish and turned away. I asked what he had said and, as my friend translated it, it seemed to be the perfect epitaph for Kemal Ataturk, the father of the Turks.

'When he came to us, we were nothing. He showed us how to do all things. He was a real father to us. God be with him.'

17

Turkey had captivated me in a way that I had never expected and I kept putting off my departure to make one more expedition – until the sight of the full moon one evening in Ankara reminded me that I had little time left. It was the tenth moon since I had left England and the next stage in my journey would have to be the last. It was time to be up and off.

So, one evening in early November, I strapped up my suitcase and the dusty old bed-roll and climbed aboard the Anatolian Express for the last long pull over the plateau and down through the pine trees and the vineyards to Istanbul. And then, after a last look round the bazaars and the mosques and the delicious shores of the Bosphorus, I was off to Athens, where there was just time to call on Mrs Xenophon to reassure her that I had survived the hazards of my brief exile in Turkey, before flying on to Rome.

After Ankara, Rome took my breath away. Remember, this was just seven years after the end of the war and all the grandeur and beauty of Rome was there, without the jerry-built rubbish which was later to surround it – and without the traffic which was to clog the streets and drown the soft music of the fountains.

I had brought a little money with me from Turkey and while it lasted I decided that I could do no better than immerse myself in this background. I took a cheap room, bought a map and set out on foot to explore Rome. The sounds in my ears as I walked through the city in the autumn sunshine were predominantly those of the old authentic Italy: the shouts of welcome or recrimination or sheer exuberance with which the Roman, like most other Italians, likes to conduct the business of every day. It was refreshing and invigorating and I revelled in it and in the casual ebullience of the architectural background – 'the finest urban landscape in the world' as someone has called it – against which this engaging pageant was performed.

I wrote to my father:

You walk down some narrow street, which winds out of sight, and when you turn the corner you suddenly find yourself in a great *piazza* whose four walls are formed by four vast palaces, each with a huge portico, a balcony over it and wrought-iron lanterns mounted on the walls on either side. As likely as not a couple of statues stand negligently by one entrance and over another there are bas-reliefs set in the stonework, or a renaissance inscription; and somewhere in the *piazza* there is a fountain with nymphs or tortoises or dolphins, an old man with a barrel, a cherub, or a boat – the variety is endless, and always the cheerful sound of water trickling or tumbling or vigorously spouting reaches your ears over the occasional traffic and the conversation of the passers-by. Then if you can gain a bit of height and look out over the rooftops, there are domes against the sky whichever way you look until over there beyond the river your eye lights on St Peter's, the most splendid of all. Fountains and domes everywhere – and steps, great wide shallow staircases of stone sweeping up to a palace or a church or a belvedere, all giving a tremendous sense of space and opulence and serving to lead the eye to one of the imposing prospects which Rome loves to offer.

It was easy to live simply in Rome, on something like the old pattern of my days in Belleville. Mostly I ate my meals in the cheaper *trattorie*, a plate of pasta, fruit and half a bottle of wine for a few hundred lire, but as I began to make friends I was entertained here and there and one day – I can't think how I attained such grandeur – I lunched in the Palazzo Massimo, the 'biggest palace', in a sumptuous apartment full of heavy antique furniture ranged between walls hung with tapestries and Spanish leather. My host, a bachelor aesthete and *bon viveur*, reminded me irresistibly of Browning's Bishop Blougram and of how proud the poor journalist, Gigadibs, had been to boast that he had:
> Dined with him once, a Corpus Christi Day,
> All alone, we two; he's a clever man:
> And after dinner, why, the wine you know –
> Oh, there was wine, and good! – what with the wine . . .
> Faith, we began upon all sorts of talk!

All this was a far cry from Ankara, but in Rome it seemed the most natural thing in the world to step from one ambience to another in this way, and from one century to the next as well, with no sense of incompatibility or self-consciousness. Best of all was the easy-going freedom of the street, where you never knew what you would meet next; a political protest or a circus troupe or a procession in honour of the Virgin Mary.

In Rome, more than anywhere else I had been, it seemed that the best things in life were free; but life itself was not, and presently reality began to intrude. I had to eat and sleep – and I could not forego the chance to hear Rubinstein playing Chopin at the Argentina or to find a place in the gods for the opening night of the opera, when every box in the house was decorated with a garland of roses and Tito Gobbi sang the title role in *Simone Boccanegra*. (In the next production, better still, Boris Christoff was unforgettable as *Boris Godunov*.) All this cost money: not a lot, but enough to remind me that unless I replenished it, my purse would be empty while there were still two or three weeks of the year to run. In my peregrinations about the city I began to look out for opportunities.

My Italian was improving, but although I tried to use it as much as I could and read an Italian translation of *Daisy Miller* (poor Daisy, she went flirting with a young Italian in the Colosseum under a full moon and caught malaria, and died of it), I could not expect it to sound convincing to a prospective employer. I tried this and that, with little success – and presently I found myself caught up in what it is astonishing to think was then the coming thing: tourism. Italy, of course, has always had its tourists: the pilgrims who took the road to Rome, the sensitive English ladies who followed in Browning's wake to Florence, the waves of artists and poets and adventurers from the cold north who found in Italy an environment in which their spirits could expand. But tourism in the modern sense was in its infancy in 1952 and it became my salvation.

One morning I sat opposite a charming Italian in the offices of ENIT, the state tourist agency. It was the opening phase of an association from which I was never confident of gaining any greater advantage than some schooling in the most elegant Italian – until there emerged at the end of it all, like an unexpected birthday present, boxed and gift-wrapped, a project so exactly tailored to my desires that I could hardly believe my luck.

Skiing was enjoying a post-war boom and the Italians were eager to develop their resorts in the Dolomites as rivals to those in the Swiss and French Alps. Could they persuade me, asked my friend from ENIT, with a winning smile, to go and stay in two or three of these resorts with a view to popularizing them in the eyes of my compatriots? How could I refuse? But on the eve of our final meeting, at which the deal was to be clinched, doubts assailed me. The bargain seemed to be all in my favour. Had I misunderstood its terms, or undertaken unawares some commitment which I should find it difficult to fulfil?

When we met the next morning, he called in his assistant to attend to the details and while this was being done something set him going on a discussion of the differences between the north and the south of Italy. Garibaldi came into it, I remember, and Gabriele d'Annunzio, and he illustrated a point with a deft quotation from Dante and was going on to compare him with Shakespeare when his assistant managed to catch his attention for a moment. Apologizing for the interruption, my friend turned to cross-question him about the arrangements, implying – if he did not actually say so – that if I were going to do Italy this service, he wanted to be sure that things were as they should be: the hotels advised, the rooms booked, the travel warrant (first-class, of course) prepared, instructions sent for someone to meet me with a car at Bolzano . . . Satisfied at last that everything was in order, he turned back to me, rounded off our conversation, and rose courteously to wish me *buon viaggio*.

Conscious of lowering the tone of our exchanges, I took a deep breath and asked what exactly he expected me to do in return. He replied with his most charming smile.

'Signor Adams,' he said, 'go to the Dolomites and enjoy yourself as much as you can. If, on your return to England, you should find an opportunity to . . .' – and here his expressive hands scribbled in the air the opening lines of an imaginary article – 'we shall be eternally in your debt.'

And that was how I came to end the year in the Majestic Hotel Miramonti at Cortina d'Ampezzo where, after an invigorating day's skiing, I saw the new year in with an Englishman I had met on the slopes. He was forty-ish, with a soldierly air about him, and out there in the snow that morning I had had the impression that his eye rested on me with a certain suspicion. I thought no more about it until I came down in the evening, exhilarated by a day in the open air and a hot bath and a general sense that fate was smiling on me, to have dinner in the Miramonti's opulent dining room. There I came upon him sitting by himself and was surprised when he invited me to join him. I was glad of his company and we ordered a bottle of wine and fell to talking.

He was an excellent companion, widely travelled and with a fund of good stories. I wondered how he came to be there, for you wouldn't get far at the Miramonti in 1952 on £30. When the wine had loosened our reserve, I put it to him. Oh, he said, it was quite simple. He had been serving as military attaché in Lisbon and he was taking a short holiday on his way to his next posting in Pakistan.

'But I've been wondering about the same thing,' he added, 'a young fellow like yourself – how do you manage to stay in a place like this?'

I explained that I was there, in a manner of speaking, on business; and when he asked what kind of business it might be that imposed on me the obligation to go skiing in Cortina at the height of the season, I tried to explain, with a feeling that I was getting into deep water, about running short of money in Rome with two weeks to go before I could return to England. Of course he wanted to know why I couldn't go back sooner – and gradually the whole story came out, of Belleville and the Orient Express and the Greek islands and Turkey, to all of which he listened intently, putting a question here and there, for he had the orderly mind of a good staff officer.

'It seems to have turned out all right,' he said when I had finished, 'but tell me one thing. What gave you the idea of going off like that in the first place?'

'Well,' I replied without thinking, 'I was a prisoner for three or four years during the war and while mostly it was a waste of time it did at least teach me how to rough it. I just wanted to make sure I hadn't lost the knack.'

He stared at me for a moment. Then he sat back in his chair and let his gaze wander over the dining room of the Majestic Hotel Miramonti: over the silver and the glass, the trolleys of hors d'oeuvres, the wine waiters scurrying beneath the chandeliers. Finally he leaned forward again and fixed on me a look of earnest enquiry.

'Tell me, old boy,' he said, as though it were important to him to get the facts straight, 'you don't mean to say you call this roughing it?'

PART SIX

American Interlude
(1954–55)

18

After a year like that I knew it would not be easy to settle down; but there was clearly no choice. I was nearly thirty-three and the next time I came to apply for a new passport I wanted to be able to enter as my profession something better than 'vagrant'.

One day, attending some forgotten press conference in London, I ran into an old acquaintance and we went off to have lunch together in a pub. He was working for *Picture Post*, one of the liveliest ventures in Fleet Street, but he had set his sights, as I had, on becoming a foreign correspondent. As a means to this end, he had applied for a travelling fellowship with something called the Commonwealth Fund, which offered young journalists the chance of a year of study and travel in the United States. I wished him luck and said that if I had not made up my mind to settle down I might have gone into competition with him.

It was a tempting idea, though, and when I heard soon afterwards that he had changed his mind and decided to get married instead, I began to take it seriously. I mentioned it to my father, who was now over seventy and living in retirement in Sussex, and to my surprise – for I knew he thought it was time I stopped messing about and got down to something – he was on to it like a shot. Whatever I intended to do with my life, he urged, there could be no better preparation for it than a year in America. In the world in which I must make my way, the Americans were going to be the pace-setters. I might as well learn to understand them, and the only place to do that was on their own home ground.

It was all I needed – and if to some it will seem odd that a man of thirty-three took such notice of an old man's counsel, I make no apology for it and have no regrets. After all, it was he who had sent me to Oxford – and persuaded me to go back there after the war; and in between it was his sensitive imagination that had kept the lamps burning for me in the twilight of the prison camp. When I wanted advice, I had no need to look further afield.

And of course the advice was sound, although that was by no means as obvious then as it might seem today. In the early 1950s, the United States was still a long way from assuming the role in the world which we take for granted in the 1980s. Nor were we in the old world ready to concede that Europe's day was done as the arbiter of international affairs. In Winston Churchill – triumphantly returned to power as head of a Conservative government in 1951 – and in de Gaulle in France and Konrad Adenauer in a resurgent Germany, Europe still had leaders beside whom a Harry Truman or an Eisenhower looked like beginners. The facts of power were there, but the appearances were still misleading; and if not many Europeans realized how decisively the balance had shifted, there were millions of Americans between the Atlantic Ocean and the Pacific who were no wiser.

I made some enquiries about the Commonwealth Fund and I was advised that the key to a successful application lay in one thing. Each candidate had to submit a programme explaining why a particular pattern of studies had been suggested. I had some trouble with this. What I wanted was a chance to travel and meet people all over the United States; but I felt I could not put this quite so baldly in my application. In the end I hit on what seemed to me a workable formula, posted off my application and in due course was summoned for an interview with a high-powered body of selectors, of which the outstanding figure was Sir Oliver (now Lord) Franks, who had recently left his post as British Ambassador in Washington. As soon as I had taken my place, Sir Oliver came with alarming directness to the point.

'Mr Adams,' he said, 'you've outlined here a very interesting programme. There's just one thing about it that puzzles me. It is clear that you would like to travel very widely, and I hope you will. But I wonder why you say you want to spend one semester at an American university studying American institutions?'

It was clear to me that I had to risk my all on a single throw. I tried to look imperturbable as I replied.

'Well sir,' I said, 'the rest of the programme looked so much like a joyride that I thought I ought to put in something serious. That is the serious bit.'

There followed what seemed an inordinately long silence and I held my breath. Then someone – I shall always bless him – laughed and as a ripple of amusement ran round the table I sensed that the day was won; but it was Sir Oliver who made the victory complete.

'On reflection,' he said, as the laughter died away, 'you might like to consider taking out that bit of the programme.' And of course I did.

And so, early one morning towards the end of September, I went on board the *Queen Elizabeth* at Southampton – for that was the normal way to cross the Atlantic in 1954 – and five days later fought my way in steaming heat through the jungle of the US customs at New York to start on another year of wandering. As I did so, I remembered that old song that I had learned in Paris.

> Snakes in the ocean, eels in the sea,
> A red-headed woman made a fool out of me;
> And it don't look like I'm ever going to cease my
> > wandering . . .

And there was another verse, whose relevance I had never considered:

> I've been wandering, early and late,
> From New York City to the Golden Gate,
> And it don't look like I'm ever going to cease my wandering,
> It don't look like I'm ever going to get me home.

Looking back after thirty years, the United States in the autumn of 1954 appears wonderfully peaceful. The Korean war was over, while America's long and dismal involvement in Vietnam still lay in the future. In Europe the Marshall Plan had been a resounding success and had helped to lay the ghost of American isolationism. Even the cold war seemed less threatening since the death of Stalin in 1953. Eisenhower was in the middle of his first term as president and I suppose that from that day to this the American horizon has never been so unclouded.

For a month or so I stayed in and around New York, trying to get the feel of things. Some days I loved it, and on others felt completely out of my element in this harshly beautiful metropolis. At such times it seemed odd to hear people speaking English all around me, in an environment which seemed as foreign to me as Anatolia – and much more so than Paris or Rome.

During my first week in New York there was only one topic of discussion and that was the World Series in which the Yankees and the Dodgers were fighting each other for the American equivalent of the Ashes. Once that was over and I began to advance with growing confidence into newspaper offices and television stations, I learned that there were other preoccupations. Two of these in particular were to claim my attention during the months ahead.

The first revolved around the unsavoury figure of Joseph McCarthy, the junior senator from Wisconsin, who for three years had terrorized the politicians and intellectuals of America with his allegations about a 'Communist conspiracy'. The other, with implications as far-reaching and roots far deeper, was the civil-rights question, which had been brought to a significant turning point by the decision of the Supreme Court, four months before my arrival, that segregation between white and black children in the public schools of the United States was unconstitutional.

There was a link between the two and, as luck would have it, my first major sortie out of New York took me into an environment where both were in the very air I breathed from one day to the next.

This, perhaps surprisingly, was in Kentucky, where I spent the last month of the year with a loose attachment to one of the best newspapers in the country, the Louisville *Courier-Journal*; and it so happened that I arrived in Louisville, the state capital, just in time for a trial in which the twin issues of race and of the Communist conspiracy combined to produce an atmosphere as sinister as anything in the casebooks of Kafka or George Orwell.

This was the Braden case, which at the end of 1954 tore the city apart, although – and this was characteristic – it made little stir outside Kentucky. And here I ought to say, since the outcome of the trial seemed to me to reflect such discredit on the people of Louisville, that it was also wholly out of keeping with the spirit of the place. Kentucky is an easy-going, undistinguished state of no easily discernible character. Situated right on the Mason-Dixon line, it belongs neither to the north nor to the south. Avoiding all extremes, the 'Blue Grass State' concerns itself with the raising of bloodstock and the Kentucky Derby and plays as a rule no significant part in the wider affairs of the nation. When I search my mind for some incident or observation which might encapsulate the ethos of Kentucky, I recall, not unfairly I believe, an elderly reporter on the *Courier-Journal* who once invited me to spend an afternoon at his cabin in the woods a few miles out of town. We went for a long walk (he carried a gun under his arm, I recall, and when I asked him why, he said people would think him eccentric if he just went out walking for no purpose) and cooked ourselves sausages over an open fire and sang a song or two and then smoked in contented silence, until at last I said I ought to be going. 'Why?' asked Joe. 'Well,' I said, 'you must have things you want to do.' To which Joe's reply was simple.

'Son,' he said, 'there ain't a goddam thing goes on here except relaxation.'

That is how I like to remember Kentucky. Nevertheless, it was in Louisville, Kentucky that Carl Braden, a sub-editor on the *Courier-Journal*, was tried for sedition, convicted and sentenced to fifteen years in the penitentiary and a fine of $5,000 – and all because he sold his house in a white neighbourhood of Louisville to a negro. Of course that is not what the indictment said; but that was Braden's real crime in the eyes of a community still deeply racist, and it was aggravated by the fact that he had in his possession, among literally thousands of books and pamphlets on social and labour questions, a number of Communist publications. An inconspicuous figure, to whose good character as a citizen and an honest journalist a dozen witnesses testified, Carl Braden had the misfortune to run up against the two salient prejudices of the day in America and he paid a heavy price for it.

The case had started six months earlier when Braden bought a house and transferred it to a negro friend. As soon as the black family moved in, their white neighbours began to make trouble. Shots were fired through the windows, a fiery cross was burned on the lawn outside and after a month an explosion wrecked the front of the house.

A grand jury was summoned to investigate the cause of the explosion and its findings turned the whole affair upside down. Carl Braden and his wife were arrested on a charge of advocating sedition and the lawyer for the Commonwealth of Kentucky declared that he had evidence of a plot to stir up racial prejudice in the state.

The case opened just after my arrival in Louisville. At first the prosecution's case looked absurdly thin, as the lawyers went through the contents of Braden's bookshelves and tried to make something damaging out of a handful of publications that might have been part of any undergraduate's library. Then came a string of witnesses whom I described in a letter to my father as 'looking intrinsically unreliable, people who have been Communists and have recanted and now go round the country acting as professional witnesses in cases like this one'.

This sort of thing went on for several days and the defence lawyer, when his turn came, had little difficulty in demolishing it, producing witnesses who were not and never had been Communists and who testified that they had bought Communist literature (including the constitution of the Soviet Union) on bookstalls in Boston and Chicago; and following them with character witnesses who spoke of the useful service the prisoner had given to the American Civil Liberties Union in averting or settling labour disputes, or who testified that in his work at the *Courier-Journal* Carl Braden had never been known to try to slant a story in favour of Communists or those who sympathized with them.

It looked as though the jury would have to acquit Braden; but there was an ugly mood abroad in Louisville and my friends on the *Courier-Journal* were uneasy. Several of them begged me not to assume that what I was seeing and hearing in that dingy courtroom in Louisville was representative of American justice. Nor was it – but unhappily it *was* representative of something equally important: of an attitude of mind which was widespread at that particular moment in American history and which is still latent today. It is not easy to define it with precision, but it finds expression in a tendency to suspect whatever diverges from the all-American norm; and to adopt, in dealing with it, methods which have nothing whatever in common with the ideals of the founding fathers of the republic.

It was this that emerged on the twelfth day of the trial, when an acquittal seemed the only possible outcome – until the prosecution produced, late in the afternoon, a surprise witness. This was a Mrs Alberta Ahearn, a friend of the defendant, who now created a sensation by claiming to be an undercover agent of the FBI. The FBI, Mrs Ahearn said, had planted her inside the Communist Party where she swore that she had belonged to the same cell in Louisville as Carl Braden; in fact it was Braden, she insisted, who had invited her to join the party and she had attended six meetings in his house during the past year.

From that moment it was all up with Braden. It was not – formally – a crime to be a Communist, but Braden had earlier sworn that he was not and never had been a member of the party. If Mrs Ahearn's testimony was accepted, there would be, at the very least, a clear case of perjury against Braden. It was his word against hers; and in the prevailing atmosphere of racist and anti-Communist hysteria she had a clear advantage, especially since the FBI refused access to its files to substantiate her testimony. In the witness box she was, as I wrote in my diary, 'cool and controlled, though one sensed something odd about her', and it was only afterwards that we learned that:

the one thing that would instantly have discredited her had been ruled out of order: she had been convicted a few months earlier for a sexual offence, ironically enough with a negro. It's all for the best, I suppose, for it's no good overcoming one prejudice with another – but here was a man's life & reputation at stake.

By this time I felt as involved in the case as the journalists reporting it and the crowd which packed the courtroom; indeed, the whole of Louisville could think and talk of nothing else. For me and a group of friends with whom I attended it, the final day of the trial had a frightful fascination. At the end of it, I wrote in my diary:

The whole of a long grey day we've been in the courtroom, where the last evidence was taken & the two sides summarized their arguments. After Mrs Ahearn's testimony the issue was clearcut: either she was a liar or Braden was a Communist & a perjurer. So when Zollinger (the defence lawyer) began his 'summation' after lunch, it looked pretty hopeless, with the FBI against Braden, as well as local feeling. But Zollinger made a hearteningly good defence, while Hamilton, the attorney for the Commonwealth, seemed weak and unconvincing – & we began to hope. Then Hamilton's assistant, Higgins, took over & blasted the jury with a horrible, rabble-rousing, ranting blend of half-truths & appeals to every sort of prejudice, & hope was gone. When he had finished & the jury retired, we tried to persuade ourselves that there was still a chance of a verdict that would save something from this wreck of ideals. While we waited, some of us went up to talk to Zollinger – a decent, unpretentious, small-town lawyer who keeps racing pigeons, he told us – & met Braden's wife Anne, small, nervous, unattractive to look at, & yet with what I felt to be sincerity all through her to her bitten fingernails. At last, after three hours, the jury came back & read out their verdict: 'We find the defendant Carl Braden guilty of this indictment', & then this cruel sentence. A single fool at the back shouted 'Bravo!' & our little group felt suddenly old & sad. Up by the judge the reporters were taking statements from the principals & a TV cameraman was taking pictures. Just behind Zollinger, who was being interviewed, sat Anne Braden, leaning her cheek on her hand, expressionless & tired & alone. I edged my way through to her & touched her shoulder & told her shyly that I was sorry. She was perfectly calm – too calm, it struck me – & said: 'I was expecting it to be twenty-one years, but it doesn't matter – fifteen years or twenty-one, the atmosphere in this country will have changed long before that' – & I wished her luck & made my way out into the blessed cold fresh air.

A week later I left Louisville and in thirty years I've never been back there. Nor have I ever forgotten the experience of the Braden trial or the effect it had in shaping my own ideas, not just about the Americans but about the world as a whole. As far as the Americans were concerned, who had shown me the same instinctive hospitality in Louisville as in New York, I felt anxious about what I described to my father as 'the steady curtailment of the freedom of the individual in this country', not through legislation or conscious direction from the top, but because of a general trend towards conformity and because the number of people prepared to oppose this trend seemed to be diminishing. That jury in Louisville, I wrote, 'was out to get Braden because he was different: he read books they did not like, mixed himself up in causes they thought disreputable (particularly the emancipation of the negroes) and was courageous enough to do something about them – including some very unwise things, but that's not a crime'. And I was not alone in Louisville in thinking that 'there is more danger to liberty in the States from the Hamiltons who prosecute them than there is from the Bradens'.

In a wider sense that experience in Kentucky gave a nudge – perhaps even a decisive one – to the shaping of my own outlook and to the way in which I was later to express it. In a community much like any other, I had seen with my own eyes how the truth could be subverted by prejudice and fanaticism, provided no one stood up to denounce the process. I did not realize at the time how deeply this lesson had imprinted itself on my mind. All I knew was that I had to find an outlet for the sense of outrage the affair had aroused in me, and I sat down the day after the trial ended to write an article about it. I sent the article to Alistair Cooke, who had shown a lively interest in my affairs while I was in New York (it was the Commonwealth Fund which had brought him to America too, just twenty years before me), asking him if he thought fit to send it on to the *Manchester Guardian*, whose correspondent he was in New York. Somewhere along the line, it got delayed, but the *Guardian*, much to my surprise, decided to publish it – exactly a year after the events it described. So the Braden case forged a link in the curious chain of circumstances by which our fate is decided; for this was the first but by no means the last article I was to write for this standard-bearer of liberalism.

Having got the thing out of my system I was able to shake off my depression. I had bought an old car in Louisville and I now set out to spend Christmas with friends in Long Island, on the far side of New York. It looks as though I was beginning to adapt to the local scale, for New York was about as far away to the north-east as Rome is from London: a long way, you might think, to go for the weekend. But these things look different in America and when I set out at 7.30 one morning under a grey sky, with the thermometer standing at $-3°C$, I switched on the radio to get the weather forecast. Out of the damp chill of the morning a voice addressed me, intimate, friendly, the voice clearly of someone with my best interests at heart.

'Did you wake up feeling tired?' it asked with deadly insight. Hurriedly I twiddled the knob and another voice moaned gently that 'There's no place like home for the holidays,' and as I was considering this the voice elaborated: 'For the holidays you can't beat home, sweet home.' I tried again and this time struck a news bulletin. A doctor in Michigan had predicted that the world would end that day. The jury in a murder trial in Cleveland had been out for four days without reaching a verdict. There were two more shopping days to Christmas. 'And in a moment,' said the announcer, 'the weather – but first here's a message for YOU! Did you wake up feeling . . .' I decided I could wait for the weather forecast and switched off.

Behind white fences on either side of the road, the rolling paddocks of Kentucky lay under a thin blanket of snow. As I drove on through Frankfort, Georgetown, Paris, school buses were discharging pupils in bright scarlet and green and blue windjackets, while at the corner of every Main Street stood a decorated creche. Fortified by a cup of coffee and two eggs, I tried the radio again.

'Now here's a message for you folks who are out on the road today,' said a new voice, friendly again but with an admonitory ring. 'Just remember that the fellow who's in too much of a hurry to get to the next town ends up in the next world.'

I stepped on the accelerator and drove at seventy miles an hour along a straight stretch of open road. The sun came out and the bare trees stood in silhouette against the sky. I was across the border into Ohio now, in a flattening landscape of farmland, corn stubble in the wide fields, white-painted frame houses and big barns with green roofs. Tired of the highway, I turned off into a miniature Alpland where the road wound up and down and round wooded hills and over frozen creeks, the snow lying evenly in the shady bottoms while each fresh rise brought me into slanting sunshine.

I drove on up a long ridge, the sky behind me brilliant with the sunset colours and clumps of trees forming purple smudges against the darkening landscape. 'Let me go, lover' wailed a woman's voice from the radio; and then, as the announcer broke in to say the temperature was –4°C and dropping, I came on to the top of the ridge and began to coil down towards the Ohio River and the lights of the little town of Marietta shining out of the darkness.

Dawn next morning found me pouring hot water over the windshield of the car – the temperature was –9°C – and watching it freeze solid. Soon I had cleared a little patch of glass and was driving up the Ohio valley in the first pale sunlight of the day. Mist was drifting over the water; frost glistened in the trees on either side of the road. The world was like a fairy tale just ready to be told.

The radio brought me back to earth. An announcer in Chicago said cheerfully that there was no sign yet of the end of the world. The Cleveland jury was starting its sixth day of deliberation. Temperatures in the Ohio valley ranged from -12 to $-9°C$ and it was snowing in New York.

I crossed the Ohio into West Virginia and skirted the industrial area around Pittsburgh. Ahead the landscape looked like a rumpled sheet and soon I was in the bumpy hills of Pennsylvania, their snowy outline sharp against a clear sky. Another fifty miles and I turned on to the Pennsylvania Turnpike and for the next five hours I drove at sixty miles an hour clear through the Alleghenies. Stopping for petrol and a sandwich, I learned that the Cleveland jury had brought in a verdict of guilty and then, as darkness fell, I returned to the queer detached world of the turnpike, a concrete conveyor belt which whirled us all along from our scattered starting points in Kentucky, Kansas, Nevada, Colorado on towards the glittering goal of New York beyond the eastern horizon.

I slept the night at Valley Forge, sifting vague memories of George Washington and early next morning (the temperature up to $-2°C$, the highest it had been) drove through Philadelphia and on to another turnpike which links the old capital with New York. The mountains were behind now and in the flat landscape the clustered oil tanks of New Jersey put an end to my dream of exploring a virgin continent. And then, rounding a concrete curve, I saw at last the topless towers of Manhattan, their cold, cruel beauty veiled in mists. For me at that Christmas of 1954 they spelled home; and as I sped towards them I was thinking to myself: there's no doubt about it – especially with 901 miles on the clock – for the holidays you can't beat home, sweet home.

The car – it was a two-year-old Plymouth for which I paid $650 – lent a splendid elasticity to my programme. I had intended to spend a long weekend in and around New York before moving on to Washington and spending a month there before I made for the Deep South and after that headed westwards across the country to the Pacific coast. Already there seemed to be so many friends to revisit that the weekend stretched into a week and then I was asked to go and spend New Year's Eve in Connecticut – and that too extended itself into three days of intermittent festivities, so that it was 3 January before I threw my things into the back of the Plymouth and drove sleepily down through New Jersey and Delaware and Maryland (where I picked up a negro sailor for company) to Washington: 270 miles, and it seemed like nothing.

Brilliant sunshine greeted me next morning and I was impatient to explore the city, but first I gritted my teeth and spent a couple of hours on the phone announcing my arrival and setting up interviews to launch me on my way. This was what I liked least about this itinerant life, but my inhibitions were falling away fast. It is difficult to remain hesitant about calling up perfect strangers when the response, four times out of five is: 'Come right on over, Mike,' or 'How's about dinner tonight?' I found myself a small apartment on 13th Street and had hardly moved in before my own telephone began ringing and it seemed as though, through the agency of the Commonwealth Fund and friends in New York and Louisville, Washington lay open to me. As I had done in Greece and Turkey ('Allah be praised who has brought guests') a year or two earlier, I marvelled at the spontaneity of this welcome for the stranger.

Washington in that January of 1955 seemed to have few worries. A day or two after my arrival, in response to a phone call from Alistair Cooke, I joined him for breakfast with Max Freedman, the astute and elusive Washington correspondent of the *Manchester Guardian*, and afterwards we watched on television the opening of the new session of Congress and saw President Eisenhower reading his State of the Union message to the nation. 'Firm and businesslike', I noted in my diary, and there was no mistaking 'the sincerity and good intentions which were plainly there'. This impression was confirmed a fortnight later when I attended one of Eisenhower's regular press conferences. He seemed well able to take care of himself and handled the questions confidently, except when he got entangled in the controversy over one of the 'security-risk' affairs which were a feature of Washington life in that last phase of the McCarthy era. On this dangerous ground, Eisenhower was ill at ease, like so many other people in Washington at the time. Otherwise, his openness and sincerity created around him an aura of idealism which was attractive; at a time when the country was prosperous and there were no major problems on the international horizon, it was also a reassuring asset for him and for the Republican Party.

Already, though, I had doubts about the extent to which this idealistic approach was representative of the mood of the country at large. It was not only the Braden case which coloured my feelings here.

There were other illustrations of the yawning gap between the theory and the practice of American democracy – and if the gap was in reality no wider in America than elsewhere, it seemed so because of the unctuous tones adopted by almost any public speaker when he came to talk about the American way of life. Platitudes were plentiful and the Americans, I wrote to my father, 'really seem to believe in their own high-mindedness, just as they believe that there's more freedom in America than anywhere else – and it's not true'.

I was anxious not to prejudge issues of which I still knew so little, but I had the advantage, thanks to the Commonwealth Fund, of getting to know many of the best political journalists of the day. In New York, I had met Lester Markel of *The Times* and Joseph Wechsler, the humorous and outspoken editor of the *New York Post* (then a liberal-minded tabloid). Alistair Cooke had taken me down to the CBS studios to watch his own show, *Omnibus*, which was generally agreed to be the best of its kind and had introduced me to other leading current-affairs men like Bob Trout, a kind of American Richard Dimbleby, and Ed Murrow, who had made a great reputation with his broadcasts from London at the height of the blitz. I had taken a trip to Boston to meet Erwin Canham, the editor of the *Christian Science Monitor*, which many people, then as now, considered the best paper in the United States. And here in Washington, besides Max Freedman, there were Dan Schorr of CBS and Douglas Cater of the *Reporter* and Joseph Harsch of the *Monitor*, as thoroughgoing an idealist as any journalist could be, and yet cautionary about the belief in human perfectibility which inspired the Eisenhower era.

Through them and others I met politicians like Paul Douglas, the splendid old-fashioned liberal senator from Illinois and one of the commanding figures in the Senate at the time. With the country at peace and the economy booming, he could afford to give rein to his principles and denounce McCarthy, who was already past the peak of his sinister career; yet even Douglas, when it came to this issue of 'security risks' and Communist 'subversion', faltered, as Eisenhower had done, and became carefully defensive.

It was through Douglas that I had an opportunity to see in action the man behind this apparent distortion of American values. Douglas had given me a ticket for the reserved gallery of the Senate and at first I thought I had struck a dull day. As someone from the mid-west droned on about agriculture, most of the other senators quietly left; but I noticed that the one man I was interested in stayed on, making notes about something that I guessed was not agriculture. I stayed too, and was rewarded by seeing the legendary Senator McCarthy turn in a characteristic performance.

At that time Joseph McCarthy was forty-five years old and I suppose it would be true to say that he was the most hated man in the United States and one of the most influential. He came from Wisconsin, a relatively unimportant state, where he had practised as a lawyer until he joined the Marines during the war. Immediately after the war he gained election to the Senate, where he made it his special concern to campaign against what he claimed to be the presence of a large number of Communist agents in positions of influence in the administration and throughout the country.

In the early fifties, with the cold war at its height, it was not surprising that this should be an emotive issue. The United States had just had thrust upon it a role for which many Americans felt it lacked the experience and the political subtlety. In the past, as Americans saw it, it had been the light-fingered politicians of the old world, not just the Hitlers and Mussolinis who had been safely disposed of, but the crafty old rogues in London and Paris as well, who between them had engineered one crisis after another and eventually called on the virtuous Americans to come and pull their chestnuts out of the fire for them. And then, to cap it all, there was Stalin pushing the might of the Soviet Union right up against the frontier of the 'free world'; and behind him that ill-defined and sinister threat of international Communism that was threatening to swallow up decadent, bankrupt old Europe and then to infiltrate and undermine the very citadel of freedom and the capitalist system: the United States itself.

This, in even cruder terms, was the gospel that McCarthy preached and which won him fame and ultimately notoriety as the leader of a witch-hunt on a national scale. For a few disastrous years America bowed to his dictation, with politicians and film stars and journalists and businessmen all scared into submission by this demagogue, who traded in threats and innuendoes and whose contempt for the truth in the end undid him – but not until he had inflicted lasting damage on the national psyche. A few – very few – courageous individualists had defied him, of whom even fewer had lived (in political terms) to tell the tale. Arthur Miller, in his play *The Crucible* (1953), had taken the story of the witches of Salem and the mass hysteria which they provoked and turned it into an immensely effective parable about McCarthyism. But for the most part, whatever their politics or their profession, Americans in public life had swallowed their pride and their convictions, if they had any, and toed the McCarthy line.

This then was the man I had come to the Senate to see, and I sensed, as I watched him scribbling on that January day in 1955, that he had something up his sleeve. Sure enough, as soon as there was a break in the debate he was on his feet and had started a diatribe against the Democrats, who had just introduced a woolly motion denouncing Communism in very general terms. He was glad to see, said McCarthy, that they were starting to take this question seriously, but then he sneered at them, suggesting that they only did so 'to wash some of the dirt off their own hands', and went on to talk about the 'twenty years of treason' which America had suffered under the Democratic adminis-trations of Roosevelt and Harry Truman. He was challenged several times to give chapter and verse for his allegations, and the chairman tried to make him sit down; but McCarthy managed each time to carry on until he had quite made his point, though without producing any evidence, and the senators who tried to give battle were worsted. It was a fascinating performance, I told my father next day:

> . . . and I could see clearly how he got to his present position – which everyone keeps telling me he is losing, but without convincing *him*. He is so agile in debate, so free from the restraints of scruple or logic, so quick on his feet, that he runs rings round the rest of them. And he has a sense of humour, which stood him in good stead that day, for he would put on an act, be rude and infuriating, pound on the desk – and then, when the others lost their tempers and their self-command, he would suddenly grin, adopt a silky tone, and flay them with sarcasm. The whole exchange took up an hour of the Senate's time and achieved precisely nothing, except to get him the headlines of today's papers.

I added that the *Washington Post* that morning had 'quoted someone as saying that "McCarthy is no longer an -ism, he's a wasm" – which is a nice crack, but it would be nicer if it were true'.

In fact it was more nearly true than I realized. Within a week I was writing of a Canadian radio programme which someone in New York had taped and brought down to Washington, where I heard it at a party. Called *The Investigator*, it ran for an hour and was a brilliant parody of the hearings into 'subversion' which McCarthy had been carrying on in the last months of 1954. Everyone in Washington, I wrote, was clamouring to hear it:

> It starts with McCarthy's death in a plane crash, after which he goes

up to heaven and is annoyed to find that St Peter won't let him in until he has been 'investigated'. McCarthy, of course, isn't going to put up with this; he organizes a palace revolution, gets Peter thrown out of his job and has himself elected as chairman of the investigating committee. He then gets the committee to look into the records, not only of new applicants but of people who have been in heaven for centuries – and in no time at all he has banished to the other place such obvious subversives as Milton, Jefferson, Luther and a dozen more. The hearings are brilliantly done, with each of the accused replying in words he actually used when he was on earth: words which have become famous, like the Bill of Rights and Milton's defence of free speech. In the end McCarthy, trying to 'get right to the bottom of this conspiracy', attacks 'the Chief'; but this time he has over-reached himself and is himself banished 'down there'. But the devil won't let him in either and for want of any other solution he is returned to earth, where he is found near the scene of the crash, wandering and demented, mumbling 'Mr Chairman . . . Objection . . . Mr Chairman' in the accents I recognized from hearing them in the Senate a couple of days earlier. The recording had been pirated and apart from the repercussions it is bound to have in Washington (I heard yesterday that the president had had a private hearing of it) there are sure to be all kinds of lawsuits about it and it will probably sell millions of copies . . .

And of course it did, and for a long time it was everybody's favourite radio programme; I heard it again months later on my car radio when I was sleeping out on a wooded hillside high in the Rockies and it took my mind off the bears and snakes I had been warned to expect to keep me company. But by that time – and *The Investigator* undoubtedly helped to complete the rout – McCarthy really had become a 'wasm', as Americans all over the country realized that this ten-cent emperor really had no clothes and that all that had held them back from saying so was fear: the fear of being different and, if they stood up to McCarthy, of being labelled 'subversives' themselves. It was a realization which few of them found flattering.

I left Washington at the end of January and drove south and west along the Shenandoah valley, stopping to see the splendid house which Jefferson designed for himself at Monticello and then going on under the Blue Ridge mountains out of Virginia, across the edge of North

Carolina and into Georgia. Already a third of my American year was behind me and if I had been going back to England instead of on across the continent I should have taken home with me a jaundiced set of impressions.

Apart from the unfailing warmth and spontaneity I had encountered at the personal level, my idea of the American dream was becoming sadly tarnished. It was not just the triviality which seemed to characterize the American approach to life: the rubbish on radio and television, the preference for machine-made substitutes over the old authentic ways of living, the standardized ugliness of most American towns, with their used-car lots and filling stations and motels. These were the outward and visible signs of some inner malaise which I tried to identify. And what lay at the bottom of it all, I was beginning to think, was the very opposite of what I had expected to find. Instead of individualism and the impulse to think and act for oneself, all the evidence seemed to suggest a society cramped and clogged by conformity, anxious at all costs not to offend against conventions as narrow and restrictive as any in the old world from which most Americans believed they had escaped.

This instinct to conform started with small things. It was considered eccentric to walk where you could ride in a car; even Joe, when he took me for a walk in the woods outside Louisville, had carried a gun, not to shoot anything but to avoid ridicule; and from there it was not such a long step to persecuting a man like Carl Braden because he read books you didn't like and associated with blacks. Once you got that far, the way was open for a McCarthy to impose on a supposedly open society the straitjacket of fear and suspicion which darkened American life in the decade after the war; and the fact that everywhere there were individual Americans who rejected this abandonment of the Jeffersonian tradition and fought against it and tried to reassert the old values, only served to highlight the decline. For it was this liberal minority, made up of people like the editorial writers of the *Courier-Journal* in Louisville, and the handful of senators in Washington who refused to be cowed by McCarthy, and the writers like Lillian Hellman and Arthur Miller who did the same in lonely isolation all across the country, who were labelled as heretics and became the targets in a nationwide witch-hunt.

I was conscious, of course, that such impressions were both subjective and superficial, based on very limited experience; but they were reinforced by the ideas I absorbed in Washington from some of those I met and who gloried in the epithet then just gaining currency as a term of abuse: egg-heads. It was one of these non-conformists who prompted me to read Sinclair Lewis and in his *Main Street*, published nearly forty years earlier, I found this concise definition of what I felt had gone wrong: 'life is comfortable and clean enough here already. And so secure. What it needs is to be less secure and more eager.'

It was in this frame of mind that I headed southwards out of Washington and found to my delight that I had entered a new world. For a month, as I zigzagged about through the Deep South, it seemed that everything – climate, appearances, attitudes, even the vegetation – was wonderfully, refreshingly different. In Georgia, among the cotton plantations and the shanty towns, people still nursed dark memories of Sherman's march to the sea, when his men had burned Atlanta to the ground less than a century before. In Charleston, South Carolina, one of the few really distinctive American cities (every American town thinks of itself as a city), they cherished by contrast a vision of a sunlit past, to be preserved at any cost and against every change – and who could blame them, with the camellias in bloom and bougainvillaea trailing over their charming old frame houses? In the pleasure grounds of Florida there were cardinal birds swooping among the azaleas and herons motionless in the swamps, and you could buy grapefruit for one cent apiece by the roadside.

When I drove up to Birmingham, Alabama to attend the sensational trial of a racketeer who had terrorized the city (he seemed to have every charge in the book against him, from murder on downwards), the judge greeted me like an old friend, gave me a cigar and asked me where I wanted to sit in court next day. It was Mardi Gras when I arrived in New Orleans and the mayor gave me the freedom of the city – and the same evening I had my first experience of tear gas when the police raided a bar where I was relaxing with a couple of acquaintances. A hundred and fifty miles up the Mississippi I came to Natchez, another delightful incarnation of the dream-past of the old south, to find there was a pageant in progress and all the girls were wearing crinolines and there were coloured lanterns gleaming through the Spanish moss draping the trees. And at last I came to rest in the little town of Greenville, in the flatlands of the Mississippi delta, where the cotton fields were protected by levees against the swirling brown river now nearing the end of its long search for the sea.

All this was balm to my soul after the sameness of the north and east, where one city looked so like another and few had any charm. My concern, though, was less with this alluring surface than with what lay beneath. In the six weeks or so that I spent between the Atlantic seaboard and the Mississippi I had one aim in view. I wanted to discover how the south was reacting to the Supreme Court's ruling on desegregation, whose wider implications threatened so much that was precious to every white southerner.

Most of a year had passed since the Supreme Court's decision, whose effect, once it was implemented, would be to end the separate education of white and black children. By striking in this way at the roots of discrimination, it was bound in the end to bring down the whole structure, with consequences which it would be difficult to exaggerate for every aspect of life in the south, and ultimately in the rest of the country as well. For that reason it was a truly historic decision, and I was conscious as I drove down from Washington that I should be seeing the south at a critical turning point in its history.

So far, the question of segregation had been for me an academic one, apart from its relevance to the Braden case. Of course, it was a frequent topic of conversation everywhere, but outside the south it had no immediate impact. On the eastern seaboard I had hardly met a black man. In New York, when I drove up late one evening with an American friend to explore Harlem (something no white man in his senses would do today), we encountered no violence, no open hostility, but no one cared to speak to us and there seemed to be no basis for communication. People simply went on with what they were doing and treated us as though we were not there: a disconcerting experience. Even in Washington, with its large black community, I had noted that there was only one negro member in the press club. Now in a flash I was transported into a world, a few hundred miles from the White House, where segregation, with all its complex of rights and wrongs, its bright hopes and dark fears, was the overridingly important issue, the keynote of every discussion, the touchstone of loyalties and passions that lay just below the surface of every encounter.

Today, after thirty long years, the battle is almost over. Then, as the bugles were blowing, the antagonists were just shaping up to each other, uncertain of the outcome but conscious that this was the decisive moment, that for both sides it was now or never. Even a spectator could see that; and it was exciting.

Out of all the diversity of the south, it was in three places that I found most clearly articulated the points of view that had somehow to be reconciled. The first of these was Charleston, which I loved at first sight – and where people's attitudes seemed to be so firmly anchored in the past that it was difficult even to approach the question of segregation without offence. That I was able to do so at all I owed to one of the introductions that had begun to serve me so well, turning the impersonal map of this vast country into a web of personal connections which reached from coast to coast. Late on New Year's Eve at a party in Westport, Connecticut, my partner of the moment had said, on learning that Charleston might be on my itinerary: 'Then you just *must* be sure to go and see Mrs Pettigrew Verner'. I could have had no better passport in Charleston, where a stranger – even if he were not a damn Yankee, but especially if he came asking impertinent questions about what Charleston considered its own business and no one else's – could expect some dusty answers.

Mrs Pettigrew Verner, as her name suggests, was the very embodiment of southern charm. She was not young, but the years can only have enhanced her elegance. She was beautifully dressed in what my mind's eye recalls as pastel shades of blue and green and she had the eyes of a friendly bird, which surveyed the world and its absurdities with amusement and an exceptional sharpness of vision. Charleston was her life and she showed me – indeed, on parting she *gave* me – a copy of her personal history of the place, illustrated with her own delicate pencil drawings of the lovely old houses and the church with its white steeple dating from 1762, where I later attended a service. When she had told me as much as she thought it right for me to know, she bravely sent me off to meet some of her friends and the vicar of the church and the editor of the *News and Courier*, warning me gently but very firmly that they would not talk to me as she had done and that, if I asked the sort of questions I had asked her, they would shut their doors in my face – 'and quite right too' – and telling me to come back before leaving and tell her all about it.

When I did so, of course she had heard all about it already: how what I thought had been my cautious and diffident approach had ruffled feathers not used to being disturbed by talk of realities, how I had shown an almost Yankee disregard for southern susceptibilities . . . It seemed that I was the talk of the town, and in no flattering sense. I hope I had not failed in politeness, but it is true that I had spoken at one point of the decision of the Supreme Court as being, when you came right down to it, a binding one (to which I received the answer 'Oh, pooh'); and true too that Charleston stands out in my mind, not just as one of the loveliest of American cities, but as the only place I remember in the whole of the United States where I encountered an unwillingness to discuss with me both the best and the worst of American life.

If the very idea of change seemed in Charleston not just distasteful but unthinkable, very different was the atmosphere in the second of my test cases. This was Atlanta, the capital of Georgia, which had not long shaken off the dreadful consequences of the Civil War but was now a bustling industrial centre, with new industries springing up and jobs for all and its eyes firmly fixed on the future. Here, only two or three hundred miles inland from Charleston, I found minds refreshingly open. The mayor, still bent on re-election after seventeen years in office and with his eye perhaps on the black vote, now that emancipation was under way, talked convincingly of the need to make progress towards a real partnership between whites and blacks. So did Ralph McGill, the likeable and enterprising editor of the *Constitution* whose policy was to make haste slowly in order to avoid a white backlash. There was clearly much to be said for this gradualist approach; the question was, would the blacks put up with it, now that they had the law as well as natural justice on their side?

Here lay the difficulty, for in this case 'the law' meant federal law, the law of the United States; but education, like so much else, lay within the jurisdiction of the individual states of the Union. The Georgia state legislature was still dominated by the 'shellback' conservatism of the old south, for which 'States' Rights' was an emotive battle-cry. In its determination to resist desegregation, the old guard was prepared to introduce, under the banner of states' rights, all kinds of reactionary legislation, even threatening to abolish the public schools altogether rather than submit to the 'tyranny' of the Supreme Court. It was a potentially explosive situation, in which much would depend on the patience of the black community and the power of its leaders to maintain control of events.

There were two of these leaders especially that I had been told I should try to meet. The first was Dr Rufus Clemens, the president of Atlanta University, who had just been elected to the Atlanta School Board and had thus become the first black office holder in the history of Georgia. A gentle, soft-spoken man, he received me gladly and spoke with convincing moderation of his hopes for the future. But it was the second man who gave me an unforgettable impression both of the difficulties the blacks had to contend with in the Deep South and of how they envisaged their way ahead.

His name was Bill Gordon and he was the editor of the *Atlanta Daily World*. I called on him at his office and found him to be a man of about thirty, self-assured, quite extraordinarily good-looking and with the most infectious laugh in the world. Within five minutes we were old friends – but when I said that I wanted to have a long talk with him, a problem imposed itself. His office was tiny and he had after all a newspaper to bring out. He would be delighted to talk to me as soon as he was free, but he could think of nowhere in Atlanta where the two of us, one black, the other white, could legally meet. No restaurant or bar would accommodate us both, we could not meet at my hotel, we would not even be able to ride in the streetcar together. There was only one solution that he could suggest and he put it forward with charming diffidence. Would I come home to supper at his house in a new housing development for blacks on the outskirts of the city?

When we arrived together, his wife was as friendly and as much at ease with me as he was, while her mother was flustered and had difficulty in shaking my hand. But then we were off, talking until far into the night about what seemed to me the extraordinary existence this highly educated American journalist led in a city where he could have no social intercourse in any public place, not just with me but with any of his fellow-citizens whose faces happened to be white. If he resented this (and how could he not?), he gave no indication of it. His interest was in the future, about which he was confident, and when we met again the following evening – this time he persuaded the owner of a small negro restaurant to let us share an inconspicuous table in a dark corner of an inner room – he talked with the same humorous optimism about a future which at that moment still hung in the balance. There was nothing frivolous or superficial about his optimism. What he had to say to me, in essentials, was what Martin Luther King was to say thirteen years later: 'I've been to the mountain top, I've looked over and . . . I want you to know that we as a people will get to the promised land.' But Bill Gordon was a realist too. If he could have looked into the future, he would not have been surprised to learn that the day after he said that in neighbouring Tennessee, Martin Luther King would be assassinated.

In Atlanta, and in Charleston before it, I had been at opposite extremes of the great debate which was sweeping the south, between those who welcomed the new tide of emancipation which the Supreme Court had set in motion and those who preferred to man the old barricades – and were even trying to erect new ones – to check and frustrate it. As I travelled this way and that in the Deep South, through the Carolinas and Georgia, Alabama and Tennessee and Louisiana, I encountered all sorts of variations of these two basic attitudes and found, as my preconceptions weakened in the light of experience, that I could sympathize to some extent with almost all of them. The eventual outcome, in a society formally dedicated to the proposition that all men were created equal, seemed inevitable; but it was not difficult to understand the hesitancy of some of those most directly concerned, when they came face to face with a prospect so revolutionary and which required from them the abandonment of attitudes so deep-rooted and instinctive.

It would have been much harder for me to make sense of it all had I not had the luck, towards the end of my time in the south, to fall into the hands of one of the most remarkable men I met anywhere in the United States. His name was Hodding Carter and he was the editor of a local newspaper in Greenville, a small town in the middle of the 'black belt' in Mississippi. It was an area where you might have expected to find the most hidebound opposition to anything new or progressive. Not far from the border with Arkansas (whose capital of Little Rock was later to be the scene of one of the bitterest rearguard actions against desegregation), the county of which Greenville formed a part was one in which seventy per cent of the population were black. All of them, of course, were the descendants of slaves – but what was astonishing to me was the realization that some of them had themselves been born into slavery, so recent was the formal emancipation brought about by the Civil War. And nowhere in the south had that emancipation remained more of a technicality than in Mississippi, the poorest of the states and the most backward by every criterion, whether of economic or of social development. That things were not what one might have expected in Greenville was largely due to the influence of a single courageous and independent-minded editor.

I had first heard of Hodding Carter in Washington, where several people had told me that if I wanted to understand the problems of the south I had to meet him. They spoke of him (these were the sort of liberal intellectuals who thought it no insult to be called 'egg-heads') with something close to reverence; whereas in Charleston, where I learned that he was to lecture a hundred miles or so down the coast at Savannah, I was amused to find that he was regarded as a dangerous firebrand. So when I drove down and slipped into my seat in the auditorium just as he was being introduced, I was not sure what to expect.

'A heavily-built, no-nonsense-about-me kind of man,' I wrote in my diary, 'and no great speaker', and at first I was puzzled to see how so homespun a character could arouse such passionately conflicting reactions. As he led into his subject (he was speaking, of course, about desegregation) I began to understand, for he had two sources of strength which served him well in this reactionary environment. He was, first of all, an insider, speaking with all the assurance of a southerner born and bred, who shared the close loyalties and affections which mean so much in the south; and he was a man of such obvious integrity that he was able, in his bluff style and with a sensitive awareness of his audience which I came to appreciate only later, to lead them out of the narrow framework of their everyday conceptions, towards conclusions which they would not have dared to envisage for themselves. Perhaps there was some verbal sleight-of-hand about it, and perhaps, too, my first impression of him is coloured in my memory by the closer acquaintance we developed soon afterwards. What I know is that Hodding Carter, this man who for some was a demagogue, a do-gooder, and for others a knightly crusader, was one of the most persuasive advocates I ever met.

When I came to Greenville two or three weeks later, he invited me to stay with him; and when he went off with his wife to New Orleans for a week, he left me his house and his friends and the freedom of this little community, so that by the time he came back I seemed to know everyone, and felt at home as I had never expected to feel in an environment so unlike anything I had known elsewhere. For here, even more than in Atlanta, whites and blacks lived side by side but in total seclusion from each other. When I visited a negro school, I provided for the children an extraordinary inversion of the normal order of things: a white man in whose presence they could remain seated, while they listened to his improbable account of a land called England somewhere across a distant and unknown sea. When I went on Sunday morning (after making discreet enquiries and being assured that I should be welcome) to a negro church, I was received with puzzled courtesy and heard the pastor halfway through the service telling his flock that 'there's a white brother among us who might like to offer testimony'; which I did with some diffidence, to be reassured as I spoke by heartfelt interjections of 'A-men' and 'Hallelujah'. At a song recital I heard 'Old Man River' as I have never heard it sung before or since, until I felt in my very bones the plaint of 'body all achin' an' racked with pain' – and in all this and in the conversatons I had with whites and blacks alike, I was aware of sympathies as well as antagonisms which have a poignancy in the light of what lay ahead for the south. In a letter to my father I tried to unravel these complexities:

Where the south has remained nearest to its own dreams, the dreams of quiet days on the plantation, of pillared porches and the scent of magnolias, and darkies singing as they return at evening from the cotton fields, you find real kindness and a graceful attitude to life which is not merely an attempt to live up to the magazine-story concept of life in the Old South. I was talking a couple of evenings ago to a man of my own age who had been brought up on a plantation in Alabama during the depression. Way back his family had been wealthy and the plantation was a large one, with more than a hundred negro families living on it. When the depression struck and the price of cotton dropped to five cents a pound (today it is guaranteed at around thirty cents) this man's father carried those hundred and some families right through the bad years, feeding and clothing them, providing for all their material wants, instead of turning them off to live on relief in the cities – and as a result had to sell off most of his land to keep going. It's a completely feudal picture: in good times the plantation owner uses their labour and does little for them beyond keeping them in condition to work – but in bad times he wouldn't think of doing less, even though their labour was no use to him when the cotton fetched less on the market than it cost him to grow it.

They were his people and he acknowledged his responsibility for them – and ruined himself in the process. His son, to whom I was talking, now sells fertilizers here in Greenville.

This was the millpond into which the Supreme Court had thrown its challenging stone and it was no wonder that many of the whites (and some blacks too) were worried about the effect the ripples might have. After enjoying the hospitality of both, I felt as eager as anyone to find a way out of a dilemma in which so much that was good as well as bad was at stake. My preconceptions gone, I felt sure of only one thing:

. . . that any change in white attitudes must come from within. They react violently to outside interference and are wild about the Supreme Court's decision for this reason, regarding it as an invasion of states' rights. Of course it is easy to point out that the violence of their reaction is due to a guilty conscience (hence the hasty building of new schools for the negroes all over the south), but still it is only realistic to say that they will never accept a solution forced on them from outside; even if the Supreme Court forces on desegregation, the south will find ways of circumventing the decision, and the sufferer in the end will be the negro. I believe that two or three big men, preferably established politicians (which presents a problem, for southern politicians by and large are as crooked and prejudiced a bunch as you could find) could provide enough of a lead to swing a revolution in southern thinking within a decade or so; at present there is no sign of their appearing. Men like Hodding Carter, who is considered a bit of a firebrand down here and has his life threatened from time to time, can help a lot – and do, by writing fearlessly and realistically – but they can't influence the backwoodsmen who hold the key to the problem in this predominantly rural area. Even Carter, by the way, wouldn't invite a negro to sit down in his house, and he is suspect as a radical among the less quick-witted of his fellow-citizens – which gives you an idea of the problem.

It wasn't quite true, I learned before I left Greenville, that Hodding Carter would not invite a negro to sit down in his house. The truth was that he would not want it *known* that he had done so, not for his own sake but for that of the negro – which in its way was just as revealing.

When Hodding and Betty Carter came back from New Orleans, we had a few days together in which they almost persuaded me that I was one of the family (they had two sons, one of whom was later to be President Carter's press secretary). We would sit on the porch in the evening, looking out at the cypress trees rising out of a lake and the daffodils and the brilliant blossom of the Judas tree (which the Americans call redbud) catching the last of the sunlight, and drinking our whiskey (Mississippi 'votes dry and drinks wet') while they answered my questions and spread out before me their own romantic, optimistic but always realistic ideas about the way the south might be brought – *must* be brought, with patience and good humour and respect for the rights and the preferences of all parties – to swallow the medicine the Supreme Court had prescribed for it. They didn't minimize the difficulties and they foresaw the kind of obstruction and heartbreak that would have to be faced and overcome. What I remember best about them, apart from their boundless hospitality, is the calm assurance with which they accepted their own responsibilities in the matter, and the risks they incurred, and the unassuming way in which they held to the course they knew they had to follow. When I left them, I carried away with me their optimism about the future of the south – provided there were enough Hodding Carters about to see it through.

In the event, it seems to me, the south did pretty well. It took longer than the 'decade or so' that I had foreseen and the story isn't finished yet; but the civil-rights battles of the 1960s were fought in the main with less bitterness than might have been expected from a society which took violence so much for granted. Gradually, thanks in the main to moderate leadership, the barriers came down and the petty humiliations in streetcars and public places were consigned to the scrapheap. Even in the backwoods of Mississippi and Alabama blacks began to exercise their right to vote, something they had not dared to do before, and in 1973 Atlanta became the first big city in the south to install a black mayor. This steady progress was reflected too in economic terms: the average family income of blacks all through the United States, which was just about half that of the whites at the time of my stay in Greenville, crept up in the sixties to close to two thirds. You couldn't say the blacks had reached the promised land, but they were well and truly on the move and when Georgia's Jimmy Carter became president in 1976 and chose as his secretary of state Andrew Young, the promised land seemed to be in sight and people began to speculate about how long it would be before there was a black president in the White House.

There was nothing inevitable about this steady progress, slow and painful as it was. It was achieved by individuals, both black and white, who took their courage in both hands and simply refused to accept any longer the old shibboleths or the clichés behind which the timid will always shelter, saying that 'this is the way it has always been' and 'you can't change human nature'. You can – but it takes some doing, for people, as Emerson said, wish to be settled, adding that 'only as far as they are unsettled is there any hope for them'.

On my last evening in Greenville, Hodding fixed us mint juleps and we cooked steaks over a charcoal fire and he and Betty helped me to get into focus all the impressions I had picked up about the south – for early the next morning I was off again, across the Mississippi and a corner of Arkansas to the Texas border. It was hot, there was little to see and the best the car radio could offer me was a programme of hillbilly and pop songs:

> I know a fellow, he's rich as a king,
> But he wouldn't give his neighbours a thing.
> When he gets to heaven, I know what he'll find:
> A rusty white halo, a skinny white cloud,
> An' second-hand wings all in patches.

At the border a sticker on the rear window of the car in front asked me: ARE YOU BORN AGAIN? and I wondered, as I drove on through a forest of oil derricks rising out of the empty plain, what Dallas would afford me in the way of mental stimulus. Luckily, as I found a room and went downtown to look for mail, I bought a copy of the *Morning News* and noticed the announcement of a concert by the Dallas Symphony Orchestra, with Rubinstein as the soloist. I arrived a moment before the orchestra launched into Prokofiev's Classical Symphony and then Rubinstein played Chopin's second concerto, following it as an encore with a revolutionary study which had him bounding off the piano stool. Exhilarated and a little remorseful over my earlier misgivings about Texas, I turned to my neighbours, a couple of middle-aged school teachers from somewhere up-state. They had driven 160 miles to attend the concert – and would have to drive 160 miles back again that night, so as to be in school at nine in the morning. I felt both chastened and impressed.

That first experience of the relish with which many Texans pursued what they liked to call the 'finer things in life' was attractive; and there was more to satisfy their appetite in Dallas than in most of the United States. Between leaving Washington and arriving at the Pacific coast, this was the only time I heard a concert or attended any sort of live entertainment — except for a lively amateur production of *Private Lives* in El Paso (also in Texas) and a splendid evening at Las Vegas, where Noel Coward was having the time of his life at the Desert Inn and bringing a breath of sophistication into the circus atmosphere of that most improbable oasis. From now on and for three or four months I was in the west; and if it was short on culture in the formal sense, it was in the west, driving immense distances over range country and deserts, through deep canyons and up and over the Rockies, into the lake country of the Olympic Peninsula in the far north-west and down through the Sierra Nevada into southern California, that I enjoyed more varied pleasures and felt myself nearer to the heart of a great country than anywhere else in the United States.

This feeling was induced partly by the sheer majesty of the landscape, which was beyond anything I had imagined; but the key to all lay in the attitudes of mind I encountered and the openness with which Americans of every kind welcomed a stranger and were ready to discuss their ideas with him about everything under the sun. If some of these ideas were narrow and provincial, they were coloured more often – and even when those who held them knew next to nothing of the world outside North America (or even beyond the borders of their own state) – by a spirit of freedom and generosity and a grasp of the fundamental decencies of life which I have found nowhere else. Best of all I found in the west the individualism that I had looked for and so seldom found elsewhere in the United States.

Here to be sure, are all the weaknesses of generalization on the grand scale; but most generalizations start from a kernel of truth and I can only say that it was not until I travelled west of the Mississippi that I was able to shake off completely that first impression, formed on the eastern seaboard and in Kentucky, of a society straitjacketed by conformity and in which people were apprehensive above all things of being seen to be different. In the west, and especially in the inland states lying east and west of the Rocky mountains – Montana, Idaho, Wyoming, Colorado – the opposite was true, and I revelled in the difference. In the shaping of this view, a hundred small incidents played their part, of which one will have to serve as the epitome, recapturing as it does in my mind's eye, after thirty years, this sense of a world entire and uncorrupted, where everything is in tune, like that vision of Flecker's of 'a garden at daybreak where all the birds are singing at the sun'.

It was in June and I was driving north-westwards through Idaho, following the route which Lewis and Clark had taken when they were the first to find a way through the Rockies and on to the Pacific coast exactly a hundred and fifty years earlier. I'd had an amusing morning when I picked up a hitchhiker who was part Cherokee Indian and weighed 295 pounds. He was that rare being, an American nomad, living nowhere special and not exactly bound for anywhere, but picking up a living as he went along, partly as a fire-eater in circuses. When I told him I was headed for Portland, Oregon, the best part of a thousand miles away, he said I ought to look up his sister. She was the fat lady in a circus up there: 'six feet tall and she weighs 350 pounds – married to a little feller about your size', he added. We bought a picnic lunch at a place called Massacre Rocks (which reminded me that I'd been told never to pick up hitchhikers) and ate it at a kind of oasis in the middle of a lonely stretch of desert, where he startled me by saying grace with some formality before falling on the food and pouring a pint of milk after it as though he were filling up a tractor.

Soon afterwards he left me and I came to the valley of the Snake River and followed it through strange lava hills where there were springs bursting up out of the rock. I thought I would camp out and I was looking for a likely place when I passed a sign saying 'Snake River Pottery'. Intrigued, I drove back and down a stony track through a meadow. At a gate there was a man fixing a new rail and I asked him if this was the way to the pottery.

'Sure is,' he said, 'and I'm the potter'. He got in the car and as we drove on down the track I told him that his sign had caught my eye but what I was really looking for was a place to put my sleeping bag. Could I camp on a corner of his land?

'You certainly can,' he replied, 'and you can have dinner with us presently – my wife's down at the beach. Maybe you'd like a swim?'

By this time we had reached the house, a bungalow built right over a great bend in the river. There was a lawn to one side and beyond it goats and a sheep and chickens and geese and a pig were all going about their business behind a series of fences. My friend introduced himself as Drich Bowler and took me into the house to show me the potter's wheel he had made out of the motor from the gun turret of a bomber. Seizing some clay he quickly threw a pot to show me how it was done, and before it was finished it was agreed that I was to stay the night, in or out of the house as I preferred, and longer if I would, and that it was clearly providence that had brought me to this spot on the Snake River and no other. But first I must have my swim.

Just then his wife came back, a lovely blonde girl called Diana, as brown as a berry and with two children in tow.

'Look here, Di,' said Drich, 'we're in luck' (it reminded me of the Turkish farmer near Xanthos), 'here's an Englishman come to see us and he's going to stay the night, but right now what he wants is a swim.'

'Fine,' said Di, as though nothing could be more natural; and as she had to get the dinner ready and Drich had to milk the goats, their six-year-old daughter was deputed to show me the 'beach', and off we went through the livestock and down to the river with a big collie bounding along beside us. I had a wonderful swim and when I came back with the child's hand in mine, she was chattering away as though she had known me all her life. The Bowler family was clearly not one that stood on ceremony.

Over dinner I learned that Drich and Di were not just farmers or potters: they were two people who had chosen the life they wanted and who enjoyed it. Just after the war they had both been aspiring actors in New York, until they decided the game wasn't worth the candle. So they bought a Jeep, loaded their things into it and drove two thousand miles across the continent to make a new start here, on this bare hillside above the Snake River. Drich could do anything with his hands and together he and Di had cleared the land, built the house, dammed a stream for their water supply and put in a little power plant which gave them electric light and drove the home-made potter's wheel on which they had both become expert. Between them they bred the animals, milked them, nursed them, made their own butter, sold some of the cream down the valley and every now and then took an animal to the butcher and brought back their meat supply for a week or two. They were building up a mail-order business for the pottery which they made at odd moments of each very full day, and to balance the budget Drich taught in the high school of a little town just up the road (I'm not inventing it) called Bliss.

The schools were on holiday when I arrived so Drich was taking the opportunity to go round fixing the gates and fences and doing a hundred and one other chores at which he was expert. I would go along and hold the nails for him and learn a lot about a lot of things, until we felt we had earned another swim. When I talked of moving on, they always found some reason to keep me: a ghost town up in the hills they wanted to show me, or some old pioneer who could tell me of the days when fortunes were made out of mining for silver – and the upshot was that I stayed with them for nearly a fortnight, sleeping in the garden and waking up early to find that Drich had already milked the goats and Di was baking bread. During the day I would help with odd jobs around the place and then retire to a barn to do some writing for an hour or two, and in the evening the three of us would gather in the pottery with a can of beer each, and while one of them threw something on the wheel we would all pull the world to pieces.

There were plenty of books in the house (Drich and Di were both college graduates) and they had the radio to keep them in touch with the outside world – and to me their life was just what a life should be, its roots deep in the piece of land they had found for themselves and which gave them almost all they needed to live, with a stream flowing out of the hillside and the splendid river sweeping below the terrace they had made with their own hands, and clay from the river bank for their pottery, and home-made butter, and the goats . . .

They hadn't forgotten the theatre either, for they had organized a travelling repertory company which toured the valley with a few bits of scenery in an old van and brought Shakespeare and Arthur Miller to communities as far off the beaten track as they were themselves.

Best of all was the fact that they had chosen all this and created it and given substance to their dreams – and they didn't give a damn what anybody else might think of it. I should have loved it anywhere, and here it provided the perfect answer to all those criticisms I had never quite been able to stop making about how regimented life had become in America and how conformity seemed to be most people's goal. Besides, as I added in trying to explain it all to my father, 'it isn't every day you make two friends for life'.

By the time I got back to New York I had driven 24,000 miles through forty-six states and seen more of their extraordinary country than most Americans will ever get the chance to see. People asked me what I made of it all and I found it very difficult to answer. Experience, I had written in my diary somewhere along the way, is settling all the time, imperceptibly, like a gentle snowfall, on the landscape of my mind', and by the end of the twelve months it was piled pretty high. How was I to sort it all out and arrive at any sort of conclusion about the Americans and what the rest of us might expect from them?

However reluctantly, I had to make the attempt, for I was required to make a report to the Commonwealth Fund on the use I had made of the opportunity they had given me. I could not simply say, as the narrator of one of Somerset Maugham's stories had said in similar circumstances: 'There was neither good nor bad there, there were just facts. It was life.' I had to do better than this and with enormous difficulty I assembled my findings and strove to give them some sort of unity. I blush now to think how superficial my judgements must have seemed. But in a general sense and to myself, or when some importunate questioner invited me to encapsulate in a sentence or two the impressions which it had taken me a year to gather, I felt more sure of my ground.

The Americans (I would say) were extraordinarily open and spontaneous and essentially fair-minded people. With their energy and their technical skills, they had every right to believe – as they did – that they were equal to any challenge. They were also, as I had found in my survey of newspapers and radio and television stations all over the country, in general ill-informed about the outside world, and so ill-equipped, as far as knowledge and experience were concerned, to play the role in the world which they must presently assume. Where moral issues were involved, they were as a nation desperately anxious to do the right thing. Provided – and it was a crucial reservation – they could be put in possession of all the facts about any given situation, you could count on them to try to come up with the right answer.

It was, of course, a very subjective judgement; but I don't think I would want to revise it in the light of what has happened in the last thirty years. For the obverse of my conclusion, although I did not state it at the time, is that if they got the facts wrong, and given their energy and self-assurance, then the answers they came up with would be wrong too – and on a monumental scale.

Baptism of Fire
(1956)

19

Thoughts like these were jostling each other in my mind as I came restfully home to England, this time on the French liner *Île de France*, and for three months I tried to put them down on paper. I had plenty to occupy me as a freelance, but the time had come for me to look for something permanent, something that might help me before long to realize that old ambition to become a foreign correspondent.

One evening I was sitting alone in my tiny flat in London when the phone rang. The caller was Dick Scott, the diplomatic correspondent of the *Manchester Guardian* and the only person I knew on the paper. He was just ringing, he explained, to warn me that later that evening I should be getting another, more formal, call from the *Guardian*, with the offer of a job. I was all ears, and when he went on to say that the job was that of Middle East correspondent based in Cairo, I did not try to conceal my delight. Scott was amused.

'That's why I thought I would warn you,' he said, 'so that when the call comes you could take it in your stride – tell 'em you'll be glad to think it over . . .'

As I sat impatiently by the telephone, all sorts of thoughts raced through my mind. What could have impelled the *Guardian* to decide to take me in off the street, as it were, and send me straight to Cairo? And why Cairo: was anything special happening there? As I asked the question, I realized how little I knew about the Middle East. My father had spent most of his working life in Egypt, the old Egypt which had been to all intents and purposes a part of the British Empire. My own experience of it had been limited to a couple of summer holidays when I was at school and those few weeks in 1940 when I was waiting to get into uniform.

Could the people at the *Guardian* have made a mistake? Perhaps there existed somewhere a Michael Adams who was an orientalist, who spoke Arabic and knew all about the tribes and the history of the Ottoman Empire and the rites of the Eastern Churches – and the oil industry. As the extent of my own ignorance unfolded itself, I became more and more apprehensive. When I had taken the awesome phone call and agreed to go up to Manchester to discuss the appointment, and even when all had finally been agreed between us, I took my anxieties seriously enough to put the question frankly to the foreign editor. Was he quite sure he had got the right man? Did he realize that, while I had knocked about a good deal, I had hardly set foot in the Middle East?

'That's all right,' he said reassuringly; 'we just wanted someone with an open mind.'

All the same, he conceded, it would do no harm if I tried to inform myself better before I undertook my new assignment. There was no one on the paper who could give me much help, for the *Manchester Guardian* had not had a correspondent in the area before; but he suggested that I should go and see the editor of the *Glasgow Herald*, who had for many years been the Middle East correspondent of *The Times* and who was willing to share with me his knowledge and experience.

So one day in January 1956 I took a train to Glasgow to consult this oracle, who gave me dinner at his club, a sooty mausoleum in the centre of the city. Over the meal he had little to say, seemed indeed averse to conversation, while I, like a subaltern in the presence of the general did not feel it was for me to set the pace. In his own good time, I assumed, he would open to me his treasure-house of wisdom. I was wrong, and when we were drinking our coffee in two huge leather armchairs on either side of a dying fire I realized that it was now or never. It was with diffidence but in desperation that I intruded on him, reminding him gently that I was about to undertake for the *Manchester Guardian* the role in which he had acquitted himself with such distinction for *The Times*. Perhaps, I suggested, there was some advice that he could give me, a few tips, one or two pointers that might help me . . .? My voice faltered in the face of his impregnable silence.

For a long time he considered my question, and at last he made a superhuman effort. 'You have to remember,' he remarked, 'ninety-five per cent of the people who read what you write don't know and don't care; but the other five per cent know more than you'll ever know – and you have to please them all.' With that the audience was effectively at an end.

At the time I remember thinking that he had given me rather short measure. On the other hand, perhaps because his advice was so compressed, I never forgot it – and it was very much to the point, as I was soon to discover. For the meantime, though, I approached my new assignment, as far as I can remember, in much the same spirit as my earlier travels. It promised to be an amusing way of seeing a bit more of the world, chalking up a few more adventures and experiences, adding one more verse to that old song about 'wandering'. I had every intention of being a conscientious correspondent and I was proud to be working for the *Manchester Guardian*, but I didn't take the whole thing too solemnly. As for my new masters at the *Guardian*, beyond sending me on that abortive expedition to Glasgow and introducing me to some bigwig in British Petroleum in London (who gave me a good lunch and showed me some incomprehensible coloured charts about oil reserves and extraction rates), they gave me no guidance that I can remember. They furnished me with a 'collect card', with which I could send messages to the paper without paying for them, but asked me not to be extravagant in using it, and the parting words of the foreign editor were: 'Don't worry if you don't hear from us very often; we like to leave our people a free hand.' With an open mind and a free hand, it all sounded very refreshing.

When I began to do my homework, I found that there was more going on in the Middle East than I had realized, although at the time very few people in England seemed to attach much importance to it. Looking back from the 1980s it is hard to recapture the mixture of ignorance and complacency with which the British public regarded events in the area. We had grown so accustomed to thinking that anything that happened there required our own prior approval, and that we had some sort of historic right to manipulate events to suit ourselves, that we tended to disregard the signs that the old order was changing, and changing fast. Less than a fortnight before I took off for Cairo, something happened that upset these easy assumptions.

On 29 February King Hussein of Jordan dismissed General Glubb, popularly known as Glubb Pasha, the British officer who for seventeen years had been the commander of the Arab Legion. A man of modest tastes and unassailable honesty, whose long experience among the tribes of Arabia had invested him with the aura of a second Lawrence, Glubb Pasha was the embodiment of a dying tradition. He was also old enough to be the father of the young king who had now so abruptly given him the sack. To the British public, ignorant of the background to the affair, Glubb's dismissal came as a shock. To many, there was something almost treasonable about it. Had not King Hussein – who at the time was just twenty years old – been to Harrow and Sandhurst? Was not his family indebted to Britain for its protection, even for its very throne? Clearly there was something sinister behind this sudden rejection of one of the most prominent symbols of British influence in the heart of the Arab world.

The leader writers, like the British government, jumped at once to the conclusion that it was the work of the man who was then on his way to becoming Britain's bugbear in the Middle East: Colonel Nasser – as the British insisted on calling him long after he had left the army to become the president of the Egyptian Republic. Nor was it altogether surprising that the British should have made this mistaken assumption – for mistaken it was.

Gamal Abdel-Nasser had been the moving spirit behind the revolution which had overthrown Egypt's decadent King Farouk in 1952, and during the next three years he had won a following in the rest of the Arab world as the rising champion of Arab nationalism. This wider reputation rested on his declared objective of liberating the Arab world from imperialist control, and on the expectation among the Arabs that he would go on to recover for them the lost land of Palestine.

To begin with, Nasser pursued his objective through negotiations with Britain, the arch-imperialist, and it was an objective which aroused a good deal of sympathy in the West. The Americans, in particular, who thought it was high time for Britain to get rid of the vestiges of empire in the Middle East, looked kindly on Nasser and even gave him a helping land with his revolution. Their good impression of him was heightened when he merely dispatched Farouk into exile with his family and much of his personal fortune, allowing him to join the other ex-kings on the Riviera (I remembered seeing him in a box at the opera in Rome a few months later, when I attended that opening performance of *Simone Boccanegra* in December 1952).

For the British government it was not easy to take such a detached view of Nasser, for at the time of the revolution there was still a very large British garrison in Egypt, encamped beside the banks of the Suez Canal. But Nasser played his cards carefully and within two years had negotiated an agreement with Britain by which the British troops were to be withdrawn in stages, until in June 1956 Nasser was to be master in his own house and Egypt would be completely rid of the imperialist presence.

At first all went smoothly; but before long the pattern was disturbed by a series of events which were all linked in one way or another to what the world tended to see as Nasser's obsession, but which was in reality his besetting problem, of what to do about Israel. When I was packing my bags to go to Cairo, the first Arab-Israeli war was a very recent thing. It had ended seven years earlier with the establishment of a Jewish state in Palestine, on territory which no Arab could doubt was a part of his historic homeland and from which a very large number of the indigenous Arab population had fled or been driven out. (It made no difference which, for in either case they had not been allowed to return.) As the largest and most important of the Arab states, Egypt felt most keenly the humiliation as well as the injustice which the war had meant for the Arabs. As the leader of a revolutionary regime whose *raison d'être* was to restore to the Arabs their self-respect, the one course not open to Nasser where Israel was concerned was to do nothing.

As to what he intended to do or should have done or was capable of doing thirty years ago there is still room for argument. But Nasser was not the only or the most powerful player on the field and to a large extent it was the behaviour of the other players which dictated his course of action. The Israelis, understandably anxious that those whom they had so deeply wounded would try to reverse the verdict of 1948, had to make a choice. Either they could try to conciliate the Arabs or they must make a sufficient show of force to convince them that further resistance was hopeless. Without apparent hesitation – and forgetting Churchill's dictum about magnanimity in victory – they chose the second course. It was a momentous decision.

Then there were the British, who had agreed with a good deal of reluctance to withdraw from Egypt but who were searching for another means of protecting what they still considered (how long ago it all seems!) their vital strategic interests in the Middle East. The idea they hit upon was the Baghdad Pact, whose aim was to provide, under Western control, a defensive alliance against the possibility of Soviet invasion or subversion of the Middle East. With Turkey and Iraq as founder-members, and Iran joining soon afterwards, they thought they had a sound basis. If they could persuade Egypt and Jordan to join too, the British felt that they would have devised a new and less offensive way of maintaining their old pattern of strategic control.

It was a tidy conception, which had one grave drawback: it took no account whatever of the preferences of the Arabs themselves or of the new climate of opinion in the Arab world. With the exception of Iraq, where the monarchy survived and the veteran prime minister, Nuri es-Said, had thrown in his lot wholeheartedly with Britain, the Arabs were not interested in the supposed Communist menace. What they cared about was Israel, and the need to arm themselves against what they perceived as a far more immediate threat to their own security. As

part of the bargain over Britain's withdrawal from Egypt, Nasser asked
the British and American governments to provide the arms without
which Egypt felt dangerously vulnerable.

In 1955, while I was far away in the western United States, from
which the Middle East at that time looked as remote as the dark side of
the moon, these various strands had come together to form an ominous
pattern. In January the Baghdad Pact had been formally constituted.
In February the Israelis mounted a major raid against the Egyptians in
the Gaza Strip. In May, in an Independence Day parade, the Israelis
showed off for the first time the new tanks and jet fighters with which
the French government had secretly been supplying them. All this time
Nasser was pressing his request for arms from the West and hinting
that if he did not get them he would turn to the East. During the
summer rumours began to circulate about an impending arms deal
with Moscow; and the British ambassador in Cairo was told to
investigate them, while the American state department sent a special
envoy to Cairo to dissuade Nasser from going through with the deal. It
was too late. In September, at an armed-forces exhibition in Cairo,
Nasser announced a 'commercial agreement' with Czechoslovakia by
which the Czechs, in return for Egyptian cotton, had undertaken to
supply Egypt with a substantial quantity of modern weapons.

Until that moment in the autumn of 1955 the Middle East, with all its
internal divisions, had been a purely Western sphere of influence. The
Czech arms deal (which of course had been authorized by Moscow)
provided the opportunity for which the Russians had been working to
break this Western monopoly. And to repair the damage the British
government in December 1955 took a step which consolidated the
Russian gain. To try to demonstrate the value of the Western alliance
and draw Jordan into the Baghdad Pact, General Sir Gerald Templer,
Chief of the Imperial General Staff, was sent to Amman with a gift of
ten Vampire jet fighters and the promise of a substantial quantity of
other arms for Jordan. The effect of the move was the opposite of the
one intended. There were riots in Jordan, where the government split
over the question of joining the Baghdad Pact and presently resigned.
There was an angry exchange of accusations between London and
Cairo, where Nasser was convinced that the British were trying to
mobilize the rest of the Arab world against him; and at the end of it all
King Hussein, instead of joining the Baghdad Pact, dismissed his old
and trusted friend Glubb Pasha, the very symbol of the special
relationship between Britain and the Arab world.

A week later I set out for Cairo, stopping briefly in Cyprus on the way to report the riots which followed the arrest of Archbishop Makarios and his deportation to the Seychelles.

When I finally got to Cairo, however, nothing could have seemed more tranquil. If this was the revolutionary capital of Arab nationalism, it certainly did not feel like it; still less was there any outward air of antagonism towards the British, who on the contrary were still treated with the same friendly deference they had enjoyed when the British embassy had been the real centre of power in Cairo – as it had been until less than four years before my arrival.

More than anything else, I got the impression that it was habit which governed the relationship between the two peoples: the habit of command on the part of the British, of subservience on the part of the Egyptians. By any reasonable criterion it was absurd and unhealthy, but it did not appear so at the time, perhaps because it was coloured on both sides by something which it is not fanciful to describe as affection.

The fact is that neither side, in that lull before the storm, took the other quite seriously. The British, for all the revolutionary fervour of the Cairo press and the speeches which Nasser made to exuberant crowds about the coming collapse of imperialism, thought it would be a generation at least before Nasser could put any stuffing into the Egyptians. And the Egyptians, patient and easy-going and long-suffering, could see that the day of the British was over and that it was only a matter of time before they would fold their tents and drift away. Characteristically, they seemed disinclined to exert themselves in order to speed the process.

Meanwhile the British stayed on, living their comfortable lives as though there had been no revolution, masters still of most of the levers of economic power in an Egypt which for so long had been a British preserve. It still wasn't easy for an Egyptian to get into the Gezira Club (and quite impossible for him to be put up for the Turf Club), and while the great majority of the Egyptians lived in crowded squalor in the tenements of old Cairo, the British in their airy houses in Zamalek were waited on by respectful Egyptians wearing turbans and scarlet cummerbunds, and when the British ambassador went out in his Rolls the traffic came to a standstill until he had gone by.

It was in this engagingly out-dated Anglo-Egyptian establishment that I found a temporary niche for myself, when an old friend of my father invited me to stay until I found more permanent lodgings. An Englishman, he had been a judge in the Egyptian courts and was now legal counsellor to the British embassy, so that he was well placed – just how well placed I was to discover before long – to brief me on some aspects of my new environment. But that was in his office, where he exercised great authority. In his own home, it was his wife who played the more dominant role. While he was small and reserved, she was large and ebullient; and if physically speaking the contrast between them was pronounced, it was even more striking when they came to express their opinions. He much preferred silence, but if pressed would say what he had to say concisely and with the most scrupulous exactitude. She, on the other hand, was a perfect rattle, and a very entertaining one. Of accuracy and precision she had no idea; nor was there an ounce of ill-will in her make-up. She simply said whatever came into her head, reinforcing it with a wealth of gesture and emphasis; and if with her gossip she demolished a reputation or provoked a crisis, she did so in perfect innocence.

We would sit over the dinner table in the evening and I would tell them what I had been up to that day and how I had called on so-and-so, naming some public figure, a politician perhaps, or a newspaper editor, whose acquaintance I had made. 'Oh, *him*,' she would say, 'I remember meeting him in Alex' (Alexandria was always 'Alex'), 'when was it, just after the war, when he was going round with that Turkish princess, the one with dyed hair and a wooden leg – and we all thought . . .' and she would be off romancing to her heart's content, until she found herself at a loss for some detail and appealed to her husband to supply it. And the judge would lay down his knife and fork and say, with just the hint of a wink in my direction: 'It was not quite as you put it, my dear; it was not in Alexandria, but in Cyprus when we were there on holiday four years ago, and the princess, as you call her, was the perfectly respectable daughter of a Turkish Cypriot who was the local agent for the Prudential insurance company . . .' and the whole story would rearrange itself in a quite different pattern, or perhaps it would emerge that his wife was thinking of another person altogether. In either case, she would hear him out and then turn to me unabashed.

'I knew it was something like that,' she would say, 'and it's so important for you to get these things straight.' And a moment later she would be off again on some new flight of fancy. It was a most enjoyable household.

The foreign press corps was very small, for the Middle East had not then assumed the importance which it was soon to have for the outside world. Of my colleagues I have a clear recollection only of one, and that was *The Times*'s correspondent, James (who has since become Jan) Morris. James lived with his family on a houseboat in a backwater of the Nile, one of those white-painted, old-fashioned paddle-steamers in which well-to-to families in the early part of the century had cruised upstream in winter to Luxor and the Valley of the Kings. It was a most enviable situation and when I took up his standing invitation to come aboard for coffee in the middle of the morning or a drink at sunset, I felt very humdrum and conventional as I sat on the deck with his children scrambling round us and heard James's sparkling account of his latest expedition to Oman or Kurdistan. Sensibly, since his time in Cairo was nearly up, he took every opportunity to explore the wider horizons of the Arab world and where Egypt itself was concerned he was more interested in the rich byways of the past than in the posturings of contemporary politics. It was an idiosyncratic approach to the job of a foreign correspondent and perhaps it helped to postpone the day when the British would learn to take Egypt seriously. Certainly the readers of *The Times* in those days were not starved of colour or romance in the picture James Morris gave them of events in the Middle East.

Fired by his example, I tried my hand one day at a piece of fancy writing, only to fall foul of the sub-editors in Manchester. Nasser at the time was the darling of the Arab world and among those who came to woo his favours was King Saud of Saudia Arabia. Casting about for some way to give an original flavour to my report of the visit, I seized on the fact that the newspapers in England were preoccupied by the wedding of the lovely Grace Kelly to Prince Rainier of Monaco. Romance was abroad in the air of Egypt too, I suggested, and Nasser, with his fairy prince from across the Red Sea, was becoming 'a kind of Middle Eastern Grace Kelly'. Alas, the vagaries of the Egyptian telephone system and an unimaginative sub-editor transmuted this into 'a kind of Middle Eastern race filly', which made nonsense of all that followed and must have mystified the readers of the *Guardian*. I resolved to play safe in future.

Meanwhile life was agreeable for an English reporter feeling his way into the Egyptian environment, and as the British garrisons were withdrawn one by one from the old bases in the Suez Canal zone the atmosphere was positively cordial. True, there were quarrelsome rumblings now and then, particularly over broadcasts by Egypt's 'Voice of the Arabs' attacking British colonial policy in Africa, and the controversy over the Baghdad Pact was still simmering. Otherwise, the cordiality seemed genuine enough; but I soon found out how swiftly it could be shouldered aside by an unforgotten grievance. Before I had been a fortnight in Egypt, there was a serious incident in the Gaza

Strip, where the activities of Egyptian *fedayin* – guerrillas – provoked severe Israeli reprisals. This time the Secretary-General of the United Nations, Dag Hammarsköld, came out to investigate and the Egyptian press was full of inflamed comment about Britain's responsibility for the tragedy in Palestine.

Reporting this – it was my first brush with the Palestine question – I reminded readers of the *Guardian* that this was a question 'on which the Egyptians and their Arab neighbours felt that a great and remediable wrong had been done to them by the West'. And I went on to make a comment that has a curiously topical ring after more than a quarter of a century. Whoever was right in the argument that was blowing up between ourselves and the Egyptians, I wrote:

> Britain's interests would be best served by a settlement of the Palestine question, without which there can be no security for anyone in the Middle East, and by the social and economic regeneration of Egypt and the Arab countries, which is the surest way to save them from falling into the Communist empire . . . Nasser is not alone in believing that Western policy towards Israel is influenced more by expediency and Zionist pressure (with the American elections in the offing) than by any true understanding of the rights and wrongs of the Palestine question.

If I was to enlighten others about the Palestine question, I needed first of all to get a fuller understanding of it myself. A week later I was off to Beirut for a briefing at the headquarters of UNRWA, the United Nations Relief and Works Agency, and then to visit the Palestinian refugee camps in the West Bank and Gaza. As it must do for anyone with any sensitivity to the sufferings of others, the trip made a lasting impression on me. From the air, as we dodged to and fro round the borders of Israel, all looked peaceful enough, I reported:

> . . . the sandy strip of land about Gaza shelving into the sea which, from emerald close inshore, shades into ultramarine; the bare brown hills between Jerusalem and Amman empty in the sunshine. But each time we landed there were faces listless or sullen and voices raised in sudden argument and glances towards an unseen line beyond which, a few hundred yards away, lay enemy territory to remind us of the passions that brood over all this land.

First impressions, I have found all through my life, are often the surest, unclouded by theorizing, uncluttered by the irrelevant. When I sat down, back in Cairo, to sort out those first impressions of the Palestine problem, I was no longer ignorant of the framework within which, if the problem was to be solved at all, a solution had to be found. But I knew nothing of the fearsome buffetings of prejudice and manipulation which await anyone who tries honestly to find that solution. I approached the issue as far as one can ever approach anything in this complex existence, objectively and with that open mind on which the foreign editor of the *Manchester Guardian* had placed his modest bet. Of this I am sure – and I feel no inclination today to change one word of what I wrote then, in the first of many attempts to set the problem fairly before an audience prepared (I hoped) with equal fairness to envisage its solution.

Dag Hammarsköld was trying once again to persuade the two sides to overcome their mutual suspicions. I tried to explain to the reader the basis for these suspicions and the particular points of controversy – the Arab blockade of Israel and Israel's attempt to divert the waters of the River Jordan – on which at that moment each was in breach of United Nations resolutions. These issues balanced each other and were the formal expression of the existing deadlock between the two. But there was one issue, I wrote, on which the UN had declared its firm verdict seven years earlier, in December 1948, 'a verdict which no amount of legal quibbling can disguise as anything but a simple statement of elementary human rights'. This was the issue of the Palestinian refugees who had left their homes (I made no mention of expulsion) during the fighting and whose return the UN had stipulated as part of any general settlement. I described their situation and the work of UNRWA in maintaining them just above the subsistence level (spending sixpence a day on each refugee). I explained that in the prevailing conditions in the Arab world – for this was long before the oil boom – there was simply nowhere else where any large number of them could go. I urged that, if the Arabs must recognize that Israel was there to stay, the Israelis too must recognize that the Arabs were their neighbours and would remain so, for the rest of time. Surely, I said:

From every point of view the problem is one which cries out for a new and urgent approach. In itself it is a monstrous injustice; but beyond that it lies at the root of the poisoned relations between the West and the Arab peoples and it is a standing challenge to the reality and the worth of the United Nations as an arbiter in world affairs. And for Britain and Israel it is something more. Those refugees on their stony hillsides and in desolate valleys, on the sandy wastes about Gaza and in hovels on the glittering fringe of Beirut, are a million witnesses to the fact that Britain failed in something to which she had set her hand, and to the further fact that it was as a result of that failure that the State of Israel came into being.

It was to be some time before I returned to the subject, for shortly after this I flew south, a long and uncomfortable journey, to Aden and on up country into what was then still the Eastern Aden Protectorate under British rule. There were skirmishes along the border between the Aden Levies, with their British officers, and the tribesmen of the Yemen, where the old Imam maintained himself in almost total isolation from the modern world; and for a couple of weeks I had an invigorating time driving about the desert in this anachronistic twilight of imperial rule. Then I went on to Khartoum, where a row was blowing up with the Egyptians about the division of the Nile waters, and by the time I was back in Cairo the country was in a ferment – well, what passed in that easy-going old Egypt for a ferment – over three events whose juxtaposition was clearly no accident. The last British troops were about to leave Egypt in fulfilment of the Anglo-Egyptian agreement of 1954; a nation-wide plebiscite was to be held to confirm Nasser's 'election' as president of Egypt (there was of course no other candidate); and the Soviet foreign minister, Mr Shepilov, had arrived in Cairo to see the fun.

All this was heady stuff and likely to provide the occasion for some jubilant tub-thumping. The withdrawal of the British, after all, meant that for the first time in three quarters of a century Egypt would be free of foreign troops; and when the Union Jack was hauled down over Navy House in Port Said and Nasser himself raised the Egyptian flag in its place, he had every right to say proudly (even if no one knew quite what he meant) that 'this generation of Egyptians has an appointment with destiny'. Some of my colleagues in the foreign press took this as the prelude to an orgy of chauvinism and recrimination about the past, but Nasser took the wind out of their sails at a popular rally in Cairo next day by putting the emphasis entirely on the future and on the internal challenges which faced this renascent Egypt. I was inclined to take what he said at face value when he:

> . . . sprang buoyantly up the steps of the platform at last night's 'liberation rally' to call on his countrymen for renewed efforts to achieve their goals of social justice and a sound democratic life and

told his audience of 250,000 from every Egyptian province and from all the surrounding Arab countries that 'we shall remember nothing of the past except its lessons and warnings'.

This seemed to me probably sincere and certainly realistic, for whatever wider ambitions Nasser might have for Egypt he could not hope to achieve them until he had transformed the passive, uncomplaining mass of the Egyptian people into an instrument more apt to keep that 'appointment with destiny'. Perhaps, I wrote, the attempt was doomed to failure. But I saw no reason to doubt that Nasser meant what he said and that his next objective was to try to hasten that transformation. I only had to use my eyes to see how difficult it would be:

Looking round Cairo during this potentially momentous week in Egyptian history, it is depressingly easy to gauge the task facing any progressive leader in Egypt. It is as though there were two entirely separate celebrations going on – one in the orbit of the Officers' Club and the various marquees raised in the public squares for government officials and visiting dignitaries, the other in the streets and coffee-houses and along the banks of the Nile. In the first you see again and again the same faces in the equivalent of the royal box: the Crown Prince of Morocco, round-cheeked and dapper in his uniform, Hajj Amin el-Husseini, the Grand Mufti of Jerusalem, with suspicious eyes darting from side to side, Russia's Mr Shepilov, acknowledging with vague and untidy gestures the applause to which he has yet to accustom himself without self-consciousness.

And in the real Cairo, on patches of grass in Tahrir Square, or along the new Corniche overlooking the river, or in the crowded streets of the disreputable Boulak quarter, there are the ordinary, unofficial Egyptians, countless thousands of them, drifting with genial unconcern this way and that, talking, joking, arguing, with tired children asleep on their shoulders or dragging at their heels, as unconcerned as they could well be with imperialism or the stern tasks ahead or pan-Arabism, and resembling nothing so much as a satiated and exhausted crowd at the end of a hot August bank holiday.

Mingling that evening, as I had come to enjoy doing, with the huge and good-natured crowds in Cairo, I was convinced that Nasser had touched an instinctive chord in the hearts of these ordinary Egyptians and that there was an opportunity at that moment to set Anglo-

Egyptian relations on a new and promising footing. I concluded my round-up of the week's celebrations on this optimistic note: 'The people of Egypt are not anti-British, and after 18 June 1956 anyone who tries to make them so will have a harder task than ever.'

A bold prophecy; but for the moment the omens looked promising. Martial law was lifted – it had been in force ever since 1939 – and Nasser appointed a new cabinet, with the emphasis on economic reconstruction and land reform. The conciliatory attitude towards Britain was maintained and it was widely remarked that one of the officers dropped from the cabinet was Colonel Anwar es-Sadat, who had recently written a series of virulently anti-British articles in the government mouthpiece, *al-Gumhuriye*. Once again, though, the actions of the other players on the field made it difficult for Nasser to hold to his new course.

In Israel there had been a cabinet reshuffle and a certain Mrs Myerson, later to become better known as Golda Meir, had been appointed foreign minister. On 2 July Mrs Myerson made a speech insisting on Israel's right to divert the waters of the Jordan – the point on which Hammarsköld's mission in April had failed to reach agreement. For Nasser this was a challenge which it would be difficult to ignore, especially since the Syrian government was pressing him to join in a united stand. It would be a cruel irony, I wrote to the *Guardian*: 'if Nasser, now that it looks as though he feels secure enough to concentrate on domestic reforms, should be forced to put his armour on again and take himself unwillingly to the battlefield. For he knows that, whatever, the result, it would mean the end of his dreams for a better Egypt'.

In the event it was something quite different that presently plunged Nasser and Egypt back into the turmoil of international politics. The rumour spread in Cairo that Mr Shepilov had conveyed to Cairo an offer from the Russians to finance the building of a great dam at Aswan on the upper Nile, a dam which was to be the lynchpin of Nasser's ambitious plans for the economic rehabilitation of Egypt.

The high dam was the largest project of its kind in the third world. The governments of the United States and Britain, in co-operation with the World Bank, had already agreed to put up the money for it, on condition that the project remained an exclusively Western one. But now, just when the barometer for Egypt's relations with the West seemed set fair, complications set in.

In Washington, where Foster Dulles as Eisenhower's secretary of state was now in charge of foreign policy, the Americans were beginning to have second thoughts about Nasser's regime. They had been upset by the Czech arms deal, despite the fact that it was their own refusal to sell arms to Egypt that had provoked it; and Dulles was incensed when, in May 1956, Nasser recognized Communist China. (The Americans, of course, were to follow suit – but not for another fifteen years.) In addition, the Zionist lobby was opposed to anything that would strengthen Egypt; and the growers of cotton in the south (my old friends in Mississippi and Georgia) saw no good reason why their own government should help the Egyptians to expand their production of excellent long-staple cotton. At the same time in Britain, where Anthony Eden had succeeded Churchill in 1955 and was eager to prove himself a leader in his own right, there was a lingering assumption that Egypt was in some sense part of the British sphere of influence and must not be allowed to get too big for its boots. This Colonel Nasser, people were beginning to say, who had somehow manoeuvred us out of the driving seat; what exactly was he? A demagogue at best, and almost certainly – for all his talk of democracy – a dictator. What if he turned out also to be a fellow-traveller? And on top of everything else there were genuine doubts on both sides of the Atlantic about sinking a very large sum of money into a country with an economy as shaky as Egypt's undoubtedly was – which, of course, was precisely why Nasser was so set on building the high dam.

With the atmosphere already soured by this confusion of prejudice and misgiving, the rumour that the Russians were competing with the West for the favours of Egypt seemed doubly sinister: and not just to a Western public which was woefully ill-informed about Egypt, but also to leaders in Washington and London who might have been expected to know better, but who showed little sympathy for the problems of the underdeveloped world. Eden's instinct was to show that he was not a man to be pushed around; Dulles thought the Russians were bluffing and could not afford the investment needed for the high dam. Both men suspected that Nasser's game was to play off the East against the West; and they decided to teach him a lesson.

And so when Nasser, after a final consultation with his ambassador to Washington, formally authorized him to accept the Western offer of aid for the high dam, the announcement that the offer after all was withdrawn had every appearance of being a deliberate snub. And that impression was heightened, as the Egyptians were quick to note, by an accompanying memorandum which threw doubt on the ability of the Egyptians themselves to handle their share of so vast an economic undertaking.

Nasser was away from Cairo when the news came of his rejection by the West. He was in Yugoslavia, where he was the guest, along with India's prime minister Nehru, of President Tito. The three of them had emerged a year earlier from the summit meeting of third world leaders at Bandoeng as the outstanding figures in the new movement of 'positive neutralism', the attempt to establish a third force of countries which refused to align themselves with either the East or the West in the cold war. There was an element of paradox here, for Nasser's neutralism was passionate and genuine; he had not got rid of one form of imperialism to submit to another. And yet it was the West's refusal of aid for the high dam which forced Nasser out of his neutralist stance. To some extent it was his own fault; there was something in that charge of playing off the East against the West. But his reluctance to turn Egypt into a Russian satellite was plain enough, I wrote, and if in fact Nasser had overplayed his hand:

> the result is as unpromising for the West as for himself. The withdrawal of the Anglo-American offer leaves these alternatives: either the high dam will be built with Russian money or it will not be built at all. If it is built with Russian money, Egypt will be economically at the beck and call of the Soviet Union for a generation. And unless it is built somehow, the present regime's plans for the economic and social regeneration of Egypt will have to be greatly modified. Neither alternative makes any sense of the withdrawal by Britain and America of their offer of assistance.

If I was right in thinking that Nasser was anxious not to fall into the arms of the Russians, the West was certainly not helping him. Both as an individual and as the leader of a newly independent nation, it was inevitable that Nasser would take up the challenge, all the more so because the Egyptians were now preparing themselves for another round of patriotic celebrations. This time the occasion was the fourth anniversary of the revolution which Nasser had led and whose target had been the overthrow, not just of the monarchy of which King Farouk had been the decadent symbol, but of 'imperialism', which Nasser portrayed in his speeches as an almost intangible juggernaut always ready to trample on the rights and the aspirations of the Egyptian people.

As we waited to see what the Egyptian response would be, the tension was heightened by a heat wave. Instead of the fresh breeze which normally blows down from the Mediterranean in summer, tempering the fierce heat of Cairo, the wind swung round to the south and the thermometer stood at 43°C, when Nasser, on 24 July, gave the first indication of what was to come. He was incensed especially by the terms of the communiqué in which the Americans had questioned Egypt's ability to undertake the building of the high dam. Speaking at the opening of a pipeline connecting a brand-new oil refinery to the port of Suez, he reminded his hearers that only a year had passed since he had laid the foundation stone of the refinery. If things were moving as fast as that, how could anyone pretend that Egypt was incapable of bringing its plans for economic development to fruition? Addressing the Americans, he said: 'If rumour in Washington tries to make out that the Egyptian economy is not strong enough to warrant American aid, I reply: "You may choke with rage, but you will never succeed in ordering us about or in exercising your tyranny over us, because we know our path of freedom, of honour and of dignity." '

It was strong stuff and the crowd loved it; but to the older hands in the foreign community in Cairo it was not to be taken too seriously. Nasser had become the victim of his own propaganda, they assured me. He could not trust the Russians, any more than he could rely on the Egyptians to play up to his new line. A few more days of this sort of thing and then he would have to swallow his pride and try to rebuild his bridges with the West. I was not convinced, but I was conscious of my inexperience – and certainly it was difficult, when I looked about me, to picture these amiable, humorous, unmistakably gentle Egyptians turning to violence, especially in the languid atmosphere of Cairo in July. And then I was reminded of the mistake made by another foreign correspondent in Cairo exactly four years earlier.

He was the correspondent of the *New York Times* and he hated the heat of the Cairo summer. Looking about him, as I was now doing, but in the July of 1952, he had persuaded himself that nothing newsworthy was in the wind and had taken himself off to Beirut, informing his masters in New York that he was going there 'to write some uncensored dispatches'. Arriving in Beirut on 23 July, he took a hotel room looking over the sea, ordered a drink and settled down with it on the balcony as the sun was setting. His peace was disturbed by the arrival of a cable from his office. There had been a revolution in Egypt, it informed him; would he be good enough to get back to base and see what was left of the story? Anxiously, he returned to Cairo, to find that Nasser and his young officers had indeed seized power. There had been no bloodshed and the revolution had not attacked or even deposed the king. All, it seemed, was safely over and perfect peace prevailed. Filing a story to that effect, our hero saw no reason not to revert to his original plan and after a couple of days he was back in Beirut, taking up where he had left off on his balcony overlooking the bay. It was there that another cable reached him on the evening of 26 July in which he thought he detected a note of asperity.

'King Farouk,' it informed him, 'has abdicated; what are *your* plans?'

Perhaps it was the memory of his discomfiture that persuaded me, when I received an invitation from the Egyptian government's press department, not to turn it down. The press department was running a bus to take foreign journalists wishing to go next day to Alexandria for the celebrations on 26 July to mark the fourth anniversary of Farouk's abdication. President Nasser was to make a speech which would contain an 'important announcement'. Would I like to go along? When I turned up at the rendezvous next morning I found myself the only Western correspondent present. There were East Europeans, an Indian and a few others whom I have forgotten, and as we travelled across the desert to Alexandria I wondered whether I had not allowed myself to be taken for a ride. It was hotter than ever and in Alexandria extremely humid as well, and after the long drive it was tiresome to have to take our places an hour before the show started, on a balcony outside the Stock Exchange in the full glare of the setting sun.

As we waited, though, there was plenty to hold our attention. In front of us was the wide expanse of Liberation Square, where a huge crowd was assembling, jovial in mood as though expecting to be entertained, but swelled all the time by contingents of men who had clearly been imported for the occasion from the villages and towns of the Nile delta and from further afield, each group with its cheer-leader and a repertoire of slogans to chant. There were banners held aloft and flags snapping in the fresh sea breeze and the atmosphere was full of cheerful anticipation, as was right and proper. For the time and the place had been chosen with dramatic precision. Beyond the square was the harbour, and it was from here that, at this same evening hour, exactly four years earlier, the last discredited king of Egypt had been dispatched into exile.

By that time, I had heard Nasser speak often enough, but never before had I been so close to the man around whom such contradictory legends of hatred and hero-worship were being woven. Four years earlier he had been just another colonel in the Egyptian army. In the fighting in Palestine in 1948 he had distinguished himself by holding on to an outpost cut off behind the Israeli lines, and from the humiliation of defeat he was almost the only Egyptian officer to emerge with any credit. There was something of a parallel here with Kemal Ataturk, whose career had so fired my imagination when I was in Turkey. Ataturk too had made his reputation in his thirties, with his successful defence of Gallipoli and it was this that had given him the strength later on to confront the Western allies when they had tried to bend Turkey to their will. Would Nasser prove to be Egypt's Ataturk? And was this July evening in Alexandria to mark a vital turning point in an equally dramatic career? It was an intriguing speculation as the tall figure, with broad shoulders straining the seams of his jacket, stood up before that great crowd in Liberation Square.

At first, as he embarked on the familiar recital of the sins of the imperialists, he seemed nervous, shuffling his notes and repeating himself. Then he gained confidence and began to speak light-heartedly, in the colloquial style which he was the first Arab leader to use in his speeches, about his dealings with the Western powers. There was nothing new in what he said, but a noticeable emphasis on self-respect and on his determination not to allow any outside power to dictate terms to Egypt. When he turned at last to the high dam, he spoke scornfully of the conditions which the West had attached to its offer of assistance, suggesting that the real motivation had not been to help Egypt but to reassert Western control over its policies. It had been the same story a century earlier, Nasser said, with the building of the Suez Canal, which had cost Egypt dearly in human lives and treasure, but whose profits the imperialists had taken for themselves.

The parallel was a telling one, for there was no doubt that the Europeans who planned and supervised the building of the Suez Canal had done so for their own advantage and not for Egypt's. It was not surprising that Nasser, who by now was in full flood, should make the most of the Suez Canal as an illustration of Western greed and hypocrisy. As he went on and on about it, though, he seemed to be in danger of losing his audience. We looked surreptitiously at our watches. The speech, like most things in Egypt, had started more than an hour late and it was now half past nine. We had been sitting there since five o'clock and it looked as though, instead of that 'important announcement', all we were to get was another lecture about imperialism. I began to wish I had stayed in Cairo.

In the end I was glad I had not, for that evening did after all mark a turning point, not just in Nasser's eventful career but in the whole relationship between the Arab world and the West. I cannot say that I recognized the turning point when it came; but then, nor did anyone else who was present that evening in Alexandria. In fact, there was only one man in Egypt besides Nasser himself who did recognize it and whose actions shared the headlines with Nasser's speech in the next day's newspapers all over the world.

That man was Mahmoud Yunis, at that time director of the Egyptian Petroleum Authority, who was listening to the speech on the radio in Ismailia. Like the rest of us, he heard Nasser recall the circumstances in which the Suez Canal had come to be built: how the project had been conceived by a Frenchman named Ferdinand de Lesseps, how de Lesseps had come to Egypt in 1854 to persuade the Khedive Ismail to join in financing the canal, and how the Khedive had later been swindled out of his shares by the British government. But while the rest of us merely thought it curious that Nasser should launch into this elaborate history lesson about the canal, Mahmoud Yunis had a much more precise reason to follow his president's words with the closest attention. For Yunis, unknown to everyone except Nasser himself, had under his command detachments of Egyptian troops at key points along the Suez Canal. His orders were, as soon as he heard Nasser pronounce a secret code word, to send those troops in to seize all the installations of the Suez Canal Company and assume complete control of the canal in the name of the Egyptian government. The code word was '*de Lesseps*'.

For us in Alexandria another half-hour passed – for there had to be time for these orders to take effect – before we learned from Nasser's own lips of the nationalization of the Suez Canal Company. Its revenues of $100 million a year would in future be devoted, said Nasser, not to enriching its British and French shareholders, who would (and did) receive proper compensation, but to building the high dam which was to be the cornerstone of Egypt's future prosperity.

By the time Nasser delivered this carefully timed bombshell, Yunis's troops were in effective occupation of the canal and all its installations from Suez to Port Said – and the telegraph wires were beginning to hum all over the world.

20

There followed the three busiest months of my life and I had good reason to be glad of the free hand the *Manchester Guardian* left me to report the crisis in my own way. My colleagues, I learned later, were kept on a much tighter rein and waited anxiously for the directions with which London began to bombard them. But by now I was accustomed to receiving only an occasional air letter from Manchester (once or twice these were inadvertently sent by surface mail and took a month or so to reach me) and since the *Guardian* was not on sale in Cairo, it was only after some delay that I learned what the paper's editorials were saying; and by that time I had made up my own mind.

It was on Thursday, 26 July that Nasser made his nationalization speech in Alexandria, ending it too late for me to file to the *Guardian* – which would have the text of the speech from the news agencies anyway. Next day, when Eden in the House of Commons deplored what Hugh Gaitskell, the leader of the opposition, called Nasser's 'high-handed action', I sent a piece describing the scene in Alexandria and wondering whether Nasser remembered what had happened to Mossadeq, the Iranian prime minister who had nationalized the Anglo-Iranian oil company in Iran in 1951.*

Saturday is the one day in the week when a correspondent for a daily paper has no deadline to meet and so before I sent a message on Sunday, 29 July, I had a chance to stand back and consider the implications of Nasser's nationalization of the Suez Canal Company† and of the rapturous reception he received on his return to Cairo next

---

* Mossadeq was driven from office a year later in a coup engineered by Kermit Roosevelt and the CIA.

† It was often said at the time that Nasser had 'nationalized the Suez Canal'. This was an error. The canal was of course a part of Egyptian sovereign territory, on which the Suez Canal Company exercised operating rights specified in its concession from the Egyptian government. What Nasser did was nationalize the *company* which in 1956 was under the control of British and French shareholders and directors.

day. The reception, I wrote, had been carefully orchestra
ted, but it would be a mistake to question its warmth and sincerity:

> With the exception of a very few wiser heads, the Egyptians were
> delighted by a step that appealed at once to their nationalistic
> feelings, their growing confidence in Nasser as the man with an
> answer for everything, and, not unimportantly, their strong sense of
> humour. The kind of joke that appeals most to Egyptians is the one
> where pride is seen clearly to go before a fall, and Nasser's riposte to
> what were considered the insulting communiqués of the American
> and British governments [over the high dam] . . . gave them just this
> satisfaction.

There were strong police guards outside the British and American
embassies, I added, but the mood of the crowd was anything but
belligerent; it was more like that of a man who had had a good day at
the races. The Egyptians were not to know that Eden had already
instructed the Chiefs of Staff in London to prepare a plan for military
action against Egypt, or that on that very day he was dictating a
top-secret message to President Eisenhower saying that the only way to
'bring Nasser to his senses' was to resort to force immediately and
without attempting to negotiate. Nor could I imagine this when I wrote
that the West's brusque rejection of the high-dam scheme, which had
prompted Nasser to make his gamble over the Suez Canal, had created
a situation full of danger to ourselves:

> It has left the West with the alternatives of protesting ineffectually or
> employing military or material sanctions whose justification would
> be doubtful. Of course, Nasser's gamble may not come off . . . The
> high dam may not be built and Nasser may be humbled, though it
> looks very unlikely. But unless the Western powers are prepared to
> take a firm step back into history and reoccupy the canal zone, they
> must reconcile themselves to uncertainty about their oil supplies and
> communications in the Middle East, and to the probability that
> Egypt will drag the Arab world with her into the Eastern camp, from
> whose threshold she was turning back ten days ago.

That dispatch appeared in the *Manchester Guardian* on 30 July and it
should have occurred to me that I was treading on the leader writer's
toes. Two days later the paper carried a report that British troops and
naval vessels were being transferred to the eastern Mediterranean as a

'precautionary' move, and on Thursday, 2 August, there was a leading article in which the *Guardian* argued that what Nasser had done might be awkward and damaging to Western interests but that it was 'not ground for military action' against Egypt.

I was relieved when I saw this, for it would have been disconcerting to find myself at odds with my own editor over an issue whose gravity was unmistakable. The rest of the British press was taking the opposite line, so it was reassuring – and exhilarating too – to know that I had the paper behind me and that the *Manchester Guardian* was setting a course of its own and one that disregarded the mood of jingoism that was coming to the surface in Britain.

It was the prime minister, Anthony Eden, who did most to set the tone in London and at the time both his words and his actions seemed unaccountably violent. I knew little about Eden at the time and what little I did know was all to his credit. His opposition to the pre-war policy of appeasement had made him into something of a hero for my generation at Oxford. He was the foreign-policy expert *par excellence*, the loyal ally of Churchill during and after the war, the embodiment of what was best in the old traditions of British public life. It was he who had authorized the negotiations with Nasser in 1954 which led to the withdrawal of the British garrison from the Suez Canal zone – that withdrawal whose final stages I had witnessed soon after my arrival in Egypt a few weeks earlier. What I did not know, what no one outside a small inner circle knew in the summer of 1956, was that Eden had made up his mind long before the start of the Suez crisis that Nasser was an enemy, a menace to British interests – and that he was determined to find a pretext to get rid of him.

Eden had succeeded Winston Churchill as prime minister in 1955. Eager to prove that his shoulders were broad enough for the great man's mantle, he had no wish to preside over the decline of Britain's imperial prestige. One area where British influence was still paramount was the Middle East, where the British ambassador was the power behind the throne in Iraq and Jordan, where Cyprus and Aden were still Crown Colonies, and where a series of treaty relationships with sheikhs and sultans masked Britain's absolute control of the Gulf and Southern Arabia. All this, or as much of it as possible, Eden was anxious to preserve; but its preservation was becoming increasingly difficult in the face of the growing impatience of the Arabs to be masters of their own destiny.

By the beginning of 1956 Eden was coming to see Nasser as the most potent threat to Britain's position in the Middle East – and he was right, so long as that position required the maintenance of British political and military domination. Nasser never tired of denouncing *istamar*, imperialism (it was one of the first Arabic words I learned to distinguish after my arrival in Egypt) and he made no secret of his determination, once he had secured Egypt's full independence, to put an end to foreign domination throughout the Arab world.

With these conflicting viewpoints, it was as though a fuse had been set which – if neither side backed down – must provoke an explosion between them; and on 1 March 1956, King Hussein of Jordan inadvertently put a match to it. When he dismissed Glubb Pasha, the English commander of his Arab Legion, King Hussein did so for reasons of his own, unprompted by anyone outside his tight little beduin kingdom. But Eden, already suspicious of Nasser as his potential adversary, at once convinced himself that it was Nasser who had prompted King Hussein to strike this blow at Britain's threatened prestige and authority. When the news of Glubb's dismissal reached London, Eden flew into a rage and, in the words of Anthony Nutting (at that time Eden's Minister of State at the Foreign Office), 'the prime minister of Great Britain declared a personal war on the man whom he held responsible – Gamal Abdel Nasser, president and prime minister of Egypt'. It was this that explained Eden's frenzied behaviour when Nasser, five months later, nationalized the Suez Canal Company; for on what Nutting called 'that fatal day' in March 1956 Eden had 'decided that the world was not big enough to hold both him and Nasser'.*

None of this could we know as we puzzled in the July heat of Cairo over Eden's intemperate response. And the response of the public in Britain, following the lead given by the prime minister and widely echoed in the press, was equally unthinking and automatic. It always amuses me when I read that this or that newspaper in Britain 'consistently opposed the British government's policy over Suez'. The fact is that some papers supported Eden from start to finish. Others started by supporting him but then, when they saw how little basis there was for his attitude, either legally or in terms of Britain's national interest, changed sides and opposed him. The only paper which made up its mind promptly and maintained its opposition from the first day of the crisis to the last, despite savage criticism and the loss of many of its readers, was the *Manchester Guardian*. I am glad to have been

* Anthony Nutting, *No End of a Lesson: the Story of Suez*, Constable, 1967.

associated with this rare example of consistency in support of principle.

At the time no such austere reflections clouded my enjoyment of life. To begin with, Cairo remained as agreeable a base as ever, and just as friendly. Most of my waking hours, of course, were taken up with the search for news or in writing the dispatches which I cabled to Manchester four or five times a week all through August. It was hot work under the summer sun, but it was also invigorating to have for the first time a story to follow: a story of importance, which grew and developed and took the most unexpected turns, and in the telling of which I could feel that what I wrote might have some marginal influence in shaping the course of events. Nor was this all. As I went about the city in search of this or that informant, chasing a rumour or pinning down some essential fact, there was Cairo itself to savour and explore, a city not yet choked by its own hasty expansion or too thickly overlaid with the veneer of Westernization, but full of life and humour and the genial roguery in which the Egyptians excel. I found it as engaging an environment as one could wish; and when I wanted to escape from the heat and bustle of my daily round, it was always a pleasurable relief to seek sanctuary in a mosque and sit there, shoeless and unregarded, with my back against a pillar in the cool twilight.

Without realizing it at the time, I can see now when I look back on that summer of 1956 that I was at a point of transition. From being a dilettante I was developing – and the development was hastened by the pressure of events – into a professional of sorts. Instead of pursuing what merely interested or diverted me, I had for the first time in my life (apart from the war) to concentrate on an objective not of my own choosing. And there was something more, an extra dimension which made it easy to sacrifice ease or leisure in pursuit of that unsought objective. I found myself becoming involved in what I was doing, involved to the point where the distinction between work and play became blurred and I could see the force of an aphorism which had pleased me when I read it in that faraway prison camp and which I had never fully understood until now. It was C. E. Montague – with whom I could now claim a kind of kinship, for had he not been one of my famous precursors on the *Manchester Guardian*? – who wrote that, 'Art is only work utterly unspoilt; drudgery is only art gone utterly wrong.' I was not so pretentious as to think of my work as art – but a craft, perhaps, one which I enjoyed and to which the same principle applied.

It was a craft in which, as I was well aware, I was still very inexperienced; but common sense dictated that the first thing to do was to establish the facts. If Eden, with what seemed to be strong backing from the British press and public, was seriously thinking of using force against Egypt, there must be some concrete offence on Nasser's part which could constitute a *casus belli*. What was it? Behind much loose phrase-making to the effect that Nasser had 'his thumb on Britain's jugular vein' or that he was 'holding us to ransom', there was what amounted to a conviction that the Egyptian leader had broken some unspecified treaty; and that, as a result, he was now in a position to prevent the free passage of ships – British ships in particular – through the Suez Canal. These were clearly issues of importance for all sea-faring nations, ourselves among them.

As to the legal position, I was well placed to get at the facts. My father's old friend, the retired judge who had been my host when I first arrived in Cairo, had worked for thirty years in the Egyptian courts and he was now legal counsellor to the British Embassy. He was also, as I have said, a man of the most scrupulous exactitude, for whom it would have been unthinkable to lean to one side or the other in the interpretation of facts which affected the interests of both his old and his new masters. And if, as a British official, he felt any inhibition about revealing to a journalist facts which might be embarrassing to the British government, I could hope that as an old family friend, he might make an exception in my favour.

I found him in the embassy, surrounded by a mass of documents and law books. As I had hoped, he received me more as a friend, one who might be expected to share his interest in a crucial point of law, than as a journalist to be held at arm's length. It was too early, he said, for him to be able to quote me chapter and verse in the matter, but there was little doubt that Nasser had put himself on the wrong side of the law. The treaty involved was the Constantinople Convention of 1888, which called for free passage through the canal at all times for the ships of all nations, so it looked like an open-and-shut case. There were just one or two points of detail to be cleared up and if I could come back the next day he thought he could give me a clear statement of the position.

When I turned up again on the following morning, I detected at once a diminished certainty in his bearing. Things were not, it seemed, quite as clear as one would have liked them to be. With anyone else I might have suspected that the facts were leading him towards a conclusion unfavourable to the British government and that he felt embarrassed to say so. With the judge this was out of the question. It was not any sense of conflicting loyalties that was disturbing him, but a purely professional impatience: the impatience of a man accustomed to be precise and to expect precision from others, but who finds himself confronted by a piece of work not merely imprecise but positively confused. The Constantinople Convention, it appeared, contained two clauses which actually contradicted each other, and the judge, who liked things to be clear-cut, was indignant. What upset him was not the fact that the contradiction made it hard for the British government to substantiate its case against Nasser, but the thought that international lawyers, when they drew up the terms of the convention, should have produced such a sloppy piece of work.

When I went back to see him a third time, his mind was made up. Although Anthony Eden and a great many other people in Britain continued to talk about Nasser 'tearing up a treaty', the judge's opinion was that, legally speaking, and provided he paid proper compensation to the shareholders in the old Anglo-French canal company, Nasser was within his rights in taking over the company's assets and in asserting Egyptian control over an institution which had always been under Egyptian jurisdiction.

That dealt with one issue. There remained the question of free passage through the canal. Eden had said in the House of Commons that Britain could not tolerate any arrangement which would leave the canal 'in the unfettered control of a single power which could exploit it purely for purposes of national policy'; and on this issue, whatever the legal position might be, there was no doubt that Eden could count on strong international backing.

It is easy to forget today, with the tremendous growth of air travel and the development of supertankers which are too big to use the canal anyway, that in 1956 the Suez Canal really was vital to the prosperity of any country – and of Britain first and foremost – which depended for its livelihood on international trade. If Nasser tried to stop British or French ships using the canal, either because they refused to pay their dues to Egypt or for any other reason, he would put himself morally in the wrong and he could expect to suffer the consequences.

So the next port of call for a correspondent was the pleasant waterside town of Ismailia, halfway between Suez and Port Said, from which the canal traffic was directed. It was a journey I was to make many times that summer and I never tired of it. Out of the heat and clamour of Cairo, the road ran under shade trees out across the verdant delta of the Nile, a bright mosaic in different shades of green, where water flashed in the irrigation channels and egrets stalked with dignity behind the peasants as they worked the land. There were bee-eaters, blue and green, perched on the telegraph wires, and donkey-carts on their way to market, and small boys tending the water buffaloes which wallowed ungainly in the mud. And then, abruptly, the green petered out, the desert encroached and there were palm trees among the shelving sands, golden clusters of dates hanging beneath the dusty fronds. And finally, as a smudge of red-brown hills was beginning to emerge out of the eastward haze, you came all at once on the canal itself, becoming aware of it for the first time, as likely as not, when you saw the tall sails of a felucca crossing your line of vision, or perhaps the superstructure of an ocean liner, its hull hidden from you by the raised bank of the canal, so that it seemed to be altogether out of its element as it carved its improbable way through this landlocked environment.

I took that road for the first time one day at the beginning of August – and at once found that among the shipping agents and ship's chandlers of Suez and Ismailia the crisis took on a quite different aspect. About its political implications they knew little and cared less. What interested them were purely practical questions about the canal dues and who was entitled to collect them, and whether the ships of the world would continue to use the canal now that Nasser had 'grabbed' it. Above all – for their livelihood depended on it – would the Egyptians prove capable of maintaining the canal and keeping the ships moving through it as smoothly as the pilots and technicians of the old company?

The last of these was a question which others were asking too, and one which many people a long way away from Suez were inclined to answer without waiting for the facts. Among my newspaper cuttings from the time there is a cartoon from *Punch*. It shows a British sea-captain covering his eyes in horror as an Egyptian (dressed, of course, in galabiyeh and tarbush) takes the wheel to pilot his ship through the Suez Canal. The drawing (by Norman Mansbridge) is brilliant and the message unmistakeable: if the Egyptians were left in charge of the canal, only catastrophe could follow.

Well, we should have to see – and I cannot pretend that we of the Cairo press corps started out with a much higher opinion of the ability of the Egyptians to meet the challenge. What we established that day was that so far – this was just a week after the nationalization – the traffic was 'normal', averaging about forty-five ships every twenty-four hours. When we drove along the canal between Suez and Ismailia, we passed the northbound convoy and saw that it included the P & O Liner *Himalaya* and ships from Italy, Portugal, Holland, Norway,

Greece, Liberia, Yugoslavia and the Soviet Union.

It was a fine sight and there seemed to be several lessons to be drawn from it. First, as Eden was saying, that not only Britain but all the sea-going nations of the world had an interest in keeping the canal open. Second, as the Egyptians were pointing out, that Egypt, if she was going to collect the canal dues, shared that interest (a liner like the *Himalaya*, for instance, would pay £7,000 for the one-way passage from Suez to Port Said). And finally that it was one up to Nasser that for the first week at least the Egyptians had been able to prevent anyone from running into the bank or colliding with a ship coming the other way.

As I pieced all this together for a report to the *Guardian*, I was hoping, along with several other Western correspondents who had converged on Ismailia, to round off the day by meeting the man to whom Nasser had entrusted the crucial job of running the canal. This was Mahmoud Yunis, an engineer and, like Nasser, a former army officer, to whom Nasser had sent that coded message in his nationalization speech a week earlier. It was Mahmoud Yunis, sitting beside the radio in Ismailia, who had given effect to the *fait accompli* by immediately taking possession of the headquarters of the old Suez Canal Company. And it was there – only now it was the headquarters of the new, all-Egyptian, Suez Canal Authority – that we assembled for his first informal press conference.

I remember the moment well and it is captured for me by a single sentence in the story I sent to the paper that day. Yunis was in a board meeting and as we waited for him to emerge I noted with amusement that 'a bust of de Lesseps looked on unmoved at the journalists sprawling on the trim lawn outside the conference room'. Among those journalists, sitting beside me on the grass, was a new arrival who had come to take the place of James Morris as Middle East correspondent for *The Times*. As luck would have it, James had come to the end of his term in Egypt just before the Suez crisis broke, and *The Times* had spent some frantic days trying to trace his successor, who was on holiday somewhere off the map in France. At last they found him and out he came hotfoot to Egypt, which we were to know together in good times and in bad for many years to come. His name was David Holden and my first recollection of him is in that shady garden at Ismailia, as we waited to meet the man to whom Nasser had allotted the principal supporting role in his carefully staged Suez Canal production.

When Yunis appeared, a lean, purposeful figure, he looked equal to the part, parrying our questions with an engaging smile and telling us nothing that we did not already know. When he said that the canal, 'as you can see for yourselves', was functioning normally, he managed to make it sound less like a boast than a private joke which we could all share. Beyond that and the fact that Egypt would fulfil its obligations to the world, why, there was nothing more to be said.

As far as we could see, the Egyptians were playing their hand very shrewdly. Nasser had promised full compensation (which was duly paid) to the European shareholders of the old canal company. He had been careful, despite the threatening noises coming out of London and Paris, not to put himself in the wrong by interfering in any way with the free passage of British or French ships using the canal. When the British and French governments ordered their shipowners not to pay their canal dues to the new Egyptian authority but to continue to pay them into the account of the old Anglo-French company in Paris or London, Nasser quietly allowed them to go on doing so.

All this contrasted strikingly with the behaviour of Eden and his French colleages. Unable to establish a legal case against Egypt, they made strident accusations of 'blackmail' and suggested that Nasser was 'holding Western Europe to ransom' and must be 'cut down to size'. They sent out invitations to a conference of maritime powers in London whose objective was to 'reassert' international control (which had never existed) over the canal, and at the same time they set on foot ostentatious military and naval preparations for an invasion of Egypt and advised their own citizens living in Egypt to return home.

To us in Cairo it was bewildering to see this evidence of what seemed to amount almost to hysteria in our own country, while the Egyptians remained surprisingly calm. When the Egyptian government was invited to attend the London conference, I wrote that it was unlikely to accept unless there was 'unequivocal recognition of Egypt's sovereignty over the canal' and that 'above all, Egypt is likely to demand that if the conference is to be held it should be held in an atmosphere free of economic or military pressures'. Meanwhile, it seemed to be important for people in Britain to understand why the Egyptians felt so sure of their ground:

Paradoxically, one reason seems to be the enduring confidence of ordinary Egyptians in British respect for international law. 'You admit that we have the right to nationalize the Suez Canal Company,' runs the argument. 'You know you would not brand yourselves as aggressors by reoccupying the canal zone unless the navigation of the canal was interrupted.' And the navigation of the canal is continuing normally, forty-one ships passing through on Saturday and thirty-five on Sunday . . .

The Egyptian government may be right in thinking that by delaying its decision [whether or not to attend the London conference] it is gaining time, for it is difficult to see what British warships can do in the Eastern Mediterranean until there is more provocation for their presence than exists at present.

It never looked likely that Nasser would have anything to do with the London conference, but Eden made his refusal a certainty when he appeared on television on 8 August to make an extraordinary attack on the Egyptian president. Eden's speech was given the maximum publicity and was relayed throughout the world over the radio by the BBC's overseas services. In it the British prime minister made plain the context of personal antipathy in which he approached the crisis. 'Our quarrel,' he said, 'is not with Egypt, it is with Colonel Nasser,' who had shown that he was 'not a man who can be trusted to keep an agreement'. He brushed aside all Nasser's assurances and the fact that navigation through the canal was continuing normally – and the further fact that it was in Egypt's clear interest to see that it was maintained. He ignored the legal aspect of the dispute, on which Britain's case had already broken down, and concentrated instead on Nasser's character and the ambitions which Eden, without substantiating the charge, imputed to him. The fact was that this 'Colonel Nasser' (as Eden insisted on calling him throughout) was a dictator. He might be 'soft-pedalling' for the moment, but if we allowed him to get away with this, 'each one of us would be at the mercy of one man for the supplies on which we live . . .'

The insulting tone of the broadcast, together with the thinly veiled threats of armed intervention against Egypt, made it impossible for Nasser to do other than refuse the invitation to the London conference. Eden's insistence that the operation of the canal must be taken out of Egypt's control highlighted what for Nasser was the fundamental issue. Either Egypt was to be genuinely independent or she was not. If she was independent, she had the right to make what arrangements she liked for the operation of the canal. If Nasser submitted to the demand – which was couched almost in the terms of an ultimatum – to accept international control, then Egypt's sovereign independence would be infringed. There was no way of squaring this circle and every threat of armed intervention against Nasser could only stiffen his resistance, especially since the rest of the Arab world (with the exception of Iraq, where Nasser's old enemy Nuri es-Said was encouraging Eden) was rallying in his support. This too seemed to be something that was imperfectly understood in London and as we waited for Nasser's decision I tried to envisage the results of an armed intervention by Britain:

> The apparent solidarity of the Arab world on the Suez question might well break down if put to the test of action, but for the moment it looks unusually firm. Certainly any military action against Egypt would lead to varying degrees of unrest in neighbouring Arab states, with attacks on Western-owned commercial and oil installations a certainty . . . and revolutions in Jordan and Iraq a distinct possibility.

When a meeting of the political committee of the Arab League was held in Cairo, both Iraq and Jordan sent delegations and I returned to the attack:

> It cannot be too much stressed that the Suez question and the Western treatment of it has drawn the Arab world together, strengthened President Nasser's position inside and outside Egypt and placed Iraq, in particular, in a difficult position. This is, in part, for spurious reasons which are not examined too closely in the Middle East, provided they carry the seal of Arab nationalism.
> But whatever weaknesses there may be in the arguments of the Arab nationalists, the fact is that President Nasser has manoeuvred Britain into an untenable position, where she appears to be clinging to material interests and shreds of political supremacy in this part of the world – and doing so at the expense and in defiance of the local desire for independence and a measure of prosperity . . .
> Only by the most scrupulous observance of her obligations as a member of the United Nations can Britain emerge with credit from the Suez Canal dispute – and in the long run that is more important to Britain than the canal.

I suppose I was straying there once again into the leader writer's territory, but I am glad the *Guardian* printed that last comment, for it encapsulated an idea that has been in my mind ever since and which was born out of my experience of the Suez crisis. Politicians have their axes to grind, and in obedience to them civil servants and diplomats have to operate within a framework which it is not their business to try to alter. But I have always thought it a cardinal mistake on the part of those who do set the framework, and who devise policies supposedly on the basis of national interest, to leave out of account what seems to me the most important asset of all: a country's reputation. In the Suez crisis I saw my own prime minister throwing away that asset and cutting in the end a poor figure by comparison with the opponent whom he so unfairly denigrated.

When Nasser at last gave his answer about the London conference, he did so at a huge press conference in Cairo which I attended along with 250 other foreign correspondents. In explaining why he was refusing the invitation, Nasser made his points with good humour. He did not refer directly to Eden's attack on him, but asked with a smile what the point would be of sitting down with a statesman who constantly repeated that 'we have no confidence in Nasser'. He had not broken his word to anyone and he would like 'to have details about any international obligation which Egypt has violated' (I thought here of my friend the judge and his fruitless search through the archives). As for the threats of military action against Egypt, he added disarmingly, 'I know we are a small country, but we have to defend our rights; we shall give an example of morale to the small nations of the world.'

He was perfectly willing, he said, to attend a conference – one that would be open to all nations using the canal, not just to a selected few – and to try to work out practical arrangements to ensure the freedom of navigation. But he was not prepared to sit down under duress to discuss limitations on Egyptian sovereignty. There was no justification, he told the assembled journalists (with just a hint of a chuckle), for headlines in the Western press like 'Nasser's Grab at Suez'. Suez was in Egypt, he reminded us and 'this is our territory, our canal'.

It was an effective performance, not only because the arguments he used were so reasonable but because it belied the image of Nasser which Eden was anxious to foist on the world. The press conference ended with a laugh when an American correspondent, picking up Eden's point, asked with refreshing bluntness: 'Are you a dictator?', to which Nasser, after a pause for thought, replied with a grin that he really didn't know.

I had to try to do better than this when the foreign editor of the *Guardian*, in one of those rare cables from Manchester, asked me to tell our readers in 1,500 words whether Eden was justified in talking of Nasser as though he were a new Hitler. At first sight, I wrote, and especially to a politician with Eden's background, the parallel was an apt one. Nasser was an absolute ruler, whose authority was not

strengthened in the eyes of the democratic world by the claim that 99.9
per cent of the Egyptian people had voted for him in the recent
plebiscite. He had used his power and the control he exerted over the
propaganda machinery of the state to pursue a foreign policy,
'vigorous' or 'aggressive' according to taste which aimed at the
removal of alleged grievances and which, in doing so, threatened the
interests of the Western powers – and of Britain in particular – in the
Middle East.

So far there was indeed a parallel – you could even say a close one –
with Hitler. But when you came to examine the grievances and the
interests, things began to look different. Hitler's starting point too had
been the removal of a grievance; but he had set out in *Mein Kampf* a
programme which required the subversion of democratic government
in Germany and the subjugation of its neighbours; a programme
accompanied by racism and bloodshed and the enforced abandonment
of the values of Western civilization. Nasser's revolution, by contrast,
had started with the overthrow of a corrupt and ineffectual monarchy
and the emancipation of a depressed peasant population. There had
been no purges and no pogroms. Foreign interests had been left
untouched and even the wealthy and influential Jewish community in
Cairo, despite Egypt's violent antagonism towards the state of Israel,
had not been subjected to any official or unofficial discrimination.*

Having achieved power, Nasser (like Kemal Ataturk in Turkey) had
set as his first objective the complete liberation of the country from
foreign control; and once the British had agreed to withdraw from
Egypt, Nasser and his associates were eager (as Ataturk had been) to
tackle the next objective of social and economic regeneration, of which
the high dam was the symbol. It was to the West that Nasser had turned
for help in laying this vital foundation for Egypt's future prosperity;
and when the British and American governments agreed to provide the
assistance he needed, the future seemed assured. When, instead – and
so abruptly – they withdrew their offer, all Nasser's old suspicions of an
imperialist conspiracy against the Arabs were revived. How else to
explain a decision whose result must be to prevent him from leading the
Arab world forward to the goal of full independence? Were they
challenging him to turn instead to the Russians? Rather than satisfy

---

* This I knew at first hand. From my father, who had been an official of the National
Bank of Egypt and a connoisseur of oriental rugs, I had inherited a useful set of
contacts among the Levantine and Jewish communities, including Greek and Italian
bank officials and the most important rug dealer in Cairo, an old friend by the name of
Cohen.

them, he had chosen what seemed a still more dangerous alternative:

The nationalization of the Suez Canal Company was plainly an act of hostile intent, planned in resentment at the Western rebuff. To Nasser, that rebuff was also a hostile act, intended to undermine his ascendancy in the Arab world, and it is difficult to dispute this judgement. But no one has yet succeeded in challenging the legality of the nationalization. It may be that its consequences for Egypt and for Nasser's own regime will be disastrous, but that does not convict Nasser as a treaty-breaker or justify us in calling him a new Hitler.

He is a nationalist leader, an opportunist, whose objectives of strengthening the Arab world and establishing its full independence of outside influences are painful to us but arouse the natural enthusiasm of his own people and the sympathy of all the ex-colonial nations in Asia and Africa. Perhaps the West's tendency to jump to the worst conclusions about Middle Eastern nationalism has its roots in our nostalgia for the days when, if we pulled the strings in the Middle East, the important people danced. Those days are gone – and gone for good.

In saying that, I was getting ahead of the game; the West still had a few more strings to pull. So far, though, Nasser was clearly getting the better of the argument – and where he scored most heavily was in the contrast between his behaviour and that of Eden. Here was Eden, the distinguished champion of old world diplomacy, who talked in high-flown terms about the sanctity of treaties and the need to subordinate national interests to the wider good – and who went about making threats, sending off warships to the Mediterranean, blocking Egypt's sterling balances (in itself a clear breach of the agreement under which these balances were held in London) and generally giving the impression of a man determined to have his way, by fair means or foul, and whatever the rest of the world might have to say. And in the other corner there was Nasser, twenty years his junior and a soldier by profession, inexperienced and unfamiliar with the niceties of diplomatic protocol, at the head of a nation ludicrously ill-equipped to confront the leading powers of Europe – who yet managed to remain outwardly imperturbable, avoiding all the traps laid for him and doing nothing to encourage (as he so easily might have done) any spirit of xenophobia against his opponent. On the contrary he saw to it that there were no demonstrations, no outward change in the friendly attitude of the Egyptians towards the European community.

Cairo remained perfectly calm.

The London conference met at last, without Nasser (who sent an observer), and while we waited to see what would come out of it, interest switched once again to the focal point of the crisis: the canal itself. Here a battle of wits was in progress between the Egyptians who were now in charge and the European employees, whose allegiance was to the old Anglo-French company.

The Egyptians seemed to have things pretty well in hand; they were keeping the ships moving, their numbers undiminished, and they insisted smilingly that everything was 'normal' and would remain so. But the pilots were still those engaged by the old company, almost all of them European and more than half British or French – and the company's spokesmen in Paris were putting it about that if they were to leave, the Egyptians would be unable either to dispense with them or to replace them in time to avert a breakdown. Much would depend on who was right.

We journalists were well aware that both sides were trying to use us for their own purposes; and it was very difficult to get at the truth. Most people thought at the time that this piloting was a very skilled business, requiring long training and all sorts of high qualifications, and at first we were inclined to take the word of the experts. Even this was not easy, for the pilots themselves were elusive. When they were not working, they had obviously been told to keep their heads down and avoid giving interviews to prying journalists. There were just over two hundred of them, of whom 120 were British or French and only twenty or thirty Egyptians. The rest came from various countries and their loyalties were unpredictable, but it looked clear enough that, if more than half of the total strength withdrew, there would not be enough pilots to maintain the service.

But if this were true, why were the Egyptians so confident? Could it be that piloting a ship through the Suez Canal was not so difficult as the old company was trying to make out? Any such suggestion was treated by the British and French as almost treasonable and someone had clearly been getting at me when I reported that a batch of Egyptian naval officers had been signed up as canal pilots. In that case, I wrote severely: '. . . they cannot have experience of handling larger ships than destroyers, since the Egyptian navy has no larger ships; and handling a large modern tanker in a crosswind along the narrow Suez Canal is an exceptionally exacting job'.

This certainly was the accepted wisdom and it sounded logical enough – until a retired captain in the Royal Navy wrote a letter to *The*

Times saying that he had been through the canal more times than he could remember during the war and that 'I just used to tell my chap to steer straight down the middle.'

Wherever the truth might lie, there was a lot of bluff and counter-bluff going on, and trying to distinguish one from the other made a welcome diversion, especially in the congenial surroundings of Ismailia, where you could generally find time for a swim and there were sailing boats racing in Lake Timsah, while further out the ships were assembling for the afternoon convoy. Even if British warships were making for Cyprus and the Foreign Office had given a second warning to British subjects to leave Egypt, it was still difficult to take the crisis seriously. Surely Eden too was bluffing? The Egyptians thought so and retained their sense of humour, although there might be a threat as well as a joke in the cartoon which one of the Cairo papers printed towards the end of August and which showed Anthony Eden in a tin hat advancing with fixed bayonet on the Sphinx – with a large bear with its mouth watering following close behind him.

If the Egyptians up to now had been relaxed in their approach to the crisis, refusing to think the worst of an antagonist for whom they still felt a good deal of respect, a series of events in Cairo now raised the temperature. A clandestine radio station started broadcasting anti-Egyptian propaganda in Arabic on a frequency very close to the one used by Cairo radio. The Egyptians jumped to the conclusion that it was being directed by the British – rightly, I believe, for this was certainly a technique much used by the British in the later stages of the Suez crisis. Coming on top of the news of troop movements, this created an atmosphere of suspicion which was aggravated by the fact that there were now hundreds of journalists in Cairo, some of them interested in the Suez Canal and others simply looking for the kind of story that would make a good headline in tomorrow's paper. It was inevitable that sooner or later someone would get into trouble with the security services, who had good reason to be on the *qui vive*. The first casualty was Sefton Delmer of the *Daily Express*, whom the Egyptians deported in the last week of August. A couple of days later he was followed by three more, including Anne ('Shapely') Sharpley of the *Evening Standard*, who had been picked up trying to interview General Neguib, the skeleton in Nasser's cupboard.*

Apart from the popular press, nobody took these adventures very

* General Neguib had been used as a figure-head by the revolutionary officers who overthrew King Farouk in 1952. He was president of Egypt until Nasser took over and put him under house arrest.

seriously; but then came a more alarming development. On 27 August the Egyptians announced that they had uncovered a British spy ring. Three British subjects were arrested (and a fourth later) and two officials from the British embassy were ordered to leave Egypt, amid the usual protestations on both sides. On the face of it, this looked like a deliberate diversion by the Egyptians, carefully timed to counter the effect of the communiqué published when the London conference broke up. This reiterated the determination of the Western powers, with the somewhat equivocal backing of the United States, to insist on the 'internationalization' of the canal. Since this was the one thing Nasser was not ready to discuss, the deadlock seemed to be complete. To try to get round it, the conference decided to send an emissary to Cairo to discuss its conclusions with President Nasser. The man they chose was Robert Menzies, the Australian prime minister, and when Nasser after some hesitation agreed to see him, Menzies flew out to Cairo, arriving less than a week after the arrest of the British 'spies'.* It was hardly an auspicious beginning to his mission, especially as it also coincided with an announcement that French troops had arrived in Cyprus to join the British expeditionary force assembling for that 'last-resort' eventuality of an invasion of Egypt.

It was at this moment, just as Menzies was stepping out of his aircraft at Cairo airport, that I had my first meeting with Nasser. Before that I had seen him in action often enough, speaking in Arabic to huge and noisy audiences who enjoyed his jokes and listened with respectful inattention to his rambling diatribes against imperialism; but I had never come face to face with him. In Alexandria, when he made his nationalization speech, I had been sitting within twenty paces of him; and a fortnight later I had attended that press conference at which, speaking in English, he had handled his large international audience so capably. I was eager to see what impression he made at close quarters.

All the journalists, of course, were jockeying to get a private interview with Nasser. There must have been a couple of hundred of us, all trying to steal a march on each other, and inevitably few of us had any success. But then, out of the blue, I got a break. An American television team had somehow managed to penetrate the defences of the Egyptian press department and had been promised an interview which was to take place on the evening of Sunday, 2 September. The arrival of Menzies on the same evening meant that the spotlight was going to be

---

* Two of them, James Swinburn and James Zarb, were later convicted of espionage and imprisoned. I attended the trial in the following May and later visited them in prison. The others, Charles Pittuck and John Stanley, were acquitted.

on Cairo again and the Egyptians saw an opportunity to get their point of view across to the Americans at a critical turning point in the crisis. To make the most of it, they invited a dozen correspondents from the more serious papers to attend as well, so as to make the occasion look more impressive. I was one of them, and while I was not flattered by the idea of being part of someone else's captive audience, I reminded myself that in Egypt the one thing you could count on happening was the unexpected. And as a forlorn hope I asked the Egyptian official who had invited me to see if he couldn't get me a few minutes alone with Nasser in the course of the evening.

The television interview started off on predictable lines: one or two questions about the spy story, on which Nasser refused to be drawn and then the interviewer asked him what sort of a reception Menzies could expect in Cairo. Nasser was not quite at ease with the television cameras, of which his experience was still limited, and he didn't sound very interested in Menzies either. He said he would listen to what he had to say, but that there could be no compromise over the question of Egyptian sovereignty – and then he referred warmly to a speech which President Eisenhower had made the day before, in which (to Eden's intense annoyance) Eisenhower had stressed America's 'full respect for the sovereignty of Egypt'.

At this point the lighting broke down and I grabbed my Egyptian from the press office and told him that this was his chance. A moment later, disbelievingly, I found myself being hurried out of the overheated atmosphere and on to a balcony overlooking the Nile, where a friendly breeze was blowing and in the shadows a burly figure was leaning against the parapet. The official withdrew, closing the french windows behind him, and I was alone with the president.

At this critical moment in his career, Nasser was thirty-eight – just a couple of years older than I was – and at the height of his powers. It was only four years since the revolution he had engineered and his self-assurance as a politician was still incomplete; but in purely physical terms he had a most formidable presence. He stood well over six feet and, as I had noticed a month earlier in Alexandria, when I was seated close behind and to one side of him as he delivered his bombshell, he had the shoulders of a prizefighter. Now, as he came forward to meet me, he seemed to loom most ominously in the half light, the very embodiment of the challenge he had thrown down to the Western world.

The swiftness with which our encounter had come about had caught me unawares and before I could say anything Nasser went into the attack. Did I work for one of the papers which were printing all this rubbish about him, he asked? I was glad to find that this was a joke, and when I told him that I was from the *Manchester Guardian* and the interview took a more serious turn, I was still intrigued by his relaxed mood. In the morning, after all, he was going to have to face Robert Menzies, a man vastly more experienced in public affairs than was Nasser himself, and who came to Egypt as a kind of super-ambassador from some of the most powerful governments in the world, with the mission of bending Nasser to their will. There were the troops mustering in Cyprus and the warships in the eastern Mediterranean, and the Egyptians themselves had now started training a kind of people's militia (very ragged and comical they looked, as one saw them drilling in Cairo's few open spaces) to confront a possible invasion. There were the American and Russian and Indian ambassadors chasing each other in and out of Nasser's office – and yet here he was, cigarette in hand, talking to a stray journalist as though he hadn't a care in the world.

He positively chuckled when he remarked to me that Menzies was bringing with him some twenty or thirty advisers; 'I have just three people who advise me on this subject,' said Nasser.

I don't remember much else that he said before the lights came on again and they took him back to the television cameras. Whatever it was, it must have reinforced the impression I already had that Eden was mistaken if he was expecting a walkover. I fancy it was Nasser's bearing, rather than anything I heard him say that night, that lent a note of assurance to my dispatch to the *Guardian* of 3 September:

> There is no reason to suppose that Mr Menzies or anyone else can persuade President Nasser to budge from his position, especially since he is assured of wide support from outside Europe, and he is sincere in saying, both privately and publicly, that if he is attacked he will fight. In their present mood, the Egyptians would fight with him; and what matters is not the question of whether they would be a match for any invading army but the fact that, with the first shot fired, the invaders would have lost the moral battle – and that, temporarily at least, they would lose their oil supplies as well.

Menzies spent a week in Cairo and after a flicker of hope in the first couple of days it became clear that he was beating his head against a brick wall. The Egyptians were very polite and even gave a dinner party for him; but Nasser's resistance seemed to become stronger – or maybe it was just more obstinate – as the pressure on him increased. We were only halfway through the week when I wrote that:

> The best diagnosis in the case of the Menzies mission seems to be that the patient has a very slim chance of survival and that relatives will know the worst by midday tomorrow. If it is any comfort to them, the patient (who has had the best of attention) was in a critical condition before he came under the doctor's care.

Once it became clear that the Menzies mission had failed, both sides made their dispositions for the next round in the contest. A shooting war still looked absurdly unlikely; but the time for diplomacy was over. The next round would be won or lost along the banks of the canal itself.

No sooner was Menzies out of Egypt than the old company issued a directive to all its employees, including the canal pilots, to leave Egypt. This meant that at any moment three quarters of the pilots and half of the administrative staff – the men who saw to signals and dredging and all the other vital parts of the operation – would stop work. Nasser, when I asked him, had said that if this happened, the canal would stay open and the Egyptians would keep the traffic flowing. But was this possible? I hurried off again to Ismailia, where I ran to earth two of the British pilots. They would be leaving, they told me, and so would all their European colleagues except the Greeks (of whom there were nine or ten) and perhaps three or four others. That would leave at most fifty qualified pilots, most of them Egyptians, to do the work of two hundred, with about the same number of apprentices who were still being trained. 'It can't be done, old boy,' was their verdict and on the face of it, it looked as though they must be right . . . unless, of course, the Egyptians had something up their sleeve.

At the headquarters of the Egyptian canal authority, the most senior officials I could find would only say that 'arrangements' had been made to ensure that 'in all eventualities navigation will continue at the same rate as at present'. That seemed categorical enough and I drove back to Cairo to relay to the *Guardian* these flatly contradictory views about what would happen in three days' time. There I learned that when Menzies had reported failure, the American secretary of state, Foster Dulles, had come up with a new formula to reconcile the interests of the West with Egypt's sovereign rights. The nations using the canal should band themselves into a Suez Canal Users' Association which would organize traffic through the canal on terms to be agreed with the Egyptians. Eden, in presenting this idea to the House of

Commons, implied that if the Egyptians refused to co-operate with the SCUA, force would be used. In other words, the ships would shoot their way through.

This bizarre idea collapsed, not so much because the Egyptians predictably turned it down but because Dulles, to Eden's disgust, disclaimed the idea of forcing a passage through the canal. By now, though, it was clear that whatever did happen when the British and French pilots withdrew, it was going to be worth seeing. I determined that, if it was at all possible, I would be there on the canal to see it.

The day on which the Suez Canal Company had told its pilots to leave, 15 September, was a Saturday. I went back to Ismailia early that morning and spent the best part of twenty-four hours pleading, cajoling, arguing with the Egyptians in charge of the canal to let me go on one of the ships in the first convoy on Sunday morning. When I ran into any of my colleagues I had to disguise my intention – which indeed, in the circumstances of the day, with the Egyptians now highly suspicious of the motives of any Englishman, be he a politician, a pilot or a newspaperman, looked absurdly optimistic; so much so that, to my anxious relief, nobody else seemed to have thought of it.

All day and halfway through the night, putting my trust once more in that old Egyptian magic, I refused to take no for an answer – to be rewarded at last when, dishevelled but triumphant, I climbed the gangway of the *East River*, a Liberian tanker, American-built, with an Italian crew and an Egyptian pilot. When I took my place alongside him on the bridge, it was a moment to savour. After the long battle with officialdom on shore, the calm air of detachment on board was like a tonic:

This is the eye of the storm whose peripheral gusts are rattling windows as far afield as Washington, Paris, Moscow and New Delhi. Here by contrast, all is quiet – blissfully so for anyone who has been involved, however remotely, in the diplomatic and political and propaganda campaigns of the past two months. Here a line of ships steams gently, silently through the desert, and instead of slogans and threats and political catchwords, all you hear is a murmured 'ten points to port* . . . five . . . steady as she goes' and the nostalgic

---

*My landlubber's translation of *dieci a sinistra*, which is what the pilot said to the Italian helmsman. It elicited a letter to the editor which read: 'Sir, if your correspondent really heard the pilot say "ten points to port", he was lucky not to finish his journey on a camel.'

plaint of a Neapolitan love song from the crew's quarters in the after part of the ship.

The pilot's name was Gamal Mongued, and if he was anything to go by the Egyptians were clearly going to win this round too. Immaculate in white shirt and shorts, he had five years' experience on the canal and as we steamed southwards in the bright sunshine he anticipated no problems. Besides the ten Greeks who had stayed on when the other Europeans left, there were seventy Egyptian pilots, half of them fully qualified and the rest nearing the end of an intensive training course. It was not many, he acknowledged, but 'we shall just have to work a bit harder for the time being'.

It wouldn't be for long, he added, since – as I had discovered for myself – the Egyptians had got something else up their sleeve:

Of all the thousand and one rumours distracting Ismailia this weekend, the wildest turned out to be true. The fifteen Russian pilots who arrived on Saturday did not have snow on their boots, but the red and white labels on their suitcases (*Aerotransport Moskva*) seemed almost as improbable to eyes screwed up against the desert glare. Gratefully shedding their heavy jackets, they showed no unwillingness to talk about themselves. Aged between twenty-eight and fifty-two, they were all experienced seamen, though only one of them had been a canal pilot – in Leningrad. But this did not cloud their optimism and Feodor Pankov, doyen of the team, declared gaily that given two days to study the regulations and signals in use on the Suez Canal he would be ready to lead a convoy of fifteen tankers piloted by his colleagues from the Mediterranean to the Red Sea.

This put a new complexion on the challenge facing the Egyptians, which took on now the aspect of a sporting event. It was as though, on the eve of a world-cup match, half of the Egyptian team – which in any case was not expected to win – had had to drop out. Could they, by bringing in these motley reserves, hope to hold their own? Captain Mongued was sure they could, and by the time we came to the end of our placid journey I felt pretty sure he was right:

Now Suez is in sight and behind it the sun is sinking, throwing deep shadows across the pink hills of Sinai on our left. In the bay the ships are gathering for tomorrow's north-bound convoy: seven or eight tankers and a couple of small freighters, past which the leading ships of our own convoy are already steaming out to sea. Up on the bridge of the *East River* Captain Mongued looks unruffled as ever as I take my leave of the friendly Italian captain and hurry down the gangway, leaping into a cutter as the ship approaches the mouth of the canal. Already I can feel that I am leaving the quiet eye of the storm and as I spring ashore I brace myself again for the storm itself. Perhaps the canal cannot long escape the turmoil; for the moment it seems the quietest place in a troubled world.

The canal was to remain peaceful for a while yet, but now everyone's attention was distracted by events on a new front. The Israeli government of David Ben-Gurion chose this moment to mount a series of 'reprisal' raids – not against Egypt, but against Jordan. The Israelis put forward the usual pretexts of infiltration by Arab *fedayin*, but even if these were genuine, the response was so disproportionate that there was much speculation about the Israelis' motives. No one, as far as I can remember, thought of the correct interpretation. We had all been so preoccupied by the crisis over the Suez Canal that even the Egyptians had put aside their more enduring preoccupation with Israel; and it did not become clear to us until much later that there was a direct connection between the Israeli attacks and the British and French designs on Suez.

Israel's part in the Suez crisis forms no part of my story. It was more than ten years before I learned from Anthony Nutting's *No End of a Lesson* how the French, who were as eager as Eden to bring Nasser down and even more impatient, had secretly agreed with the Israelis on a concerted attack; how, at a series of secret meetings in Paris, a plan had been worked out which would require the co-operation of Britain; and how Eden and Selwyn Lloyd were eventually brought into the plan. If I had known all this, I might have guessed that the Israeli raids on Jordan were intended to divert attention from Israel's real purpose of mounting an attack on Egypt and that this would provide the pretext for Britain and France to seize control of the canal. At the time it merely looked to us as though the Israelis were fishing in troubled waters; and this explanation seemed plausible, for the raids (in which nearly a hundred Jordanians were killed) caused a wave of anxiety and recrimination all through the Arab world which pushed the Suez crisis into the background.

Not so for Eden. For him, the canal was everything – and what was so infuriating was the fact that at every point the game seemed to be going against him. The Egyptians had succeeded in keeping the canal open – and they had done nothing to prevent anyone who wanted to from using it. Despite the withdrawal of the British and French pilots, despite the continuing refusal of the British and French ships to pay their canal dues to the Egyptians, despite all the threats and the rumours and the pressures, Nasser – with the help of Captain Mongued and his colleagues – had succeeded in denying Eden any pretext that would justify armed intervention against Egypt.

But the ships were there in Cyprus and the paratroopers, while landing craft were assembling in Malta. All Eden wanted was more time, and it was to gain time as well as to try to take advantage of the uncertainty in the Arab world that he decided, after much hesitation, to take the dispute to the United Nations. At the request of the British and French governments, a meeting of the Security Council was arranged for 5 October.

With the prospect of a lull for two or three weeks while the issues were thrashed out in New York, it seemed a good moment to take a breather. It had been the most stimulating summer of my life; it had also been very hard work in the heat of Cairo, and I found Manchester sympathetic to the idea that I might snatch some rest before the story came home to Egypt. Keeping a wary eye on events, I flew home, compared notes with the foreign editor, tasted the highly-charged atmosphere of London – which came as a shock after the calm of Cairo – spent a refreshing week in Sussex, and then took up a long-standing invitation to visit friends in Munich.

For three months my world had been a narrow one and here I found myself on the fringe of a wholly different crisis: three hundred miles to the east, in Budapest, huge crowds of Hungarians were shouting defiance to the Russians. The friends I was staying with were Americans who had befriended me in Louisville two years earlier. Now they were working for Radio Free Europe and they took me to the studios to meet Hungarian emigrés and hear their warnings that an invasion of Hungary was imminent. The atmosphere and the slogans were familiar; only here the enemies were the Russians while in Egypt . . . It was all very confusing.

I could not wait for the denouement, for the lull in 'my' crisis was ending. I had planned to be back in Cairo on the 27th, but an airline strike stranded me in Athens and it was not until five o'clock in the morning of 29 October that I stepped out on to the tarmac at Cairo airport. After a sleepless night I thought I would go to bed for a couple of hours before starting to pick up the threads again. Luckily I decided first to make one or two phone calls, to reassure myself that there was nothing in the rumours I had heard in Athens of an Israeli mobilization. From the first call I learned that the American embassy had advised American citizens to leave Egypt immediately – and it was some time before I caught up on that missing sleep.

The reports were confusing. Official sources in Washington were saying that 150,000 Israeli troops were deployed along 'the Arab borders'. But which borders? At first, it looked as though the Israeli threat was directed against Jordan, which had been the object of the recent Israeli raids and where a strongly pro-Egyptian government had been elected while I was away in Europe. But the possibility could not be overlooked that the Israelis felt tempted to make a strike against Egypt while the Egyptians were preoccupied with the Suez crisis. Was this what the American warning implied? And if so, how would either the Americans or the British respond to an Israeli attack, whatever its target?

At that time, in the autumn of 1956, both governments, together with the French, were parties to a Tripartite Declaration, signed only four years earlier, by which they undertook to come to the aid of Israel or any of its Arab neighbours, if either should attack the other in violation of the 1949 armistice agreements. So here was Britain (and France too) poised to attack Egypt and at the same time committed to come to Egypt's assistance if it should be attacked by Israel. A pretty conundrum! And to add to the confusion, Russian tanks were warming up their engines for the invasion of Hungary, while Washington (as so often) was paralysed by the closing stages of a presidential election campaign. Were the Israelis counting on all this to provide them with the opportunity to snatch a quick victory – and if so, over whom?

On the evening of 30 October I was sitting in the office of the Arab News Agency in Cairo, where conflicting reports were coming in of fighting in the Sinai desert. The Reuter ticker machine was chattering incessantly, and suddenly Tom Little, the chief of the ANA bureau, put in front of me a scrap of paper containing a news flash. When I read it, I thought I must have misunderstood its sense. It said that Eden had sent an ultimatum to both Egypt and Israel, ordering them both to withdraw their forces ten miles behind the Suez Canal. Unless this order was obeyed within twelve hours, said the announcement, an Anglo-French force would attack and occupy Port Said, Ismailia and Suez.

Others joined us – David Holden was there, I remember, and Bob Petty of ANA – and as telephones rang and typewriters clattered we tried to make sense of what seemed on the face of it to be incomprehensible. How could the Israelis withdraw from the Suez Canal when they were nowhere near it? And how could the Egyptians be expected to do so when the canal lay deep inside Egyptian territory? It seemed to us that our government had taken leave of its senses. Even if every concession were made to Eden's point of view, even if one shared his hatred for Nasser, his obsessive memories of the 1930s, his disregard for the Americans' position and the rest of world opinion, it was still inconceivable to us that anyone in authority in London could fail to realize the fatal consequences of an intervention that seemed – but could it be true? – to range Britain on the side of Israel, and an Israel engaged in open agression at that.

It was true, though, and for a week we continued mechanically to function as correspondents, while the Israeli tanks swept across Sinai and British bombers systematically destroyed the Egyptian air force. Our usefulness was gone, we could not travel outside Cairo – least of all to the canal, in which the Egyptians, acting on a plan long prepared for such an emergency, had swiftly sunk a dozen blockships. All we could report were the rumours that swept the capital and the defiant pride of the man in the street and our own sense of humiliation as we watched officials of the British embassy burning their files, the ashes floating out on the fresh breeze over the Nile, while the Canberras of the RAF circled overhead. It was an odd and unhappy experience, and what gave it an added air of unreality was the fact that the Egyptians behaved towards us almost as though nothing had happened. Friends remained constant, even the officials with whom we had to deal treated us with a sort of shy sympathy. It was not our fault, they managed to convey, if our government had engaged in an aberration for which no one could hold us responsible.

The first week of November 1956 was a black one for an Englishman in Cairo. But life has taught me that nothing we have to endure ever turns out to be quite as bad as it seemed at first sight, and when I look back on the experience after nearly thirty years, what I remember about it and about the rest of a month in which I was as unhappy as I have ever been, is a series of improbable encounters which were characteristic of the Egypt I had begun to know and was to come to know better.

One evening, for instance, from the balcony of a penthouse flat in the centre of Cairo, I had been watching a British bombing raid on Cairo airport. I had not relished the experience, but I was reluctant to leave because I knew that when I reached home I should be interned. In fact,

I had no right to be out at all. I had received earlier that evening, at second hand, an order to stay indoors and I had at once slipped out again to prolong my freedom by at least a few hours. So when I left to make my way home through the blackout, with my hosts' embarrassed farewells ringing in my ears, I knew that I was in a weak position.

I hadn't gone fifty yards before a shambling figure with a rifle loomed out of the darkness and challenged me.

'Who are you?' he asked in Arabic.

Never in my life have I found the question so hard to answer. Nor, on the face of it, was this a moment for frankness. If you find yourself at large in the capital of a country with which your own government has just gone to war, you do not expect to be treated with a great deal of ceremony. Fumbling in my pockets as though for the identity card I did not possess, I thought hard.

'Who are you?'

What did the man want me to say? 'Friend' would have taken a bit of proving, and 'Foe' – even if I had known the Arabic for it – seemed an unfair simplification of my estate. But the Egyptian solved my dilemma for me. '*Ingleezi*?' he asked, thrusting his unshaven face close to mine. 'Yes,' I said simply.

He looked round him into the darkness to see if he were observed, and seeing no one he handed back the assortment of letters and bills that I had proffered, knowing he would not be able to make anything of them. 'Ya'allah,' he said, with a jerk of his thumb, 'hop it.' And I did.

I forget whether it was on the same day or the day before that I had paid a visit to the bank. The British ultimatum, which genuinely astonished President Nasser, had also taken me by surprise; I had returned from Munich with hardly any money. Clearly the course of everyday life in Cairo, particularly for such an enemy alien as I had now become, was liable to be disrupted. It would be useful, it occurred to me, to have money in my pocket against emergencies and each morning, as I set out to gather the day's news, I determined to get to the bank before it was too late.

But these were busy days and I was down to a few piastres (and those British bombers had become a part of the Cairo scene) before I found myself one morning passing the door of Barclays and slipped in, to find that the British manager had been ousted and an Egyptian installed in his place. With expectations less than great, I asked to see him.

The manager received me with courtesy. What could he do for me? Well, I explained diffidently, I had just looked in to see if I could have some . . . money. 'Yes,' said the manager. 'How much?' 'Oh,' I replied, 'not a lot, say ten pounds – or perhaps twenty?' The manager indicated that this would be quite in order and I wrote out a cheque, which he handed to an underling, asking him to bring the money to me. When the man had left the room, the manager looked at me intently, 'May I ask how much money you have in this bank?' he asked. I said that I thought there must be something like £150 in my account. The manager looked down at his desk for a moment. Then he leaned forward and said quietly: 'Mr Adams, my advice would be: take the lot.'

It was an uncomplicated gesture of goodwill. The next day all British accounts were placed under sequestration and that money came in useful when I found myself interned, along with eight other British newspapermen, in the incongruous luxury of Cairo's Semiramis Hotel. There for the next three weeks we lived in a curious limbo of humiliation – not that anyone by even the smallest gesture, tried to compound our distress.

Ostensibly, we were guests of the hotel like any others. Our security guards behaved more like gentlemen's gentlemen, sitting always a little apart from us and intervening only when someone tried to get into conversation with us – and then with a mixture of deference and geniality.

Segregated in this way, we ate self-consciously in the dining room (where I remember with gratitude how an Egyptian newspaper editor one day broke through our *cordon sanitaire* to wish me a friendly good day) and drank, with less inhibition, in the bar. The hotel staff, to their credit, made absolutely no distinction between us and the other guests, treating us all with the same courteous inefficiency. For the rest, we read or argued in our rooms or sang songs like 'Lloyd George Knows My Father' and the 'Blaydon Races' to David Holden's guitar.

To us, in this gilded cage, came the muffled echo of great events. The paratroops landed in Port Said, gained ground, and were halted by the cease-fire. Mr Khrushchev rattled his rockets, the American Sixth Fleet manoeuvred ambiguously off Alexandria and presently the first units of the United Nations expeditionary force landed in Egypt. The canal, of course, was blocked and remained so until the following March. For journalists it was galling, among all this, to rust in idleness. It was a relief when we were ordered to leave.

At my home, when I was taken under escort to collect such of my belongings as I could carry, a small crowd gathered – a few local shopkeepers, the laundryman from over the road, casual acquaintances, street urchins – who came not to jeer or to throw stones, but to give me a surely incomprehensible godspeed; and then we were off to the airport.

Here all was not so amicable. The emigrants, British, French, Jewish, polyglot, were hot and anxious; the Egyptian customs officials were hurried and suspicious of smuggled valuables. Before we set out with our rumpled hand-luggage to walk to the aircraft, more than a few tempers had been lost on both sides.

Ahead of me walked an elderly Englishwoman, who had made her home in Egypt for more than thirty years. She had just been stripped and searched. Halfway across the tarmac, the string broke which she had tied about a makeshift hatbox and the hats went rolling haphazardly among the feet of the travellers. An Egyptian policeman and I helped her to corral them again.

This must be the last straw for her, I remember thinking, and when I took my seat in the plane next to her I braced myself to accept with patience her pent-up indignation. She was silent for a time, and then, as the plane climbed up over the desert she said: 'He shouldn't have done it.' 'Who?' I asked. 'Eden,' she replied. 'It was wrong and it was stupid. And now it's all over.'

And so it was for her. But there were a few loose ends for others to tidy up.

Epilogue

By 1956 I thought myself reasonably well armed for life; and yet I was unprepared for the shock of disillusionment I felt over Suez. It was as though all my defences, like those of Singapore when the Japanese attacked it in 1941, were pointing in the wrong direction. I was ready for a frontal assault of the kind with which Hitler had made us familiar, and I felt I should know how to withstand the more insidious methods which McCarthy had used to browbeat his fellow-Americans a few years later. What took me by surprise at Suez was the fact that the skullduggery came from our own side: the realization that where political manipulation was concerned a democratic leader and an Englishman could be just as unscrupulous as any foreign dictator.

It only shows how much I still had to learn, and in that sense the Suez affair marked for me as distinct a watershed as that pre-war dawn on the Glandaz seventeen years earlier. Indeed, its effect on me was even more decisive and far-reaching, so that my life, now that I come to look back on it, falls clearly into two halves, with Suez as the crucial frontier between them. The first half was an adventure, which had its ups and downs and in which – at Oxford and in the prison camp, and through those subsequent wanderings from Finland to Anatolia and across the wide expanses of the United States – I had been half-consciously equipping myself for the pursuit of some objective as yet unidentified. Suez put an abrupt end to this phase of apprenticeship, leaving me bitter and despondent; but it marked also the opening of another phase in which, as I emerged from the twilight of disenchantment, I was conscious of a new sense of purpose stirring inside me which was presently to shape my life.

Out of the jumble of past experience I began to detect at last the semblance of a pattern emerging, into which Browning and Ataturk, with my companions in the dinghy and the Russian prisoners at Luchenwald and Deligny in Paris and the one-legged Englishman at the monastery on Mount Hymettus, had all woven their individual threads. 'I am a part of all that I have met . . .' That was what Tennyson's Ulysses felt as he looked back on a life spent 'always roaming with a hungry heart' – and that was how I felt: that there was something vital to be extracted, something of endurance and resolve to be distilled, from the windfalls that life, with such seeming waywardness, had dropped in my path. And this distillation, I sensed, would prove its worth when I resumed my wandering, not as an apprentice now but a participant in events for whom:

> . . . all experience is an arch, wherethro'
> Gleams that untravell'd world, whose margin fades
> For ever and for ever when I move.

Of the fading margin and all that it encompassed I hope to tell in due course.

Index